Oxford Secondary English 4

John Seely

A GCSE Course

Oxford University Press

Oxford University Press, Walton Street, Oxford OX2 6DP

Oxford New York Toronto
Delhi Bombay Calcutta Madras Karachi
Petaling Jaya Singapore Hong Kong Tokyo
Nairobi Dar es Salaam Cape Town
Melbourne Auckland

and associated companies in
Beirut Berlin Ibadan Nicosia

Oxford is a trade mark of Oxford University Press

© Oxford University Press 1985

First published 1985
Reprinted 1986 (twice)

ISBN 0 19 831151 6

Phototypeset by Tradespools Limited, Frome, Somerset

Printed and bound in Great Britain by
Butler & Tanner Ltd, Frome and London

The Teacher's Book is an integral part of the course:
ISBN 0 19 831153 2

Contents

Part A
Themes and stories

5. *I'll fight you for it*

6. *The way ahead*

Story: The white trousers

Part B
The craft of writing

1. *Your writing* 128

2. *Aspects of writing* 146

3. *Ways of writing* 174

4. *The technicalities* 208

PART A

Themes and stories

1. *Starting*

The ages of man

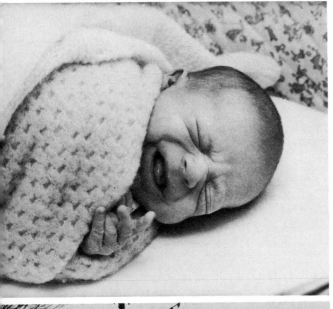

All the world's a stage,
And all the men and women merely players.
They have their exits and their entrances,
And one man in his time plays many parts,
His acts being seven ages. At first the infant,
Mewling and puking in the nurse's arms.
And then the whining schoolboy, with his satchel
And shining morning face, creeping like snail
Unwillingly to school. And then the lover,
Sighing like furnace, with a woeful ballad
Made to his mistress' eyebrow. Then a soldier,
Full of strange oaths, and bearded like the pard,
Jealous in honour, sudden, and quick in quarrel,
Seeking the bubble reputation
Even in the cannon's mouth. And then, the justice,
In fair round belly, with good capon lin'd,
With eyes severe, and beard of formal cut,
Full of wise saws, and modern instances,
And so he plays his part. The sixth age shifts
Into the lean and slipper'd pantaloon,
With spectacles on nose, and pouch on side,
His youthful hose well sav'd, a world too wide
For his shrunk shank, and his big manly voice,
Turning again towards childish treble, pipes
And whistles in his sound. Last scene of all,
That ends this strange eventful history,
Is second childishness and mere oblivion,
Sans teeth, sans eyes, sans taste, sans everything.

William Shakespeare   *As You Like It*

The Fleet Street ages of man

The Ages of Man as seen by Fleet Street may begin with a 'miracle baby', which becomes a 'babe-in-arms', grows into a 'toddler', 'tot' and then a 'kid'. If his parents are divorced and disputing custody, he may turn into a 'tug-of-love' baby, toddler, or kid – with horrific suggestions of two people tearing out his arms as in a tug-of-war. Schoolchildren are sometimes described as school 'students', especially in the left-wing and sociological press while still 'teenagers'. Girl teenagers who become pregnant are 'gymslip mums' when they are still at school, but mere 'mums-to-be' as soon as they have left, even at the age of fifteen and still wearing their gymslips. An illegitimate baby is a 'love-child', and the place in which it is thought to have been produced, a 'love-nest' – for love is apparently thought never to enter into married relationships. A 'boy' becomes a 'youth' at about sixteen and a man at nineteen; but he may remain a 'boy-friend' even into his seventies. Women can be called 'girls' into their mid-thirties and 'girl-friends' up to any age. When actors, actresses or ballet dancers are the subject of a story they remain 'boys' and 'girls' for ever. There are also compound terms which can be made into almost any permutation, such as 'teenage fathers', 'gymslip muggers' or 'singing bachelor' etc. The subject's marital or professional status ('bachelor', 'businessman', 'housewife', 'divorcee'), his or her age, whether germane to the story or not – and, if a woman, her hair colour, breast, waist and hip measurements and some indication of her attractiveness, with carefully graded euphemisms ('blonde, vivacious have-a-go housewife, Eileen Grunge, 38, 44, 49') – are considered essential information. So are the existence and number of children, if any; and even the knowledge that the subject's children have proved their own fertility ('battling grandfather of four, Bert Snodgrass, 73'). But from the age of sixty to sixty-five Fleet Street Man's decline is rapid – into plain pensioner, sans teeth, sans dignity, sans everything.

Fritz Spiegl   *Keep taking the tabloids!*

Memory of childhood

A young kid is sitting on a low wall. He is chewing and staring into the distance, beyond the heat haze. He suddenly crouches low, produces his imaginary 'pistol' and picks off three baddies. He returns the gun to his belt. He sits and continues his chewing.

*Behind him we see another kid (**George**) appear. He creeps up, and as he does so he unpins an equally imaginary 'grenade' and lobs it at **Chris**. He waits a moment before making the sound of the explosion.*

GEORGE: [*As **Chris** looks round*] You're dead.
CHRIS: No I'm not.
GEORGE: Yis y'are. I got y' with a grenade, at point blank range.
CHRIS: Well –
GEORGE: Well what?
CHRIS: Well, that means you're dead as well, cos you didn't move out of range.
GEORGE: I don't have to. A grenade wouldn't injure me. I've got super powers.

CHRIS: Which ones?
GEORGE: All of them. I'm indestructible.
CHRIS: No, y'not. None of the Super Heroes is indestructible.
GEORGE: The Hulk is.
CHRIS: No, he's not. Even Superman's not indestructible an' he's the most indestructible Super Hero there is. But even Superman can't face Kryptonite.
GEORGE: [*Shrugging*] D'you live round here?
CHRIS: [*Indicating*] Down there.
GEORGE: What y' doin' round here?
CHRIS: I've been the shops.
GEORGE: What for?
CHRIS: [*Immediately defensive*] Nothin'.
GEORGE: [*Goes into the sound of a police wah-wah siren. Suddenly stops*] Gis a sweet.
CHRIS: I haven't got any. [**George** *looks at him.* **Chris** *turns away and begins to make the sound of a bleep phone*]
GEORGE: Which shop did y' go to?
CHRIS: Supermarket.
GEORGE: What for?
CHRIS: What?
GEORGE: What did y' go the supermarket for?
CHRIS: For me mam. I was on a message.
GEORGE: What did y' get?
CHRIS: Nott'n. It was closed.
GEORGE: [*Sceptical, but not to be put off*] It's dead lucky for you it was closed.
CHRIS: Why?
GEORGE: There's rats in that supermarket. An' y' know if y' bought somethin' from there, somethin' to eat, like sweets, an' y' ate them, y'd get the fever.
CHRIS: The fever?
GEORGE: Yeh. Y' die if y' catch the fever. There's three kids died from our street, y' know.
CHRIS: [*Pause*] Y' wouldn't die if y' just ate one sweet from there, though. Would y'?
GEORGE: Y' would. Y' don't even have to eat them. Just havin' them in y' pocket – that's enough. The germs travel up t' y' mouth. They fly. It's best if y' throw them away.

CHRIS: [*Looking at him*] Listen, y' know somethin' eh?

GEORGE: What?

CHRIS: Isn't it lucky for me the supermarket was closed.

GEORGE: [*Disgusted*] I seen you chewin'.

CHRIS: Y' never, cos I wasn't chewin'.

GEORGE: Y' were. I seen y' goin' like that. [*Exaggerated chew*]

CHRIS: I wasn't chewin' nott'n though. I was tryin' t' bite off a piece of loose skin in me gum. Like that. [*Shows him the chewing action*]

GEORGE: [*Pause*] I get that sometimes, inside me mouth.

CHRIS: Yeh, well so do I.

GEORGE: Look. [*Opens his mouth.* **Chris** *peers in*]

CHRIS: Oh yeh . . . I can see it. That's just like mine was.

GEORGE: Let's have a look. [**Chris** *opens his mouth.* **George** *peers in.* **George** *suddenly pointing, accusing*] See . . . I told y' you had sweets, there's all yellow over y' tongue . . . You've got sweets.

CHRIS: I haven't got sweets. I had some, but that was the last one. An' I didn't get it from the supermarket, I got it from the paper shop. [*He gets up to go*] I'm goin'. [*Making police wah-wah sound before zooming off*]

GEORGE: Where?

CHRIS: Home.

GEORGE: Down there?

CHRIS: Yeh.

GEORGE: Y' know who's down there?

CHRIS: [*Coming back a step*] Who?

GEORGE: Tommo!

CHRIS: Tommo? [**George** *nods*] Tommo isn't down there. Tommo got sent away. Tommo's in a home cos of bullyin' little kids an' murderin' dogs.

GEORGE: Look. [*Points*]

CHRIS: Is that Tommo?

GEORGE: [*Nods*] Tommo's back now. [*He walks away leaving* **Chris** *worried and anxious, gawping down the road*] With an air pistol as well.

Willy Russell   *Politics and terror*

Leaving home

The stooping figure of my mother, waist-deep in the grass and caught there like a piece of sheep's wool, was the last I saw of my country home as I left it to discover the world. She stood old and bent at the top of the bank, silently watching me go, one gnarled red hand raised in farewell and blessing, not questioning why I went. At the bend of the road I looked back again and saw the gold light die behind her; then I turned the corner, passed the village school, and closed that part of my life for ever.

It was a bright Sunday morning in early June, the right time to be leaving home. My three sisters and a brother had already gone before me; two other brothers had yet to make up their minds. They were still sleeping that morning, but my mother had got up early and cooked me a heavy breakfast, had stood wordlessly while I ate it, her hand on my chair, and had then helped me pack up my few belongings. There had been no fuss, no appeals, no attempts at advice or persuasion, only a long and searching look. Then, with my bags on my back, I'd gone out into the early sunshine and climbed through the long wet grass to the road.

It was 1934. I was nineteen years old, still soft at the edges, but with a confident belief in good fortune. I carried a small rolled-up tent, a violin in a blanket, a change of clothes, a tin of treacle biscuits, and some cheese. I was excited, vain-glorious, knowing I had far to go; but not, as yet, how far. As I left home that morning and walked away from the sleeping village, it never occurred to me that others had done this before me.

I was propelled, of course, by the traditional forces that had sent many generations along this road – by the small tight valley closing in around one, stifling the breath with its mossy mouth, the cottage walls narrowing like the arms of an iron maiden, the local girls whispering, 'Marry, and settle down'. Months of restless unease, leading to this inevitable moment, had been spent wandering about the hills, mournfully whistling, and watching the high open fields stepping away eastwards under gigantic clouds . . .

And now I was on my journey, in a pair of thick boots and with a hazel stick in my hand. Naturally, I was going to London, which lay a hundred miles to the east; and it seemed equally obvious that I should go on foot. But first, as I'd never yet seen the sea, I thought I'd walk to the coast and find it. This would add another hundred miles to my journey, going by way of Southampton. But I had all the summer and all time to spend.

That first day alone – and now I was really alone at last – steadily declined in excitement and vigour. As I tramped through the dust towards the Wiltshire Downs a growing reluctance weighed me down. White elder-blossom and dog-roses hung in the hedges, blank as unwritten paper, and the hot empty road – there were few motor cars then – reflected Sunday's waste and indifference. High sulky summer sucked me towards it, and I offered no resistance at all. Through the solitary morning and afternoon I found myself longing for some opposition or rescue, for the sound of hurrying footsteps coming after me and family voices calling me back.

None came. I was free.

Laurie Lee   *As I walked out one midsummer morning*

Night watch

FATHER: Four o'clock.

MOTHER: Not quite four, dear. . . . More like half-past three.

FATHER: My watch says four o'clock precisely.

MOTHER: Are you sure you set it properly?

FATHER: I set it by the clock.

MOTHER: Then it can't be four o'clock precisely.

FATHER: Why not?

MOTHER: Because the clock hasn't struck four yet. (*The clock strikes four*)

MOTHER: It feels like half-past three.

FATHER: (*pointing at the clock*) Four o'clock.

MOTHER: You said that before.

FATHER: And I'll say it again. Four o'clock.

MOTHER: My nerves are in a twitter just waiting. You don't improve them by charging up and down muttering four o'clock.

FATHER: In another hour I'll be muttering five.

MOTHER: Oh, she won't be another hour.

FATHER: At twelve o'clock you said she would be another minute.

MOTHER: That was at twelve o'clock. It's four now.

FATHER: What is my daughter doing out until four in the morning?

MOTHER: I don't know, dear, I've been here all the time. With you.

FATHER: What is she doing? What can anybody do in this benighted dump at four in the morning?

MOTHER: There are lots of things she could be doing.

FATHER: Such as?

MOTHER: I'd rather not think about them.

FATHER: I'm thinking about them.

MOTHER: So am I. But I'd rather not.

FATHER: A girl of her age.

MOTHER: It would be different if she were our age. She couldn't get into any trouble if she were our age.

FATHER: No, she couldn't. . . . (*pointing at the clock*) Four o'clock!

MOTHER: You're repeating yourself. Why do you keep repeating yourself? I never repeat myself.

FATHER: What did you say?

MOTHER: I said I never repeat myself.

FATHER: (*pointing at the clock*) Four o'clock. It's got to stop. When I say eleven o'clock I mean eleven o'clock.

MOTHER: I thought you said four o'clock.

FATHER: At her age I was never allowed out after ten.

MOTHER: Oh, but you were, dear.

FATHER: When?

MOTHER: Whenever you took me home. You would kiss me goodnight on the doorsteps as the clocks were striking twelve.

FATHER: I didn't say that I was never out after ten. I said that I was never *allowed* out after ten . . . Just wait until she comes in. She won't stay out again in a hurry. I can promise you that.

MOTHER: Thank you dear.

FATHER: I shall have a few words with that young lady. A few well chosen words.

MOTHER: What words, dear?

FATHER: I haven't chosen them yet. (*he points to the clock*)

MOTHER: Four o'clock.

FATHER: Five past . . . Who does she think she is?

MOTHER: Your daughter dear.

FATHER: What did you mean by that?

MOTHER: She *is* your daughter.

FATHER: She's *our* daughter.

MOTHER: What's bred in the home, they say. Remember what you were like at her age.

FATHER: At her age? At her age I was in the Air Cadets.

MOTHER: Exactly.

FATHER: At her age I was serving King and Country. Two nights a week at Air Training classes.

MOTHER: You only joined the Air Cadets so that the girls would run after your uniform.

FATHER: No girl ever ran after my uniform.

MOTHER: I did.

FATHER: At her age I had no time for that sort of thing.

MOTHER: What sort of thing?

FATHER: The Air Training Corps was all I had time for. Two classes a week and square-bashing on Sundays.

MOTHER: You weren't at Air Training classes that night we spent in the air-raid shelter.

FATHER: We had to take cover.

MOTHER: Father could never understand why he never heard the sirens.

FATHER: If I had been your father you'd have been too tender to sit down.

MOTHER: What did your father do?

FATHER: I was too tender to sit down . . . and it was your fault.

MOTHER: Mine.

FATHER: You led me on. I was a model Air Cadet, but you tempted me. I was just weak and foolish.

MOTHER: Then what were you doing all night in the air-raid shelter?

FATHER: Uniform mad you were at her age. Always after the Yanks.

MOTHER: Yanks.

FATHER: I only hope my daughter does take after me. I don't want to see her chasing after chewing-gum and Chesterfields.

MOTHER: I wasn't with a Yank the night you took me to a hop and the lorry broke down miles from anywhere.

FATHER: Petrol was rationed in those days.

MOTHER: I'm not blaming you. Just reminding you.

FATHER: I don't need reminding. I have a perfect memory. You in bobby-sox with a guy named Joe.

MOTHER: His name wasn't Joe. It was Urwin. Besides, he was fighting for me.

FATHER: He was fighting for you, was he? And what was I supposed to be doing?

MOTHER: You were losing your stripes over Valerie Pringle.

FATHER: I never even knew Valerie Pringle. At least not more than once. The Flight Sergeant was jealous. That time he caught us alone in Cadet Headquarters. I was teaching her morse code.

MOTHER: You never told me you were teaching her morse code.

FATHER: Anyway, what has all this to do with our daughter?

MOTHER: It's four o'clock.

FATHER: What does she think she's doing at this time of the morning?

MOTHER: I only hope it's nothing we might have done.

FATHER: Hark!

MOTHER: Her key!

FATHER: Now for it. Now we'll see who's head of this house. Now! (**Daughter** *comes in, weary but starry eyed. She wears a polo-necked sweater and carries a pole with a C.N.D. device on top*)

DAUGHTER: (*ecstatically*) Wonderful! We sat on the Town Hall steps until after midnight, and I've been kicked all over, and thrown into the gutter, and dropped on my head.

MOTHER: I'm glad you've had a nice time.

DAUGHTER: Night. (*she goes out.* **Father** *realises that he is still pointing at the clock and lowers his arm*)

MOTHER: Now . . . what?

FATHER: Oh, come to bed.

David Campton   *On stage*

Away from home

I was late leaving my dormitory again, so that by the time I had reached the Methodist High School, the Assembly had already begun. They were singing. The voices echoed along the Assembly Hall, and reverberated against the grey walls between the front of the school and the yard opposite. Everywhere there were young voices; everywhere there was the determined military tune, the tune that was making the khakied uniformed girls inside into pilgrims of Christ.

It was a little odd – a little nostalgia-making – standing outside, late, listening to an orthodox church hymn. The girls sang in tune – Miss Davies, their Welsh Music Mistress, saw to that – but you could tell that the voices were African. You could hear in these voices something of their grandparents: the grandparents who had once used their voices in village music – singing ballads or stories – or possibly in forest calls to accompany the rhythms of the cone-shaped talking drums. These girls, the modern girls of twentieth-century Africa, still possessed their grandparents' voices. They were voices full of strength and vigour, but they were also voices full of hope and pride. It was the hope and pride of believing that they were going to be the new women of the new Africa. They had been told that they were special, that one day they would be rubbing shoulders with the likes of Miss Davies from Wales, Miss Osborne from Scotland, Miss Humble from Oxford, Miss Walker from Australia, plus many, many other white missionaries who had left their own countries to come to Lagos to teach the girls here to value their own importance. There were a few black mistresses – one in the needlework department and the other in the domestic department – but you could tell that they really didn't count.

I, though, was not really among these new women. In part it was because I was shy and sensitive – too shy and too sensitive to be able to forget myself among a crowd of people. Even though I craved company, I always seemed to act like a fool when with people. And so I lingered or walked alone or read or memorized what I read. In part, it was because I was different. Although I could recite works by Shakespeare or Keats or Rupert Brooke, I was the daughter of parents who had scant education, who had simply emerged out of their innocent (and yet exotic) bush culture. They were innocents in the so-called civilized world. Maybe a little crude. But in their world – in terms of communal caring and support, in expressions of language and in the making of music – they could not be surpassed in their sophistication. But they had to leave all this, my parents, in search of this New Thing. They left their village homes which had been the homes of their ancestors for generations and generations, and they came to the city. And it was in the city that they had me, and they said I was clever. They said I was clever because I won something called a scholarship and which my mother called 'sikohip'. I was to be brought up in the new way. That was why instead of being in the village – claying the mud floor of my ancestors – I had to stand in front of this school compound feeling guilty for having read too late into the morning, hearing the voices now of my already assembled school friends singing.

I often gave the village life a good deal of thought. My people made sure I

never lost touch with it. I had to go through all the rituals. Even so, even then, I knew that, like my parents, I was already trapped in this New Thing. But of course to all my friends and even to me, it wasn't a New Thing any more. It was becoming a way of life.

However much I may have admired or thought about village life, I knew that, just to survive, I had to make a go of the education I was being offered. I was at a school where all the girls had to pay, but I was going for free. And because I was not paying for my education I ended up spending more and more time by myself, without friends. I was not of course given a scholarship out of charity but it made no difference. Although I was also aware that my parents could not have paid the high fees if they had been asked to do so. How could they? My father had been dead for some time. And my mother even though a Christian, had to return to being a native in our village town Ibuza. She had to return for survival. So I was, in a funny way, guilty for being on a scholarship, and grateful for being on a scholarship.

Buchi Emecheta *Head above water*

Assignments

The ages of man (6)

Writing about the characters
Jaques lists seven 'ages'. Read the speech and try to get a clear picture of each one in your mind. Write one sentence for each of the seven ages, describing each character in your own words.

Descriptive writing
Shakespeare was writing in the reign of Elizabeth I and his 'ages' were all character types from that period. Write your own 'Seven ages of man' using character types from today. You may find the illustrations on pages 6 and 7 useful in deciding on your 'Seven ages'.

The Fleet Street ages of man (7)

1 What exactly does Fritz Spiegl object to in phrases like 'gymslip mums'?
2 Why do journalists use such phrases?
3 Do all newspapers use such language or are some more 'guilty' than others?
4 Should newspapers try to avoid such language and 'stick to the facts'?

Memory of childhood (8)

Writing dialogue
Write a short dialogue between two or three children. Either continue the conversation printed in the book, or make up a conversation of your own based on one of your memories of childhood.

Leaving home (10)

1 When and where do these events take place?
2 Why was Laurie Lee leaving home?
3 Where did he think he was going?
4 How do you think he felt as he set off?
5 How did he feel by the end of this extract?

Writing dialogue
Suppose that at this point in the story Laurie Lee met someone travelling back towards his home. How would he have described his thoughts and feelings? Write an account of the meeting and the conversation they have.

Photographs (11)

Free writing
Use the photographs as the starting point for a piece of writing. Write in whatever form seems to you most suitable.

Night watch
(12)

Directing a script

Imagine that you have been given the task of directing this short sketch. Read it carefully and decide how you would work on it. In particular, think about these points:

1 *The characters*   What are Mother and Father like?   What advice would you give to the actress and actor about how the characters should be presented?

2 *The setting*   Where are the characters?   What furniture and props (if any) are needed?

3 *Tempo and timing*   What are the main laugh lines you would go for in the script?   How could you use timing and pauses to get the laughs?   In what other parts of the dialogue would timing and pauses be particularly important?

4 *Movement*   When and how should the characters move?   Make production notes summing up your conclusions.

Writing dialogue

Write a conversation between the same three characters, starting:

DAUGHTER: Hullo Mum, hullo Dad.
MOTHER: Oh hullo dear, you're early this evening.
FATHER: For a change.
DAUGHTER: I've something to tell you . . . something important.

Away from home   (14)

1 What impression do you get of the school that Buchi Emecheta attended?
2 What was her background?
3 What does she mean by 'this New Thing'?
4 What conflict did she feel at her school?
5 Why did her mother have to go back to the village?
6 Why do you think she says of her parents that, '. . . in their world . . . they could not be surpassed in their sophistication.'?

Narrative writing

Many people experience the feeling of being separate or different from those around them. This can be for a great number of different reasons: home background, race, religion, different beliefs or ideas. Think of a situation in which you might find yourself to be such an 'outsider'. Write an account of the experience. Make sure that you describe not only what happens to you, but also how you think and feel about the experience.

The unit as a whole

Writting assignments

The writing topics that follow are based on the ideas in the unit as a whole. Treat them freely, using them as starting points rather than restricting 'titles'.

1 All the world's a _____
2 When I'm 64 (or 24, or 44, or 104)
3 Partings
4 If I meet that journalist again, I'll . . .
5 Loner
6 'Leave home? The day you leave home, I'll . . .'

★ GOLDFINGER ★
PRODUCTIONS ★
★ Shepherds Bush • London W12
★ ★ ★

<u>NEW TEENAGE TV STAR IS BORN</u>

Comprehensive schoolgirl gets big break in prime time romance series

Sharon Peterson, 16-year-old schoolgirl from Camberwell, has landed the chance of a lifetime in the new Goldfinger/Channel 6 production, <u>Younger than Springtime</u>, due to start filming in October and to be screened next autumn.

Director, Goodall Adams (remember <u>Rotten Apple</u>, <u>Cops at the Kop</u>, <u>The Death of Senorita Blom</u>?) auditioned over 650 actresses for the part of Ellie in his new down-to-earth teenage romance series. Many of the hopefuls were experienced stage and TV actresses, but Adams was looking for something different: 'Someone with that special quality needed for this script. It's difficult to define in words, but it has to do with a kind of nagging raw-edged honesty. I wanted to sum up the reality behind today's teenagers. Sharon has got precisely what I was looking for. I could never have found that sort of painful sincerity in a trained actress.'

The story of <u>Younger than Springtime</u> is set in

Press release

Interview between Sharon Peterson and Simon Crudder of the *Camberwell Mercury*

CRUDDER: Sharon it's very good of you to give me this interview.

SHARON: That's all right.

CRUDDER: What does it feel like to suddenly be a star?

SHARON: I'm not yet, am I?

CRUDDER: No, but -

SHARON: I've only just got the part. How can I be a star?

CRUDDER: But you will be, won't you, I mean once the series is made and running on TV.

SHARON: We'll have to wait and see, won't we?

CRUDDER: Can you tell me how it all started?

SHARON: The director –

CRUDDER: Goodall Adams?

SHARON: Yeah ... wrote a letter and he sent a copy of it to all the schools in London – he wanted to set this play in London, see. Well we were having drama and Mr Jamieson had a copy of this letter –

CRUDDER: Mr Jamieson – he's your drama teacher at school?

SHARON: That's right.

CRUDDER: And he suggested that you should do an audition?

SHARON: Yeah. An' I thought I might as well have a go, after all, there wasn't anything to lose, was there?

CRUDDER: And what happened?

SHARON: Well ... I got myself some new stuff, clothes y'know, 'cos I thought I ought to look good for it and Mr Jamieson he coached me in a speech.

CRUDDER: What was that?

SHARON: Oh, it was a speech from St. Joan, when she's in prison. So I practised that and then when the day came, I went along for this audition.

CRUDDER: Tell me about the clothes you wore. Where did you get the money for them?

SHARON: Well we haven't got much money at home because my Dad's out of work at the moment, but I had a bit of savings from something I had for Christmas, so I spent that.

CRUDDER: Ah yes. And so you went to the audition?

SHARON: Yes. I was a bit scared at first of course, specially when I saw how many people there were there, but once I got going it wasn't too bad really. And when I'd finished, Mr Adams asked me a few questions about what I'd done before and that and then later on they said they'd let me know what was going to happen.

CRUDDER: And how did you feel when you got the letter?

SHARON: Well, it wasn't a letter it was a phone call at school. I couldn't believe it – I thought some of my friends were having me on at first.

CRUDDER: So when do you start making the series?

SHARON: At the beginning of next term, and it takes until the Spring.

CRUDDER: So what's going to happen about school? You were due to go into the sixth form weren't you?

SHARON: Yes, that's right. But Miss Baines –

CRUDDER: The Headmistress?

SHARON: Yes. She says that I can miss a year and then come back and start the lower sixth then. So I won't miss any school really, I'll just be a year older.

CRUDDER: And what were you going to do in the sixth form?

SHARON: I don't really know, I'd like to become an actress but I shall just have to wait and see how I get on in this programme.

CRUDDER: So you might go to Drama School?

SHARON: That's right. I hope so.

Photographs taken by the local newspaper photographer

Sharon's bid for fame

Schoolgirl abandons family and school career to star in TV series

Sharon Peterson — Camberwell's new TV star

Sixteen-year-old Camberwell schoolgirl Sharon Peterson has been chosen out of thousands of hopefuls to star in Goodall Adams' (remember *Rotten Apple*?) new TV series *Younger than Springtime*.

Sharon takes the part of a teenage misfit whose troubled love life leads to a crisis for her family.

Sharon Peterson, whose only experience of acting so far has been in the annual school play, plans to throw up a promising school career in the hope of making the big time in show business.

Sharon's father is on the dole but this did not stop her lashing out on an expensive new outfit specially for the audition. 'I had to look good so it was worth it,' she said.

If Sharon's bold bid succeeds she will leave the two-bedroomed council house in Camberwell way behind her as she makes for a career as an actress in films and TV.

Extract from the Camberwell Mercury

Assignments

1   There are three different accounts of the selection of Sharon Peterson for a part in the new TV series: a press release, an interview and a local newspaper report. There are also some photographs. Study all the material and then comment on the ways in which the *Camberwell Mercury* presents the story. Why do you think it tells the story in this way?

2   Suppose you had been sent to interview Sharon Peterson. The only information you have about her is the press release on page 18. What questions would you have asked her? Make a list of the questions and then write a version of the interview that you have with her.

3   Imagine that you are Sharon Peterson. How would you feel about the version of your story printed in the *Camberwell Mercury*? Write a letter to the editor expressing your feelings and commenting on the news story.

4   Using the information in the press release and the interview write your own version of Sharon's story. Which picture of the three available would you choose and why?

5   Choose one of the headlines in the extract from the *Camberwell Mercury* and write up a story based on it in the style of the newspaper.

2. *Moon and June*

Love is just a four-letter word.

Make love not war.

Love and marriage, love and marriage
Go together like a horse and carriage.

Love is not love which alters when it alteration finds.

By the time you swear you're his,
    Shivering and sighing,
And he vows his passion is
    Infinite, undying –
Lady make a note of this:
    One of you is lying.   **Dorothy Parker**

Song

I take a jewel from a junk-shop tray
And wish I had a love to buy it for.
Nothing I choose will make you turn my way.
Nothing I give will make you love me more.

I know that I've embarrassed you too long
And I'm ashamed to linger at your door.
Whatever I embark on will be wrong.
Nothing I do will make you love me more.

I cannot work. I cannot read or write.
How can I frame a letter to implore.
Eloquence is a lie. The truth is trite.
Nothing I say will make you love me more.

So I replace the jewel in the tray
And laughingly pretend I'm far too poor.
Nothing I give, nothing I do or say,
Nothing I am will make you love me more.

James Fenton

Sonnet

My mistress' eyes are nothing like the sun;
Coral is far more red than her lips' red;
If snow be white, why then her breasts are dun;
If hairs be wires, black wires grow on her head.
I have seen roses damask'd, red and white,
But no such roses see I in her cheeks,
And in some perfumes is there more delight
Than in the breath that from my mistress reeks.
I love to hear her speak, yet well I know,
That music hath a far more pleasing sound.
I grant I never saw a goddess go;
My mistress when she walks treads on the ground.
   And yet by heaven I think my love as rare
   As any she belied by false compare.

William Shakespeare

Love is a many-splendoured thing

Mickey and Dawn are in the same class at school. Their English teacher has set them the task of interviewing members of their families on the topic of 'Young love'. Mickey doesn't want to do this homework – nor does he want to work on it with a girl.

Scene: *Dawn's grandad's flat* [**Grandad** *is pouring tea*]

GRANDAD: How many sugars, young man?

MICKEY: Two please, Mr Darnell. . . . See you support Liverpool then? That's some collection of programmes.

GRANDAD: A lifetime's hobby, lad. Now then . . .

DAWN: We want to ask you some questions, Grandad.

GRANDAD: What is this – 'Mastermind'?

DAWN: No, really, we just want to know what you think . . . how you feel . . . [*Beginning to feel ill at ease*] . . . about, well, young love.

GRANDAD: [*Laughs*] It's too young for me.

MICKEY: [*Quietly*] An' me.

GRANDAD: Ah, but there was a time, there was that . . . what!

DAWN: So you didn't think it was soft when you were younger?

GRANDAD: Oh well, when I was Mickey's age, I had better things to do . . . [*Laughs*]

MICKEY: See, Dawn.

GRANDAD: . . . that is, I thought I did. If you'd have told me when I was fourteen that I'd be courting strong at seventeen, I could have laughed in your face. And to think I was married a year later.

MICKEY: At eighteen?

GRANDAD: First World War, lad: 1917, heading for the trenches in France. Most who went there never came back . . . a lot of us who went got married beforehand . . . you know . . .

DAWN: Undying love?

GRANDAD: Aye. Thought we might never see each other again. Three days before I was called up, we got married. Our honeymoon was a weekend in North Wales. I can remember it as if it were yesterday. First night we got there, we decided we wanted to go somewhere sort of romantic and, you know, exchange rings. Well, we walked up this lane heading for the top of a hill; the first snow of winter at the very top . . . an' when we got up there, we stood together, me and your grandmother, holding hands, looking down at the lights in the houses in the valley. The moon was shining on the sea, and the stars were in the sky, and I gave her my ring and she gave me hers, like we had done in church, and we stood there for ages, thinking the whole world was ours, till in the end the moon went behind the clouds and it got too cold to stand. And then I took two paces down the hill in the dark and fell over a dead sheep.

MICKEY: [*Laughing loudly*] That's brilliant.

GRANDAD: Yes, even then it was funny.

MICKEY: I'm going to use that in the project. Liven the lesson up a bit tomorrow.

DAWN: But what about *today*, Grandad? What do you think about young people falling in love now?

GRANDAD: Things are different now, aren't they? More freedom for your generation, more money, more time an' all. I worked twelve-hour shifts for nowt more than a couple of bob.

DAWN: Do you think that's a good thing, Grandad? You know, all the freedom that courting couples have today. All the discos and the clubs, staying out late, not having to be chaperoned if you go out with someone. It seems much easier than before from what I've been told.

GRANDAD: You're right, it is. It's easier to fall in love, and easier to fall out of love as well. When things are easy, you sometimes don't value them as much as you should. That's my only complaint, Dawn. That, and the fact that I'm not young today. By God, I wish I was.

MICKEY: But y'know, a lot of old people – well, not even the really old ones like . . .

GRANDAD: Like me, you mean?

MICKEY: I'm sorry, I wasn't being funny or anything . . .

GRANDAD: Go on lad, it's all right.

MICKEY: Well, even our parents, they go on about how lucky we are, and how ungrateful we are, and if only we knew what they had to put up with. They make you feel guilty just to be young.

GRANDAD: And you know what this is, Mick? Because they're jealous, a lot of them: not just jealous of what you've got, but jealous because of what you are. You're young, and they're not. [*Pause, then deliberately cheerful*] Right then, has that answered your questions?

DAWN: Yes thanks, Grandad.

MICKEY: I've got one more question for you.

GRANDAD: Fire away then.

MICKEY: Are you going to the match tonight?

GRANDAD: [*Laughing*] I wish I was.

Scene: *The street* [**Dawn** *and* **Mickey** *talk above the traffic noise*]

MICKEY: He's great, your grandad, isn't he? I mean, you can talk to him, like.

DAWN: I thought you would get on with him.

MICKEY: Well, he supports the right team, doesn't he? Okay, where next?

DAWN: My married sister, Janet. That is, she used to be married.

Scene: *Dawn's sister's house* [**Janet** *answers* **Dawn's** *question*]

JANET: [*Rapid*] Young love? You want to know about young love? I'll tell you about young love, I'll tell you about all kinds of love. *It's all lies*, from beginning to end.

DAWN: But Janet . . .

JANET: You don't know, Dawn, you're too young. When I was your age I was starry-eyed as well. I believed in true love and romance and knights in shining armour and the sugar candy mountains. And as far as I'm concerned, they're all fairy stories. [*Pause for breath*]

MICKEY: Er, y'know, if I'm in the way, I'd be happy to . . .

JANET: I don't mind.

MICKEY: As a matter of fact, I'm not really interested in, er, young love . . . or any sort of . . . anything like that.

JANET: Well, take a tip from me, stay that way.

DAWN: Right . . . er, that was . . .

JANET: Short and sour?

DAWN: Something like that.

JANET: You shouldn't have asked me. You know how I feel. I'm not going to be once bitten, twice bitten.

DAWN: That's why we did ask you. We wanted as many opinions as possible. Anyway, we'll be going . . . I'll come over tomorrow.

Alan Bleasdale *Love is a many-splendoured thing*

(i)   (ii)   (iii)

Strip-cartoon romances

A 'love comic' is a magazine consisting mainly of love stories in the form of a series of pictures in which the characters reveal their thoughts in balloons of words. After reading any of them regularly for six weeks, one has a good idea of their vary narrow range of stock situations and characters.

The central figure with whom the reader is expected to identify herself is almost invariably a young girl of conventionally attractive appearance. The name, the place and the occupation may change from week to week, but of one thing the reader can be certain: the girl heroine is obsessively eager to bring the man of her choice to the altar.

Very often, in the first picture, the heroine – Susan, let us say – is introduced to us as an exceedingly lovelorn maiden. Why? A glance at the caption tells us that the hero – Matthew, for example – (a strong-jawed, clear-eyed, well-built, 'sincere guy') is apparently oblivious of Susan's presence. She thinks, 'If only he'd look at me – smile at me . . .' From this point, the author's task is to move Susan from tears of sadness to tears of joy, through a succession of difficulties and misunderstandings calculated to hold the attention of the reader without too much mental effort.

The stories do vary, of course, but the manner in which the theme is treated does not. Here are a few of the standard devices from this ragbag of romance stories:

(i) Prolonging the agony. Two or three pictures in which Matthew is shown to be extremely busy in a 'manly' way, organizing big deals, flying all over the globe or sliding through the traffic in his Jaguar, with Susan in the background of his activities as miserable and adoring as ever. She thinks, 'If only he . . .'

(ii) Jealousy. Off duty, Matthew is revealed as being not entirely blind to the charms of the opposite sex – at times, almost wolfish, in fact – for we see him skilfully embracing another conventionally attractive, but in this case noticeably sulky female. Susan thinks, 'He's got eyes only for Marcia', and from the looks of it, he certainly has.

(iii) The 'flashback' – to scenes of childhood or teenage courtship when Susan and Matthew were innocently unaware that the seeds of love were being planted. (Marcia, of course, is in the background, in a gym slip, waiting her turn). Susan is now clutching desperately some carefully treasured souvenir – a cigarette card or a bag of marbles perhaps, that he once gave her – and she thinks, 'If only he . . .'

(iv)

(v)

(iv) Another gambit is the picture of Susan and her present makeshift boyfriend, a working-class lad of undistinguished appearance, who looks as if he needs a correspondence course in conversation skills. Susan thinks, 'What a drip he is compared to Matthew. If . . .' She obviously prefers riding in a Jaguar to sitting on the pillion of a motor bike.

(v) Susan may, perhaps, discover that Matthew is not such a marvel after all. In which case she is allowed the pleasure of refusing his hand in preference for her 'temporary' boy friend who now turns out to be noticeably more handsome from picture to picture.

Whatever the means of developing the story, Susan, like the Canadian Mountie, is bound to get her man in the end.

In real life, girls often do marry the man of their choice, and in doing so they may experience that elation and joy which is described as 'being in love'. It is a genuine feeling that ought not to be dismissed lightly or to be sneered at cynically. In love comics, however, it is nearly always falsified and cheapened, thereby arousing in the mind of the reader an entirely misleading conception of love and happiness in courtship and marriage.

In the first place, the choice of a partner ought not to be based exclusively upon income and status. Just as surely as people who are not good-looking and are without wealth may experience deep feelings of love, in some circumstances good looks, great wealth and high social status may be a barrier to happiness. Far too often in these stories, love is equated with passion of a very superficial kind. There is rarely any tenderness and warmth, or discovery and revelation of some delightful aspect of the other person's character. The stories are too brief and simplified for that. Instead there is an undue emphasis on jealousy, often over the most trivial matters, which is presented as something inevitable and acceptable in a boy-and-girl relationship.

The awakening of love in the breast of the hero occurs in a most mysterious and baffling fashion. Almost as if he had suddenly acquired a set of perspex lenses, he notices that the heroine is desirable. In the lovers' quarrels, the hero's inconsiderate and sometimes brutal disregard of the girl's feelings is in sharp contrast to the way she throws herself at his feet. There is very little attempt to suggest that it is admirable for a girl to have independence of spirit, dignity of manner, or capability of intellect in her relationships with the opposite sex. It is implied that girls should have no other interest in life than the pursuit of men, and that most of the time it is expected that she should wait around in a melancholy state until the man decides that he would like to settle down happily with an uninteresting and easily dominated girl like this. Happiness in marriage is there not for the taking but the making.

It happened like this . . .

'**C**an I help you, young lady?'
Sue jumped and turned to find Alan Evans towering over her.

'No – no, just looking thanks.'

Sue could feel she had just flushed eight shades of crimson and the more she thought about it, the redder she grew. Now it matched her T-shirt. Of course, she had no intention of buying anything at all.

Alan was the assistant manager of Shreads Boutique. He'd worked there since he'd left school, two years ahead of Sue. It seemed as if all the girls had fancied him then. He was tall and athletic. His dark hair had one of those fringes that fell mysteriously across one eye whenever he spoke to anyone shorter than himself.

The much-disliked bully about town, Jennifer Jarvis, once went out with him because she reckoned he looked like Bryan Ferry. She still claims to have chucked him first, but the truth is, he couldn't take much more of her bossiness so he put his foot down.

Despite his obvious appeal it was only recently Sue found herself compelled to visit Shreads every Saturday, under the pretence of 'Just looking.'

'I see you round here quite a lot these days,' Alan said. Sue didn't know what to say to that.

Just Seventeen
December 1983.

'**N**ERVOUS, Lyddie?' Brian, our manager, leaned across from the front seat of the car and took my hand, giving it a squeeze. I tried to smile back at him, but it was an effort, especially when the landscape all around me was becoming more and more familiar with every mile we covered.

Home . . . How long had it been? Nearly a year now, I calculated; a year since I'd seen my family, the friends I'd left behind and, especially, Martin . . .

I could still remember the shock and scorn in my mother's voice the day I'd told her I was leaving home to join a rock band. 'A rock band, darling? Don't be ridiculous! I've never heard such nonsense in my life!' she protested, gazing anxiously at my father for support.

'Oh, let her go,' Dad had said indulgently, smiling at me as though I were a little kid. 'It's only a phase. She'll grow out of it and come running home soon enough, when she hasn't got enough money for a decent meal.'

'But just think of the kind of people she'll be mixing with!' Mum argued. 'All those hippies and drug addicts and degenerates . . . I don't like to think of our daughter mixing with people like that. Anyway, what on earth will all our friends think?'

True Magazine
February 1984

'**A**NNE!' The slim, fair-haired man in the light grey jacket quickened his pace to catch up with me. 'It is Anne, isn't it?' he enquired eagerly.

It took me a moment to place him – and, when I did, my friendly smile faded. 'Hello, Roger. Have you been to meet Abigail again?' I greeted him flatly.

Amusement glinted in his eyes. 'Not round here. This is far too near home!' he replied with a chuckle.

'Yes, it would be,' I agreed, bitingly sarcastic, but he was unperturbed by my obvious coldness towards him.

'I'm just going to lunch.' He paused for a moment. 'Maybe you'd care to join me?'

'No, I would not!' I responded vehemently.

He cocked his head to one side and smiled winningly. 'Please, Anne . . . ,' he wheedled. 'I hate to eat alone.'

I hesitated for a moment, recalling all the things I'd promised myself I'd say to him if I ever met him alone. 'All right,' I accepted grudgingly, 'but I can't stay for long.'

True Magazine
February 1984

Sometimes it happens

And sometimes it happens that you are friends and then
You are not friends,
And friendship has passed.
And whole days are lost and among them
A fountain empties itself.

And sometimes it happens that you are loved and then
You are not loved,
And love is past.
And whole days are lost and among them
A fountain empties itself into the grass.

And sometimes you want to speak to her and then
You do not want to speak,
Then the opportunity has passed.
Your dreams flare up, they suddenly vanish.

And also it happens that there is nowhere to go and then
There is somewhere to go,
Then you have bypassed.
And the years flare up and are gone,
Quicker than a minute.

So you have nothing.
You wonder if these things matter and then
As soon as you begin to wonder if these things matter
They cease to matter,
And caring is past.
And a fountain empties itself into the grass.

Brian Patten

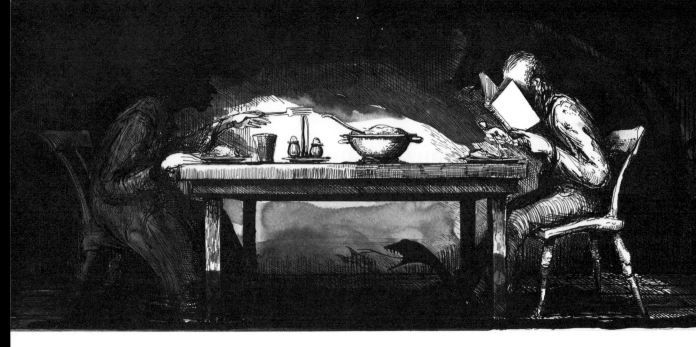

Breakfast time

FIRST VOICE: In the blind-drawn dark dining-room of School House, dusty and echoing as a dining-room in a vault, Mr and Mrs Pugh are silent over cold grey cottage pie. Mr Pugh reads, as he forks the shroud meat in, from *Lives of the Great Poisoners*. He has bound a plain brown-paper cover round the book. Slyly, between slow mouthfuls, he sidespies up at Mrs Pugh, poisons her with his eye, then goes on reading. He underlines certain passages and smiles in secret.

MRS PUGH: Persons with manners do not read at table,

FIRST VOICE: says Mrs Pugh. She swallows a digestive tablet as big as a horse-pill, washing it down with clouded peasoup water. (*Pause*)

MRS PUGH: Some persons were brought up in pigsties.

MR PUGH: Pigs don't read at table, dear.

FIRST VOICE: Bitterly she flicks dust from the broken cruet. It settles on the pie in a thin gnat-rain.

MR PUGH: Pigs can't read, my dear.

MRS PUGH: I know one who can.

FIRST VOICE: Alone in the hissing laboratory of his wishes, Mr Pugh minces among bad vats and jeroboams, tiptoes through spinneys of murdering herbs, agony dancing in his crucibles, and mixes especially for Mrs Pugh a venomous porridge unknown to toxicologists which will scald and viper through her until her ears fall off like figs, her toes grow big and black as balloons, and steam comes screaming out of her navel.

MR PUGH: You know best, dear,

FIRST VOICE: says Mr Pugh, and quick as a flash he ducks her in rat soup.

MRS PUGH: What's that book by your trough, Mr Pugh?

MR PUGH: It's a theological work, my dear. *Lives of the Great Saints*.

Dylan Thomas   *Under Milk Wood*

A poison tree

I was angry with my friend:
I told my wrath, my wrath did end.
I was angry with my foe:
I told it not, my wrath did grow.

And I water'd it in fears,
Night and morning with my tears;
And I sunnèd it with smiles,
And with soft deceitful wiles.

And it grew both day and night,
Till it bore an apple bright;
And my foe beheld it shine,
And he knew that it was mine,

And into my garden stole
When the night had veiled the pole:
In the morning, glad I see
My foe outstretched beneath the tree.

William Blake

Assignments

Title page (22)

Look at the quotations on page 22. Choose the one that you agree with or disagree with most, or that makes you angry or laugh, or that you find most striking for some other reason. Think about your reaction and then write brief notes describing and explaining it.

Personal writing

Write a short piece commenting on the ways in which different people react to the word *love*.

Song (23)

Behind this poem there is a *relationship*. Think about the poem and work out what you think that relationship must have been like. Ask yourself questions such as:
1 How did these two people meet?
2 Were they both attracted to each other at first?
3 If so, how did things begin to go wrong?
4 Why does the writer sound so hopeless now?

Narrative writing

Write a story based on the relationship described in the poem.

Sonnet (23)

The first twelve lines of this poem don't seem very complimentary. The writer says that his mistress' hair is like wire, her breath reeks and her voice is unmusical – among other things. The key to all this is in the last two lines.
1 The last line is difficult, but becomes easier, if you replace the original words as follows:

she	by	girl
belied		wrongly described
compare		comparison

2 So what do the last two lines mean?
3 How does this explain the way in which the poet talks of his mistress in the first twelve lines?

Writing dialogue

Write a conversation between two men or two women about a person of the opposite sex. One of the speakers is like the writer of this poem and the other is like the people he or she is satirizing.

Love is a many-splendoured thing (24)

Personal writing

Not everyone would agree with either what Grandad or what Janet has to say. Study their opinions carefully and choose some that you agree or disagree with strongly. Write your views, explaining why you hold them.

Strip-cartoon romances (26)	1 In the second part of the article the writer gives a number of reasons to explain why he objects to strip-cartoon romances. Make a list of them. 2 Do you think that the readers of these magazines come to believe that love and marriage are really like the stories they read? 3 If you do not agree, why not? 4 If you do agree, what, if anything, do you think should be done? **Narrative writing** Make up captions for the story illustrated on pages 26–27, and then invent a conclusion.
It happened like this . . . (28)	One of the criticisms of stories like these is that they are full of clichés: **Cliché:** a word or expression that has lost much of its force through over-exposure Examples of clichés from the third story are: . . . he enquired eagerly . . . . . . I greeted him flatly . . . . . . bitingly sarcastic . . . . . . and smiled winningly . . . 1 Find similar examples from the other two extracts and list them. 2 Explain why you think they are clichés. **Narrative writing** Either continue one of the extracts imitating the writer's style, or write a similar story of your own.
Sometimes it happens (29)	1 Read the poem letting the words and images work in your head. 2 Jot down on a piece of paper all the thoughts and ideas that occur to you about the poem. 3 Read the poem again and write down any further ideas you have. **Personal writing** Organize your ideas into a written expression of your reaction to the poem.
Breakfast time (30)	1 Read the dialogue through and note which words are actually spoken aloud by Mr and Mrs Pugh. 2 Observe how the writer lets us know their thoughts *and the moments at which he does so*. 3 What effect do you think the author was trying to achieve by putting speech and thoughts side by side in this way? Is he successful? **Writing dialogue** Either write another conversation between Mr and Mrs Pugh – on a different occasion – or copy this technique to write a similar 'speech and thoughts' conversation of your own.
A poison tree (31)	Explain in your own words what you think this poem is saying about friendship, anger, and hatred.

HOW IT ALL BEGAN..

In 1886, a new flavoured syrup went on sale at Jacob's Pharmacy, Atlanta, Georgia. The syrup was the invention of John S. Pemberton, a pharmacist whose other products included 'French Wine Cola – Ideal Nerve Tonic'.

Legend has it that fizzy water was accidentally added to the syrup instead of plain water, and so Coca-Cola's potential as a soft drink was discovered.

Pepsi-Cola appeared a few years later. The syrup was also the invention of a pharmacist, Caleb D. Bradham of North Carolina, and was first known as 'Brad's Drink'. In 1898 Bradham renamed it Pepsi-Cola.

Since those early days, many other cola drinks have come onto the market, and colas are sold all over the world.

WHERE COLA COMES FROM

Cola extract comes from the nut of the cola tree. The tree is native to West Africa but is grown in other parts of the world too. Cola extract has a bitter taste because the nuts contain caffeine.

WHERE THE 'COCA' COMES FROM

Flavour prepared from the coca leaf was used in the original Coca-Cola. Minute traces of cocaine may have been present in the early days, but soon after 1900 steps were taken to make sure that any such traces were removed from the flavour.

WHAT MOST COLA DRINKS ARE MADE OF

FIZZY WATER (water and carbon dioxide. About 90%, though, of course, it's not shown in proportion here).

SUGAR (about 5 to 11%) and/or **ARTIFICIAL SWEETENERS**.

CARAMEL (for colour).

FLAVOURING (including cola nut extract).

ACID (usually phosphoric).

EXTRA CAFFEINE

Preservatives and **other permitted additives** may be included.

The exact flavouring that goes into cola drinks is a closely guarded secret among manufacturers. You probably won't see cola extract mentioned on the label. That comes under the heading 'flavouring' and manufacturers don't have to be any more specific than that. All cola drinks should contain some cola extract. If they don't, they should be labelled 'cola flavour' drink. Other things used for flavouring cola drinks include citrus oils, vanilla, and spices like cinammon and nutmeg.

WILL COLA DRINKS HARM YOUR TEETH?

Dentists worry about cola drinks because of the sugar and acid they contain.

The colas in our tests contained up to 11 per cent sugar. Sugar promotes tooth decay. It does this because the bacteria in dental plaque feed on sugar and produce acids. (Plaque is a sticky film that forms on the surface of teeth.) These acids attack the enamel surface of the tooth and eventually break through and cause decay. But cola only stays in your mouth for a short time. Chewy toffees and biscuits, for example, stick to the teeth and so the sugar in them has longer to do its damage.

Even if you choose a sugar-free cola instead of a 'normal' one, your teeth will still be under attack, from the acid in cola drinks. Phosphoric acid is the usual one used – it adds flavour and 'bite'! Acid erodes enamel, although erosion is a very slow process.

The more frequently you drink cola, the more damage you'll do to your teeth. So that's one reason for not drinking too much. But you can reduce the damage by going for a cola that's very low in sugar or sugar-free.

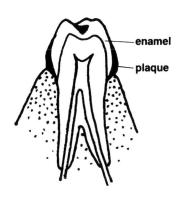

- enamel
- plaque

ARTIFICIAL SWEETENERS

In low calorie colas all or nearly all the sugar is replaced by artificial sweeteners. Until last year the only one allowed was saccharin. Now some others are allowed, including aspartame which you'll find in some colas.

Aspartame shouldn't be used by the few people who suffer from a rare illness called *phenylketonuria*. But the UK government says that aspartame is safe for everyone else, despite controversial claims to the contrary.

Aspartame is said to leave less of an aftertaste than saccharin, but our own taste tests were inconclusive.

HOW MUCH SUGAR THEY CONTAIN

We analysed 18 different brands of cola to see how much sugar they contained. Five of these were low calorie colas. The results are shown below. As a rough guide one level teaspoon of sugar = 4.9gm.

One gram of sugar contains 4 Calories. The calorie content of low calorie colas is usually given on the label.

Sugar (gm) per 170ml (6fl oz) glass*	
Coca-Cola	17
Diet Coca-Cola	—
Corona Coola Cola	17
Fine Fare Cola	17
Fine Fare Low Calorie Cola	2
Fine Fare Yellow Pack Cola	9
Pepsi-Cola	18
Diet Pepsi-Cola	—
Rola Cola	13
Sainsbury's Cola Drink	19
Sainsbury's Caffeine Free Cola Drink	18
Spar Economy Cola	10
Spar Sparkling Cola	8
Tesco Sparkling Cola	10
Tesco Sparkling Low Calorie Cola	2
Waitrose Cola Drink	16
Waitrose Low Calorie Cola Drink	2
Wells Cola	10

(*Amounts based on those found in our samples)

CAFFEINE IN COLA DRINKS

West Africans have been known to chew cola nuts for their stimulating effect since the eighteenth century. The reason for this effect is that cola nuts contain caffeine. Extra caffeine is added, too, to cola drinks. Other popular drinks throughout the world, like tea and coffee, also contain caffeine.

Caffeine keeps you alert, but too much can cause sleeplessness in some people. Several questions have been raised over the long term effects of caffeine on health. But recent work suggests that, in moderation, caffeine won't do you any harm.

You still might want to know how much caffeine there is in different brands of cola. We analysed 17 colas to find out. Right, we show how much each contained.

This compares with about 85mg of caffeine in a cup of coffee, 50mg in tea, and 5mg in cocoa, all depending on the strength of the brew.

If you want to avoid caffeine altogether, you can buy caffeine-free cola. We found two: Sainsbury's, and the new Energen One-Cal. New Energen One-Cal Cola came onto the market too late to be included in our taste tests.

Caffeine (mg) per 170ml (6fl oz) glass*

Coca-Cola	15
Diet Coca-Cola	15
Corona Coola Cola	16
Fine Fare Cola	14
Fine Fare Low Calorie Cola	14
Fine Fare Yellow Pack Cola	12
Pepsi-Cola	8
Diet Pepsi-Cola	10
Rola Cola	11
Sainsbury's Cola Drink	15
Spar Economy Cola	14
Spar Sparkling Cola	20
Tesco Sparkling Cola	14
Tesco Sparkling Low Calorie Cola	15
Waitrose Cola Drink	10
Waitrose Low Calorie Cola Drink	7
Wells Cola	11

(*Amounts based on those found in our samples. These should only be used as a guide, as caffeine content may vary within colas of the same brand.)

THE COLAS WE TESTED

All the colas we included in our taste tests were bought in either 1, 1½ or 2 litre plastic bottles. We did this to minimise any effect that type or size of container might have on fizziness and taste. But some supermarkets use more than one manufacturer for their own-brand cola, and the cola that goes into a 330ml can, for example, may be different from that inside a plastic litre bottle. Our taste tests, and the sugar and caffeine analyses, were carried out on the plastic bottles listed.

Brand	size of bottle
Coca-Cola	1.5l
Diet Coca-Cola	1.5l
Corona Coola Cola	1l
Fine Fare Cola	1l
Fine Fare Low Calorie Cola	1l
Fine Fare Yellow Pack Cola	1.5l
Pepsi-Cola	1.5l
Diet Pepsi-Cola	1.5l
Rola Cola	2l
Sainsbury's Cola Drink	1l
Sainsbury's Caffeine Free Cola Drink	1l
Spar Economy Cola	1.5l
Spar Sparkling Cola	1l
Tesco Sparkling Cola	1.5l
Tesco Sparkling Low Calorie Cola	1.5l
Waitrose Cola Drink	1l
Waitrose Low Calorie Cola Drink	1l
Wells Cola	1l

THE RESULTS

We set out to see how our panel would compare different types of cola – 'normal' cola, low calorie cola, and caffeine-free cola – and how they would compare different brands. But our panel didn't find any big differences. No one type or brand of cola came out well above or well below average on any of the individual characteristics we asked about, or on preference. Our panel preferred Pepsi-Cola slightly above average, and Spar Sparkling Cola and Fine Fare Low Calorie Cola slightly less than average.

But the differences weren't great. **So even if your family claims a preference for one of the more expensive brands, why not give them a cheaper one to try?**

HOW WE DID OUR TASTE TESTS

We asked 50 cola drinkers from our specially selected taste panel in Hertfordshire to try 18 different colas. Over half our tasters were teenagers, and the rest were between 20 and 35 years old. We gave each taster two cola samples at a time, in coded beakers. We asked them if either left an aftertaste, and if they could tell a difference between the two colas. If they could, they were asked to assess the two colas for sweetness, flavour, fizziness, bitterness and body. We also asked them which of the two they preferred. All the drinks were served at the same temperature, and to make sure none of the drinks went flat between tastings, we used new bottles each time.

DIFFERENT PRICES YOU CAN PAY

The biggest selling colas in this country are Coca-Cola (about 50 per cent of the market) and Pepsi-Cola (about 17 per cent). But there are many other, cheaper brands. Here's our price list for 18 different colas.

Generally, our price surveys show that for each brand, the bigger the size you buy the cheaper each glass will cost.

Brand	Biggest size available	Target price*	Price per 170ml (6fl oz) glass
Coca-Cola	2l	69p	5.9p
Diet Coca-Cola	1.5l	59p	6.7p
Corona Coola Cola	2l	62p	5.3p
Fine Fare Cola	1l	33½p	5.7p
Fine Fare Low Calorie Cola	1l	34½p	5.9p
Fine Fare Yellow Pack Cola	2l	45p	3.8p
Pepsi-Cola	2l	65p	5.5p
Diet Pepsi-Cola	1.5l	54p	6.1p
Rola Cola	2l	42p	3.6p
Sainsbury's Cola Drink	2l	52p	4.4p
Sainsbury's Caffeine Free Cola Drink	1l	29p	4.9p
Spar Economy Cola	1.5l	36p	4.1p
Spar Sparkling Cola	2l	49p	4.2p
Tesco Sparkling Cola	2l	49p	4.2p
Tesco Sparkling Low Calorie Cola	1.5l	39p	4.4p
Waitrose Cola Drink	2l	52p	4.4p
Waitrose Low Calorie Cola Drink	1l	29p	4.9p
Wells Cola	2l	42p	3.6p

(*Prices are based on a survey carried out in May 1984.)

Which? *August 1984*

Assignments

1   After reading the information on pages 34–37, which brand of cola would you buy, and for what reasons?

2   Write a short informative article based on the information in this unit, entitled *What is cola?*

3   In what ways could drinking cola be harmful to your health, and how serious are the risks? Write a short report entitled *Cola and health.*

4   Find advertisements for cola drinks in/on newspapers, magazines, hoardings, radio, and TV.
Think about how the advertisements try to sell the product. In the light of the *Which?* report, what do you think of these advertisements?

Trust

Lynne Reid Banks

At the time of this story I was living in Canada. It was towards the end of the Second World War, and I was nearly sixteen – a rather uncomfortable mixture of child and woman, Canadian and English. My mother and I had been evacuated five years before to Saskatoon, Saskatchewan – euphemistically known as the Hub City of the Prairies – and had only during the last two grown accustomed to the flat sameness of the wheatfields, the vast space between towns broken by the stark, jutting grain elevators, white in the dry clear air.

We had even grown fond of Saskatoon itself; but it was always with relief that we escaped, during the baking hot months of the summer holidays, to one of the scattered lakes north of Prince Albert. Pushed like thumb-prints into the all-but-unexplored Northern forest, the sheltered rims of these lakes accommodated occasional groups of log cabins in which farmers, woodsmen and summer visitors shared the peace and beauty of the woods with the teeming wild life that belonged there.

In these magic surroundings we used to spend the long summer days in the open air, swimming and canoeing, walking, reading, or just lying dreaming in the sun. In the evenings the three-foot pine logs would burn with their blue flames and sweet smell, and we would sit and talk, listening to the piano students playing in the next cabin and the bitterns creaking in the reeds, or watch the fireflies, millions of them, dancing in the fringe of trees between our porch and the Lake, which was always a bright, luminous grey after the unbelievable sunset colours had faded.

That last summer before we returned to England was particularly enchanted. For one thing, I was in love for the first time. No one will ever convince me that one cannot be in love at fifteen. I loved then as never since, with all my heart and without doubts or reservations or artifice. Or at least, that is how I loved by the end of the summer. When we left for the Lake in June, it was all just beginning.

My boyfriend worked in Saskatoon, but the Lake was 'his place' – the strange and beautiful wilderness drew him with an obsessive urgency, so I cannot claim it was only to see me that he got on his motor-cycle as many Fridays as he possibly could, and drove three hundred-odd miles along the pitted prairie roads to spend the weekend with us.

Sometimes he couldn't come, and then the joy would go out of everything until Monday, when I could start looking forward to Friday again. He could never let us know in advance, as we were too far from civilization to have a phone or even a telegraph service, so that it wasn't until noon on Saturdays that I had to give up hope. Three hundred miles in those conditions is quite a journey. Besides, Don was hard up, and sometimes worked overtime at weekends.

But except for those lost and empty Saturdays and Sundays, I was deliriously happy. So happy that I began to think, for the first time in years, quite a lot about God. After Don had managed to come for several consecutive weekends, I came to the conceited conclusion that God was taking personal care of me. I talked to Him as if to a companion, and somewhere in that maze of hot, contemplative days, when God, or nature, or whatever you care to call the abstract Power of the world, seemed almost tangibly close, I conceived the idea that if I posed a direct question the first answer that came into my mind would be the correct one.

The childishness of this faith-game is easy to deride now; the fact remains that it worked. I used to try it out on simple things; 'Will it rain tomorrow?' 'Will there be a letter from England today?' – and, most often of all, 'Will Don come this week?' At first I used to be a little confused by the jumble of negative and affirmative thoughts that would rush through my mind, but after a while there would be a little space of whirling blankness, and then a yes or a no would flash forth quite clearly, and if it ever proved wrong, I don't remember it. Except for the last time.

One Monday morning I was sitting at the end of our little canoe-jetty with one foot trailing in the warm water, watching the tiny fish prodding at it inquisitively with their transparent noses, when my mother came down to me, stepping over the gaping holes in the planking.

'Did you borrow a five-dollar bill out of my cash-box?' she asked.

'No . . .' I replied, stirring idly with my foot and watching the little fish flicker away.

'Funny,' she said. 'I must have put it somewhere else.'

She went away, and I lay back on the planking, feeling it warm and rough through my shirt, and behind my sun-baked eyelids relived the past two days, moment by moment. After a while, my mother came back. Her hollow footsteps behind me had a worried urgency that made me sit up.

'I can't find it,' she said. There was a little knot of muscles between her eyebrows.

'I'll come and help you look.'

'It's no good,' she said, pushing me back. 'I remember now, I *did* put it in the box. There's nowhere else it could be.'

'Well, what's happened to it?'

'I don't know,' she said. She stood beside me, frowning across the bright, flat water.

I should explain that Don was not the only person who used to visit us. We had many friends, and weekends at the Lake during the heat of July were considered well worth the long train journey and the uncomfortable truck ride involved in reaching us. Lots of local people used to pop in too, as well as neighbours from nearby cabins. During the weekend just past, there had been a good half-dozen people on the premises besides Don.

I find it quite impossible to this day to understand why the thought that Don might have taken the five dollars should even have crossed my mind. But it did, and at once a cold pall of self-loathing fell on me. I shivered in the glittering heat, and my mother bent and put her arm round me.

'Don't worry, darling,' she said. 'We can't be sure anyone took it.'

'But they're all friends,' I mumbled. What had occurred to me would never in a hundred years have occurred to her; she would as soon have suspected *me* of stealing as Don. She said: 'Anyone could have come in and taken it while we were over at the reef.' But there were no strangers, and she knew it. The lakeside population is a tiny, isolated community, which no tramps or wanderers ever invade.

Five dollars was a respectable sum to us in those days, with only our meagre allowance from England to live on. But my mother was never one to cry over spilt milk, and she told me to forget all about it.

But I couldn't. I think it was guilt at that flash of involuntary disloyalty that kept the thing alive in my mind. I hated myself for giving it a first thought, let alone a second, and as the days went by the silly, groundless suspicion grew, and my guilt with it, the one feeding the other. The happiness of our surroundings was utterly spoilt, and so was the former delight of forward-looking; I felt I couldn't look Don in the face again, and almost dreaded the coming weekend. And yet I could not shake off this feeling of doubt, which lay on my spirit like a guilty burden.

At first I refused to apply my newly found 'test', because to do so would be to admit the doubt to myself, at a time when I was still desperately trying to pretend it was not there at all; and then, when I reached the stage of having to admit it, I was afraid to 'ask' because I knew I would believe the answer.

But by Friday I was so wretched in my self-created hell that I could bear it no longer. I went away by myself onto the shore; the evening air was unusually heavy, and the placid water had an almost ominous beauty. I stood looking at the dying sunset, beyond the trees' ragged silhouette. It was beautiful – too beautiful for me, at that moment. I didn't feel fit to look at it. I started to cry in great, dry sobs, and suddenly I said aloud:

'Did Don take the five dollars?'

And the answer came quite clearly, 'Yes.'

The storm broke with the uncanny abruptness of all weather changes in that land of extremes. One minute the accentuated reds and lemons of the sunset were smeared across the west; the next, the blackness of thunderclouds had obliterated them, and the leaden bowl of the sky was fissured with lightning which spread in infinite detail, like the veins of a leaf. It vanished, leaving me blinking in the sudden darkness; then came the thunder, and the next second the flat face of the lake was dancing in angry peaks and the pines were lashing like whips.

I tried not to expect Don that night. I felt that my thoughts might have communicated themselves to him somehow, and that, sensing my treachery, he wouldn't come. But it was ironic that, convinced, irrationally, as I now was, of his guilt, I should nevertheless have longed to see him as I never had before.

I lay in bed under the sloping roof of the cabin and listened to the rain beating like multiple hammers over my head, feeling the wind shake the cabin to its foundations with one ferocious impact after another, watching the black square of window light up with blinding suddenness and frequency. Once I got up and stood looking out over the treetops, shivering; when the flashes came, they showed the solid forest swaying with the flexibility of a wheatfield.

I experienced a loneliness of spirit unequalled by anything I have felt since. My strange betrayal hurt in a sharp and basic way which would be impossible now, through the layers of self-protective insulation the years have laid on my heart.

I crawled back into bed, trying to close my throat against the tears. But when my mother, prompted by the sweet deep affinity between us, came in to me, she kissed my cheek and found it wet.

'Don't cry, sweetie,' she said softly. 'He may still come.'

'I don't want him to!' I sobbed before I could stop myself, and when, startled, she drew back and said 'But why?' I had to lie, and say it was because I was afraid for him, riding through the storm over bad roads which the rain would now have reduced to sheets of yellow mud.

When she had tucked me in and gone, the lie became true. I lay thinking about the very real danger of those roads . . . you couldn't walk along them safely after heavy rain; your feet would slip from under you on the crude camber. Would he have enough sense to stop and wait until the storm ended? But the roads in Northern Canada are not like the friendly well-populated English ones, where there is always a town or at least a farmhouse within walking distance. You can travel a hundred miles with nothing but the rough road itself to show that you are not the first human being to go that way.

I imagined Don fighting the storm, unwilling to stop in the middle of some sodden wilderness. The strength of the wind buffeting the cabin made the motor-bike, which had always looked to me so heavy and solid, seem in my frightened thoughts frail enough to be blown onto its side by the first gust that struck it. I thought of Don pinned under it, skidding, his face pressed into the yellow clay; I saw the rain beating onto the stillness of his young neck above his leather jacket; I heard the coughing of the disabled machine above the fury of the storm.

It was hours later, when I had relived the scene a hundred times, that I suddenly realized the sound of the roaring engine was real. The storm was dying; the wind was no more than a sullen, spasmodic growl through the trees and a steady patter of rain on the roof. I lay absolutely still, relief and pain fighting for ascendancy within me, each in itself overwhelming enough to freeze the breath in my lungs as I heard Don's heavy, tired footsteps on the wooden stairs.

He stood in the open doorway. The faint early-dawn light from the window gleamed on his wet black hair, his wet face and the streaming, shiny jacket. He stood for a long moment, his breath labouring, not knowing whether I was awake or asleep. His arms hung wearily at his sides; I could make out his stooped shoulders and hear the faint tapping as water ran off him onto the plank floor.

Then I whispered to him, and stretched out my hand. He came and bent over me, pressing his cold wet face against my hot one. The rain from his hair dripped onto my pillow. He tried to keep my hands under the bedclothes, saying 'No, you'll get so wet –' laughing under his breath, holding my hands down with one hand and trying to struggle out of his soaking jacket. But I got free and threw my arms round his neck, pulling him down to me, and he gave in. I felt the wet stiffness of the jacket through my thin pyjamas; his hands, freezing cold, held me close; his icy wet ear was against my cheek, his lips pressed on my shoulder . . . The guilt and the doubt broke up all at once within me, the way the solid surface of the frozen Saskatchewan River breaks up in the spring. The released water rushes along, carrying its broken bonds of ice along in a crashing torrent. That was the sort of *exulting* freedom I felt now I knew the absolute stupidity of my fears.

Most truths are learned gradually, through many small lessons. But the truth about love – or one of the truths, for there are many, and none is absolute except for the person for whom it is real – came rushing in on me in that wet, close, relieving moment. It was this: that it isn't until you have truly doubted someone that you can truly and finally believe in them.

'Don –' I whispered, into his cold ear, all my recent fear in my voice.

'Fathead,' he whispered back tenderly. 'You know I can drive Matilda through an earthquake . . . Go to sleep.' He dried my face with a distant corner of the sheet, turned my pillow over to the dry side, and tucked the bedclothes snugly round me. My hands kept creeping out to touch him, and he kept firmly pushing them back into the warmth. 'Close your eyes,' he ordered. When I did, the long exhaustion swept over me blackly. I fell asleep half-way through his kiss.

The next morning the sun shone brilliantly from a cloudless sky. The Lake was a sheet of luminous glass, and every pineneedle glistened in its cleanness like a shred of green silk. From the earth rose an overwhelming smell of bruised freshness.

The three of us sat on the wired-in porch and drank our morning coffee, watched our almost-tame chipmunks rejoicing on the steaming woodpile, and laughed at the awfulness of the night behind us. My mother, too, it seemed, had lain awake letting her imagination run riot until she heard Don arrive. And the drive, for all Don's pretended nonchalance, had been no pleasure-trip.

'Was it raining when you left Saskatoon?' I asked, and when he said it had been, heaven's hardest, I burst out 'Oh, then why did you come? You needn't have. It was too dangerous . . .'

He pooh-poohed this, and repeated that Matilda could weather the raging Atlantic if she had to. 'Besides,' he added after a moment, 'I *had* to come this weekend.'

Before I could ask why, my mother asked us if we'd walk up to the store for the groceries. It was a rhetorical question; we were holding hands and

looking at each other, and she could see it didn't matter to us what we did, so long as we were together. She went into the living-room to collect money and her shopping list. While she was gone, I noticed that Don's eyes had black rings under them; the expression on his face was sober and grown-up. He started to tell me something and then kissed me instead, leaning across the coffee-cups. The sun was blissfully warm on my closed eyelids and on our clasped hands.

My mother called me. Her voice had a funny note in it.

I went in to her. My eyes, unused to the darkness inside the cabin, could not see how she looked; but she was holding the moneybox.

'Look,' she said, holding it out to me.

Inside, lying on top of some one-dollar bills and small change, was another bill for five dollars.

'It's back!' I exclaimed. 'How funny! When do you suppose that could have happened?'

'It wasn't there last night,' she said. She sounded as if her throat were dry.

I laughed at her. 'What nonsense!' I said. 'It must have been. Nobody's been in the house since last night, except us and Don. I'll bet it's been there the whole time.' She didn't answer, and I went on: 'Well, come on, let's have the list and we'll be off before it gets too hot.'

She handed me the list in silence, and then picked out the five-dollar bill. She held it a moment, as if in doubt about giving it to me; impatient to get back to Don I almost grabbed it from her hand, kissed her, and ran back onto the sun-flooded porch.

Don had his back to me. He was hunched up a little, staring with concentration into his empty coffee-cup. As I stood looking down at him, feeling the sun's warmth glowing on my skin like a blessing, I thought: to love someone is lovely, but incomplete. It's trust that rounds love out, making it perfect. I thought of my child's asking game, and shrugged tolerantly at myself as I had been yesterday. I had the answers to all the questions now.

I dropped a kiss on the smooth black head. 'Come on,' I said. 'I've got five dollars. Let's go buy the world.'

Assignments

Thinking about the story

Immediate reactions

1 Write down your immediate reactions to the story. Don't bother about planning your writing – just write down your thoughts and feelings as they come to you.

2 *Without reading the story again*, answer these questions:
   a) What had happened to the five-dollar bill?
   b) Was she right to have trusted Don?
   c) What had she learned from this experience?

3 Is there anything about the story that you do not understand? If so, write down a list of questions that you would like to have answered.

Reading in more detail

Now read the story through again. As you read, try to answer the questions you wrote down for number 3 above. In addition, work out the answers to these questions:

1 What strikes you most about her descriptions of the places where she lived and had holidays?

2 What do you think she means when she says that she 'loved . . . without artifice'?

3 What was her 'faith-game'? What does it tell us about her age, her character and her ability to trust?

4 What does she think of herself as soon as she has the suspicion that it might have been Don who took the money?

5 After that she experiences conflicting thoughts and feelings. How would you describe them?

6 Why doesn't she try out the faith-game at this point?

7 Describe her feelings during the storm.

8 How do her emotions change as soon as she sees Don?

9 What has she learned about love from this?

10 At the end she says 'I had the answers to all the questions now.' Do you think she had?

Thinking about the author

The author says that this is a true story about herself. She tells the story in the first person as 'I'. But the author is clearly a much older, more experienced woman than the teenager she is writing about. How do you think she feels *now* about how she felt, thought, and acted *then*? In particular, how does her conclusion now about what had happened to the money compare with what she thought and felt then?

Writing from experience

Starting points

The starting point for this story was something that actually happened to the author. You may think that she was lucky to have travelled and had experiences that were 'easy to write about'. On the other hand, it's only the scenery in this story that is unusual. The experience she describes is common to many people. The quality of the story lies in the way in which she has described it.

Thinking and remembering

The author used the single word '*Trust*' to describe her main subject matter. Choose one of these words as your starting point:

betrayal   truth   despair   panic
loss   rejection   honesty   exhaustion

Think about your understanding of that word. Remember your own experiences of it. Recall as vividly as you can the occasions when you have really understood the meaning of that word *first hand*.

Preparatory writing

Now just **write**. Write about the experiences you have remembered. Don't worry about the order, or even if you are writing proper sentences. Just get down, as quickly as you can, everything you can remember about what you did, thought, and felt on those occasions.

First draft

Look at the preparatory writing you have done. Choose from it the idea or ideas that seem to you most promising. Now make up a story based on those ideas. It may be very close to something that really happened to you, or it may be completely invented. Tell your story. Use a first person narrator ('I'). Don't worry too much about the shape now – just tell your story as vividly and as convincingly as you can.

Polishing and rewriting

The next stage is best done after a gap, so that you can leave the first draft and then return to it later, when you have forgotten a little of what you wrote.

1 Read your first draft as if you were a reader to whom the whole story is new.

2 Make a note of things that need to be made clearer, more vivid, more detailed.

3 Think about the order in which you tell the story – should it be changed?

4 Does the story contain passages that go on too much about the same subject? Could these be cut down? Or removed altogether?

5 When you have made all the necessary alterations to your story, write out the final version of it.

3. *Who am I?*

1. ...THANK GOD IT'S FRIDAY. ONLY ONE MORE DAY OF PRETENDING TO BE NICE, SELLING ....

... for ten nights on the Costa del Sol. Very good value, only...

2. ... BORING HOLIDAYS...

.... a twenty-one-day cruise. All cabins are first-class, with...

3. ... To BORING PEOPLE...

... No, Tenerife isn't in Spain, it's...

4. ... WHO DON'T EVEN LISTEN TO A WORD YOU'RE SAYING...

5. ... IF ONLY I COULD JUST BE MYSELF FOR A WHILE...

Advertisement in
The Times,
12 October 1972

How sad it is to be a woman!
Nothing on earth is held so cheap.
Boys stand leaning at the door
Like Gods fallen out of Heaven.
Their hearts brave the Four Oceans,
The wind and dust of a thousand miles.
No one is glad when a girl is born:
By her the family sets no store.
When she grows up, she hides in her room
Afraid to look a man in the face.
No one cries when she leaves her home –
Sudden as clouds when the rain stops.
She bows her head and composes her face,
Her teeth are pressed on her red lips:
She bows and kneels countless times.
She must humble herself even to the servants.
His love is distant as the stars in Heaven,
Yet the sunflower bends towards the sun.
Their hearts more sundered than water and fire –
A hundred evils are heaped upon her.
Her face will follow the year's changes:
Her lord will find new pleasures.
They that were once like substance and shadow
Are now as far as Hu from Ch'in.
Yet Hu and Ch'in shall sooner meet
Than they whose parting is like Ts'an and Ch'en.

Anon

Bridges

Beatie Bryant was born and brought up in Norfolk, but has moved away to live and work in London. There she has met her boyfriend, Ronnie. She has returned to her parents' home where Ronnie is going to visit them. In the first extract she is telling her family about Ronnie. In the second it has become quite clear that Ronnie is not, after all going to arrive.

Extract A

BEATIE: Once I was in between jobs and I didn't think to ask for my unemployment benefit. *He* told me to. But when I asked they told me I was short on stamps and so I wasn't entitled to benefit. *I* didn't know what to say but he did. He went up and argued for me – he's just like his mother, she argues with everyone – and I got it. I didn't know how to talk see, it was all foreign to me. Think of it! An English girl born and bred and I couldn't talk the language – except for to buy food and clothes. And so sometimes when he were in a black mood he'd start on me. 'What can you talk of?' he'd ask. 'Go on, pick a subject. Talk. Use the language. Do you know what language is?' Well, I'd never thought before – hev you? – it's automatic to you isn't it, like walking? 'Well, language is words,' he'd say, as though he were telling me a secret. 'It's bridges, so that you can get safely from one place to another. And the more bridges you know about the more places you can see!' [*To* **Jimmy**] And do *you* know what happens when you can see a place but you don't know where the bridge is?

JIMMY: [*angrily*]: Blust gal, what the hell are you on about.

*   *   *   *

Extract B

BEATIE: Shall I tell you what Susie said when I went and saw her? She say she don't care if that ole atom bomb drop and she die – that's what she say. And you know why she say it? I'll tell you why, because if she had to care she'd have to do something about it and she find *that* too much effort. Yes she do. She can't be bothered – she's too bored with it all. That's what we all are – we're all too bored.

MRS BRYANT: Blust woman – bored you say, bored? You say Susie's bored, with a radio and television an' that? I go t'hell if she's bored!

BEATIE: Oh yes, we turn on a radio or a TV set maybe; or we go to the pictures – if them's love stories or gangsters – but isn't that the easiest way out? Anything so long as we don't have to make an effort. Well, am I right? You know I'm right. Education ent only books and music – it's asking questions, all the time. There are millions of us, all over the country, and no one, not one of us, is asking questions, we're all taking the easiest way out. Everyone I ever worked with took the easiest way out. We don't fight for anything, we're so mentally lazy we might as well be dead. Blust, we are dead! And you know what Ronnie say sometimes? He say it serves us right! That's what he say – it's our own bloody fault!

JIMMY: So that's us summed up then – so we know where *we* are then!

MRS BRYANT: Well if he don't reckon we count nor nothin', then it's as well he didn't come. There! It's as well he didn't come.

BEATIE: Oh, *he* thinks we count all right – living in mystic communion with nature. Living in mystic bloody communion with nature (indeed). But us count? Count Mother? I wonder. Do we? Do you think we really count? You don' wanna take any notice of what them ole papers say about the workers bein' all-important these days – that's all squit!

'Cos we aren't. Do you think when the really talented people in the country get to work they get to work for us? Hell if they do! Do you think they don't know we 'ont make the effort? The writers don't write thinkin' we can understand, nor the painters don't paint expecting us to be interested – that they don't, nor don't the composers give out music thinking we can appreciate it. 'Blust,' they say, 'the masses is too stupid for us to come down to them. Blust,' they say, 'if they don't make no effort why should we bother?' So you know who come along? The slop singers and the pop writers and the film makers and women's magazines and the Sunday papers and the picture strip love stories – that's who come along, and you don't have to make no effort for them, it come easy. 'We know where the money lie,' they say, 'hell we do! The workers've got it so let's give them what they want. If they want slop songs and film idols we'll give 'em that then. If they want words of one syllable, we'll give 'em that then. If they want the third-rate, *blust!* We'll give 'em *that* then. Anything's good enough for them 'cos they don't ask for no more!' The whole stinkin' commercial world insults us and we don't care a damn. Well, Ronnie's right – it's our own bloody fault. We want the third-rate – we got it! We got it! We got it! We . . .

[*Suddenly* **Beatie** *stops as if listening to herself. She pauses, turns with an ecstatic smile on her face* –]

D'you hear that? D'you hear it? Did you listen to me? I'm talking. Jenny, Frankie, Mother – I'm not quoting no more.

MRS BRYANT: [*getting up to sit at table*]: Oh hell, I hed enough of her – let her talk a while she'll soon get fed up.

[*The others join her at the table and proceed to eat and murmur*.]

BEATIE: Listen to me someone. [*As though a vision were revealed to her*] God in heaven, *Ronnie!* It does work, it's happening to me, I can feel it's happened, I'm beginning, on my own two feet – I'm beginning . . .

[*The murmur of the family sitting down to eat grows as* **Beatie**'s *last cry is heard. Whatever she will do they will continue to live as before. As* **Beatie** *stands alone, articulate at last* –]

THE CURTAIN FALLS

Arnold Wesker   *Roots*

The golden bough

As the interview progressed I became convinced that I would not get the job. My considerable experience of such events had made me almost preternaturally sensitive to the unspoken truths that lay behind their neutral formality, like snipers behind a battlement. In the early days, I had blamed myself for my failures: I must have been wearing an unacceptable jacket, there was a spot on my tie, I had interrupted a question on two occasions. I did my best to overcome my faults – careless dressing, over-eagerness, a certain insolent air of being too good for what was being offered. I became tidy, polite, humble. But the outcome of the interviews was still the same. So I decided to try arrogance. I went into the interview rooms with my hair deliberately unbrushed, my shoe-laces untied, the zipper of my fly left half-way down. I sneered at the suited, expressionless adversary across the desk, and told him what was wrong with his firm and what I would do about it, given two days and a free hand. Sometimes I snapped my fingers under his nose. My luck refused to change. Next I tried hypocrisy. I started making eloquent, testamentary statements to my inquisitors, vowing my eternal commitment to the great work of photocopying invoices, packaging bone-shaped dog biscuits, selling farm machinery, bottling a synthetic orange drink that, I was told, 'contained no harmful oranges.' My eyes goggling with sincerity, I pleaded for a chance to show my dedication to such work. It was never given to me. At length I despaired. I continued to go to the interviews, to prove that I was still alive, but I no longer expected anything. I was staring into the bland face of my latest interrogator – the same face I had seen behind a hundred such desks and above a hundred such blank white shirts – fully persuaded that I was about to fail yet again, when the reasons for all my troubles came into my head. It was so simple that I was furious with myself for not having seen it before.

The same face. At every interview the same bland features. It could not be – but it was. I was sure of that. And finally, unable to conceal my triumph, I came right out with it, 'It is you, isn't it?'

'I beg your pardon?' Frostily.

But I had no intention of letting him off the hook. 'It has always been you,' I insisted. 'I'm right. I know I am.'

His face changed, acquiring a sly, contemptuous look. 'Yes,' he admitted, not in the least abashed. 'Most of you fools never realize.'

'But why?'

He ignored my question. 'I'll say this for you,' he said reflectively. 'You've given me a busy life. Some people make it too easy; I like a challenge. Look at it from my point of view. I have to know in advance where you're going to turn up next. I always have to be one jump ahead, to make the proper arrangements, so that I can be here, behind these desks, when you walk in. There are nights when I get no sleep. Oh, yes. Credit where it's due.'

I wanted to ask how the proper arrangements were made, and other things, but I was sure he would not reply. Instead I said, 'Now that I've unmasked you, I suppose you'll go away and . . .'

'Don't bank on it,' he snapped. 'It makes no difference at all.'

'You've failed,' I taunted him. 'You'll lose your job, you'll be out on the scrap-heap like me, they'll probably assign an interviewer to deal with you!'

'This interview is concluded,' he told me, his face smooth and meaningless once again. 'I'm afraid I don't think you would be happy here, Mr . . . Mr . . .'

'Good-bye,' I crowed, sure of his defeat, filled with insane joy.

On the day of my next interview, I was still in a state of elation. I dressed neatly (I had decided to revert to this strategy for a while), and whistled in the lift as it carried me to the room in which I would have to duel for a job. When I was called into the room, it was as if I had been punched on the nose.

'Next!' The voice came through the half-open door, and I knew that I was finished. He did not permit himself the luxury of a smile when I entered. Every inch the professional, he began to comment on my curriculum vitae. I think that was when I realized that I would have to kill him.

I planned the murder for weeks, weeks during which I attended four more interviews with my merciless antagonist. At least, I tried to plan: but I could not think of a single way of doing the deed and getting away with it. There were desk diaries, letters, files. Everyone would know who had been in the room with him, even if I did manage to kill and flee without being caught. There were moments when I considered abandoning the scheme, but they passed, because I knew that the only alternative to murder was suicide, and I liked being alive.

So one day I thought, 'To hell with it,' and went to my interview with a bread knife in my inside pocket. 'Next,' the voice called, and I went in and slit his throat. The blood went everywhere, and the receptionist, hearing his death-gurgles, came and stood in the doorway, blocking my escape route. I tried to decide whether or not I should kill her, too.

A door opened in the wall behind the interviewer's desk. I had never noticed such a door in any of the rooms before. A white door set in a white wall. But maybe it had always been there, because how could anyone have known that I would pick this day, this room? Yes, the problem was just my own stupid lack of observation.

The interviewer lay twitching, frothing, etc, on the floor with the bread knife stuck in his gullet. The new man stepped over this dying marionette and extended his right hand. I took it, automatically. I was covered in blood – not a pretty sight, I assure you.

'We are now in a position,' the man said, 'I'm happy to say, that is, if you're interested, to offer you a job.'

Orderlies came in and carried out the corpse. Two cleaning ladies entered and started scrubbing the walls and the carpet, which, being blood-red, would not show the stains. My new friend opened a desk drawer and got out some clean clothes and held them out to me. 'What job?' I finally managed to say.

The new man went to the interviewer's chair and stood behind it.

'A vacancy has arisen,' he said, in a regretful but resigned way. 'It is well-paid work.'

I sat down in the chair and composed myself. My face became bland, smooth, devoid of all expression. I wondered how long it would be before someone came to see me with a bread knife up his sleeve.

Salman Rushdie

The mask

In the novel, The Lord of the Flies, *a group of boys has been cast away on a tropical island. One of them, Jack, has become the leader of a group of hunters who are trying to catch wild pigs for food. So far they have always been unsuccessful and the pigs have escaped.*

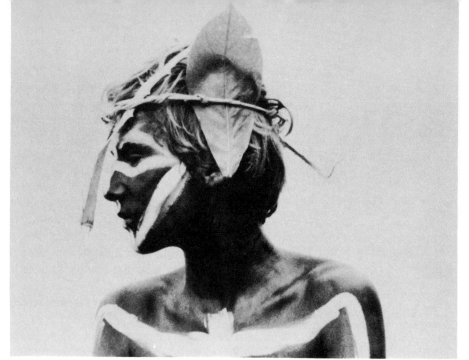

There was a pool at the end of the river, a tiny mere dammed back by sand and full of white water-lilies and needle-like reeds. Here Sam and Eric were waiting, and Bill. Jack, concealed from the sun, knelt by the pool and opened the two large leaves that he carried. One of them contained white clay, and the other red. By them lay a stick of charcoal brought down from the fire.

Jack explained to Roger as he worked.

'They don't smell me. They see me, I think. Something pink, under the trees.'

He smeared on the clay.

'If only I'd some green!'

He turned a half-concealed face up to Roger and answered the incomprehension of his gaze.

'For hunting. Like in the war. You know – dazzle paint. Like things trying to look like something else –'

He twisted in the urgency of telling.

' – like moths on a tree trunk.'

Roger understood and nodded gravely. The twins moved towards Jack and began to protest timidly about something. Jack waved them away.

'Shut up.'

He rubbed the charcoal stick between the patches of red and white on his face.

'No. You two come with me.'

He peered at his reflection and disliked it. He bent down, took up a double handful of lukewarm water and rubbed the mess from his face. Freckles and sandy eyebrows appeared.

Roger smiled, unwillingly.

'You don't half look a mess.'

Jack planned his new face. He made one cheek and one eye-socket white, then he rubbed red over the other half of his face and slashed a black bar of charcoal across from right ear to left jaw. He looked in the mere for his reflection, but his breathing troubled the mirror.

'Samneric. Get me a coconut. An empty one.'

He knelt, holding the shell of water. A rounded patch of sunlight fell on his face and a brightness appeared in the depths of the water. He looked in astonishment, no longer at himself but at an awesome stranger. He spilt the water and leapt to his feet, laughing excitedly. Beside the mere, his sinewy body held up a mask that drew their eyes and appalled them. He began to dance and his laughter became a blood-thirsty snarling. He capered towards Bill, and the mask was a thing on its own, behind which Jack hid, liberated from shame and self-consciousness. The face of red and white and black, swung through the air and jigged towards Bill. Bill started up laughing; then suddenly he fell silent and blundered away through the bushes.

Jack rushed towards the twins.

'The rest are making a line. Come on!'

'But –'

' – we –'

'Come on! I'll creep up and stab –'

The mask compelled them.

William Golding　*The Lord of the Flies*

Make the most of yourself

Assignments

Title page (46)	1 Think about the ways in which you speak and behave in each of these social situations: 　　a) with your parents 　　b) with close friends 　　c) with your teachers Are these ways of behaving the same, or different? 2 If they are different: in what particular ways? For what reasons? 3 Is any one of them closer to the 'real you' than the others? 4 What would happen if people attempted to behave in the same way in every social situation?
Teaching a girl . . . (47)	This advertisement was published in 1972. Do advertisers still make the same assumptions about women today? 1 Try to find examples of similar types of advertising. 2 Comment on any examples you find. **Writing a letter or exposition** 1 If you find any offensive advertisements, write a letter to the company which published it/them, expressing your views clearly and articulately. 2 If you think that such advertising is now rare, write an explanation of how and why you think the situation has changed since 1972.
How sad it is . . . (47)	**Writing exposition** Read the poem carefully and try to work out the kind of society about which it was written. Its family life and the roles of men and women were clearly very different from those of our society. Write a short account of what you have learned about the society from your reading of the poem.
Bridges (48)	1 What kind of person is Beatie? What are your reasons for thinking so? 2 Sum up briefly in your own words what Ronnie was trying to tell her in the conversation she describes in Extract A. (In particular you should explain what you think he means by 'bridges'.) 3 Sum up what you think Beatie is saying in the big speech in the second extract. 4 This play was written in the 1950s. Is what Beatie is saying still true today? **Writing an argument** Prepare a written or spoken reply to Beatie's argument in the second extract, as given by one of the following: 1 The editor of a popular newspaper 2 The head of a local radio station 3 A pop star

The golden bough (50)

Writing narrative

1 '. . . he began to comment on my curriculum vitae. I think that was when I realized that . . .'

Suppose the story had a conclusion that was different from the one that follows these words. Think of different ways in which the author could have ended it. Write your own version of the ending from the words quoted above.

2 If the story ends in the way in which the author wrote it, there must be a whole organization behind the interviewer and the man who appointed him. Presumably the narrator now becomes part of that organization. Tell the story of what happens to him now that he has 'joined the organization'.

The mask (52)

1 What was Jack's original purpose in painting his face?

2 Draw a diagram of what you think his face looked like when he had finished.

3 What unexpected result did painting his face like this have?

4 Can you think of any occasions when people in our society put on 'masks' like this?

5 How does this affect their behaviour?

6 Does wearing some kinds of uniform have the same effect as putting on a mask?

Writing narrative or argument

Write an expression of your opinions on one of the following titles:

1 The mask

2 Men in uniform

3 The face behind

Make the most of yourself (53)

1 Describe the products being advertised.

2 A hairdrier is a fairly simple machine: it is just a heater and a fan which blows out a stream of hot air. What have the advertisers done with:

    a) the machine

    b) the advertisement

to make the products more interesting?

Writing an advertisement

Choose a haircare product for men. Design a magazine advertisement, serious or flippant, to sell your product.

The cowboy of the American wild west is a figure who has been much glamorized in films and books. But there were many differences and some similarities between the legend of the cowboy and the reality of the men who did that particular job. The legend and the reality are summarized as follows.

Legend

The cowboy was a heroic, larger-than-life figure, tough and manly. He had an alert mind, perfect eyesight, was very strong and muscular, and indeed was admirable in every respect.

1 He was a white-skinned, honest, morally strong American.

2 He was a brilliant horse-rider and there was a strong bond of affection between a cowboy and his horse. He depended on the horse for his living and he would never neglect or ill-treat his horse.

3 He was intelligent, perceptive and a shrewd businessman, who could not be swindled in any financial deal, and who well understood the law relating to cattle-trading, land-claims and the rights of settlers as well as those of the free-range cattle-trader.

4 His job was to breed and tend cattle and then drive them in great herds from the vast plains of the Mid-West to the cattle-markets on the East coast.

5 He was generous to his friends and knew how to enjoy himself, spending his wealth on strong drink, gambling and women, and being physically robust and aggressive.

6 Cowboys lived a long, healthy life because of the fresh air and exercise, and wise old veterans

taught their tough, keen young followers all they knew.

7 He was an expert with a gun, whether rifle or revolver. He could draw a revolver from a hip holster and shoot a moving target with lethal accuracy. He could draw the gun speedily, take perfect aim and had the perfect eyesight, ice-cool nerves and strong wrists and arms necessary for this. His gun was above all the symbol of his power and virility.

8 Above all, he was a man of honour, a 'good' man who always triumphed over the crook, cheat or cunning Indian. Even the gunfights had their strict rules of fair play.

9 He bore any hardship manfully without flinching.

10 He was attractive to and attracted by glamorous women who were always waiting for him at the end of the trail.

Reality

Most cowboys were dirty, overworked and underpaid labourers who worked in terrible conditions: the climate was too hot, the land too barren and the cattle were stupid and panic-prone.

1 Many cowboys were Mexican, Indian or black. Most white-skinned ones were discharged Confederate soldiers.

2 Some did break in wild horses but few owned their own horse – it was supplied by the employer. Obviously the cowboy could not do his job without being an excellent horseman.

3 Cowboys were not intelligent. There were few schools. The cowboy would probably be able to draw and do simple arithmetic but was normally illiterate.

4 Cowboys were employed in any substantial numbers only from the end of the Civil War in 1865 to 1885. There were about 40,000 of them in total. They did indeed drive great herds of between 500 and 2,500 longhorn cattle from the great central plain to the markets in the East: at home the cattle were worth $4 each, but at the sale $40 each. The cowboy would work seven days a week for eighteen hours a day for the three or four months it took to ride about 1,800 miles, with little food or sleep.

5 For the long trail of three or four months he would get paid only $100 – hardly enough for a new hat and boots. He certainly had the comradeship of the trail. It was all a great adventure and challenge. When on the range he lived in a bunkhouse, which was a wooden slum, stinking of sweat, cow manure, boots and smoke from tallow lamps.

6 The average cowboy was 24 years old and he worked an average of seven years before settling down on his own ranch.

7 Cowboys knew of the romantic associations of guns, but could not handle them and did not wear them, for they got in the way when they were riding and working. No-one can shoot accurately from the hip.

8 There was no code of morality. Any man who survived on the great plains had to look after himself and trample on others.

9 Cowboys were proud men, who did not complain, though it was a very hard life. They were caught in fires, thrown and kicked by horses, charged by cows, and often killed by pneumonia brought on by the extremes of the weather.

10 He was always on the move and simply did not meet the very few girls that there were. After the long trail, when the town lights were in sight, what he longed for was not a drink or a woman – but a bath.

EMREB 1983

Gunfight at the Crown and Leek

LIKE a lot of inner city pubs, the Crown and Leek in Spitalfields lacks a distinctive clientele. On different nights of the week, different groups hold centre stage. Young male Bangladeshis sit and discuss local and international politics. The blacks strut around to the heavy 'dub' music, pumped out by a massive sound system. The Irish liven up things with their accordion and fiddle players. Local white youths dance to the soul and jazz-funk sounds of a conventional disco.

But Wednesday night at the Crown and Leek is something very different indeed. The blue and white stickers on the J-registration Ford Escort Estate parked outside offer a clue to the activities within: 'THIS CAR STOPS AT ALL POW WOWS', 'OFFICIAL INDIAN CAR' and 'CUSTER HAD IT COMING'. Yes, tonight is the meeting of the 2-2 Winchester Club, when 20 or so British citizens don the clothes and warpaint that magically transform them into 'Indians' and 'Westerners'. ('Cowboy', as I soon found out, is not a term than meets approval.)

Eagle is their leader. A small, thin man, 50 years of age, his real name is Tom. He works as a postal clerk at BP and lives in Stoke Newington. He is dressed as a Sioux chief. His gear consists of a spectacular war bonnet made from white eagle feathers and red binding, a blue cotton shirt, white

trousers, a bowie knife, brown moccasins, and a blue breach-cloth round his waist designed 'to protect me private parts from freezing when I ain't got no trousers on. See, we've got a sense of humour,' says Eagle with a grin.

How did the club start? Eagle explains: 'We go back about two years now. We started off as a Country and Western evening in a pub up Stepney Green. My son, Steve, over there,' he says pointing to a lean, ginger-haired youth in western gear, busy lining up the next Loretta Lynn record on his turntable, 'was asked by the guv'nor of the pub to come down and do the music. As we went on, we got more Indians and Westerners joining in. But then the guv'nor packed in the pub business, and the new people didn't want us. They turned the place into a disco pub,' he says with an air of disapproval. 'So we came here last September.'

'But it goes back before that, Eagle,' says his wife, Joleen (real name Eileen), a plump and friendly redhead dressed as a Westerner in black skirt, blouse and cowboy boots. She sits on one of the plastic-covered chairs, munching a bag of crisps. 'Would you like a cheese and onion, love? Yes? Here you are then.' She returns to her story. 'Right, well, Pontin's at Hemsby—that's just outside Great Yarmouth—they do an annual Country and Western holiday. We went there three years

ago and got into the whole thing—the guns, the clothes, the lot. After that we formed a little group and we got the name when a Western friend from another club came along and gave us a mirror which had these two crossed Winchester rifles on it. We thought it was a nice design, so we took the name for our club.'

Understood. But if you two are married, how come Eagle is an Indian and Joleen is a Westerner? 'It's like this,' says Eagle. 'When I was at Pontin's, I met the Black Crow Dancers. They're from south London. Well, I always like dancing and I really liked what they were doing. So I went along to their chalet afterwards and got talking about Indian stuff: how they make shields, moccasins and beadcraft. But it was the folklore that really got me,' he enthused, stroking the feathers of his war bonnet. 'You know everything the Indians do is *so* significant. There's nothing plastic about it. It's all down-to-earth—the Indian religion, the laws of smoking a peace pipe. All those kinds of things. But Joleen wasn't so interested at first.'

'That's right,' says Joleen. 'At the moment I'm more of a Westerner than an Indian, although Eagle's always trying to convert me.' She giggles. 'But first I'll need all the proper Indian clothes. We get most of our stuff from Ken's Western Store, up Manor Park. But it's so bloomin' expensive. It'll take a while before I go the whole way.' . . .

Are there conflicts between the Westerners and the Indians in the club? 'Yeah, we have conflicts,' says Ironhand. 'Normally it's between me and Rebel. That's Dixie's husband. He's a Confederate, see. He says things like, "They shouldn't allow Indians in a place like this", and I say, "Shut up, you damn Yankee, Rebel!" What effect does that have on Rebel? 'Hang on a minute and I'll show you. Just watch the expression on his face.'

Ironhand gets up and walks over to where Rebel is standing with a group of fellow Westerners at the bar. He interrupts their drinking and he and Rebel stand toe to toe. The immortal words are uttered. Rebel's jaw visibly tightens. All denim and cavalry hat, he says, 'What did you call me a damn Yankee for?' 'Cos that's what you are,' answers Ironhand. 'With a big yellow streak down your back,' he adds, for good measure. 'It looks like a shootout's necessary,' says Rebel. He reaches deep into a Sainsbury's plastic bag, pulls out an imitation Colt 44 and straps it round his waist.

Very wisely Ironhand decides to opt out because, as he tells me, his ear won't stand the noise. He gets Eagle to act as his deputy. A space in the centre of the floor appears from nowhere. The two men face each other. They draw. The noise is deafening. Ironhand gives a painful grimace. It's the best of three. Rebel gets three out of three. Dixie tells me he always does. But why didn't Eagle fall down dead? 'Not enough room. We only do that when we do a show outdoors,' she explains.

Sean Carey *New Society* 21 June 1984 (adapted)

Assignments

1 Write a conversation between a 'Westerner' and someone who is only interested in the reality of the cowboy's life.
2 You have been invited to speak at a meeting of the 2-2 Winchester Club on the topic: 'The cowboy – the legend and reality'. Write your speech, selecting and arranging the material in the Datafile as you think appropriate.
(Adapted from East Midlands Regional Examinations Board 1983)

4. *Places and people*

In the high rise Alice dreams of Wonderland

She received a parcel through the post.
It had everything she wanted inside it.
Sometimes when she touched it
a planet-sized man would come to the door
and say exactly the right kind of thing.
The parcel kept her happy.
Provided all she needed.
Her children blossomed,
grew fat and pink and healthy.
The high-rise in which she lived shrank,
became a neat house –
a swing on the lawn, a driveway, etc.

A bill for the parcel arrived on Monday
On Tuesday came a reminder.
On Wednesday came a solicitor's letter.
On Thursday came a court order.
On Friday the jury gave a verdict.
On Saturday the parcel was taken.
Most days
Alice can be seen in the high-rise,
mouth twisted, weeping.

Brian Patten

The ash tree

When William was growing up, the family moved from the Bottoms to a house on the brow of the hill, commanding a view of the valley, which spread out like a convex cockle-shell, or a clamp-shell, before it. In front of the house was a huge old ash-tree. The west wind, sweeping from Derbyshire, caught the houses with full force, and the tree shrieked again. Morel liked it.

'It's music,' he said. 'It sends me to sleep.'

But Paul and Arthur and Annie hated it. To Paul it became almost a demoniacal noise. The winter of their first year in the new house their father was very bad. The children played in the street, on the brim of the wide, dark valley, until eight o'clock. Then they went to bed. Their mother sat sewing below. Having such a great space in front of the house gave the children a feeling of night, of vastness, and of terror. This terror came in from the shrieking of the tree and the anguish of the home discord. Often Paul would wake up, after he had been asleep a long time, aware of thuds downstairs. Instantly he was wide awake. Then he heard the booming shouts of his father, come home nearly drunk, then the sharp replies of his mother, then the bang, bang of his father's fist on the table, and the nasty snarling shout as the man's voice got higher. And then the whole was drowned in a piercing medley of shrieks and cries from the great, windswept ash-tree. The children lay silent in suspense, waiting for a lull in the wind to hear what their father was doing. He might hit their mother again. There was a feeling of horror, a kind of bristling in the darkness, and a sense of blood. They lay with their hearts in the grip of an intense anguish. The wind came through the tree fiercer and fiercer. All the cords of the great harp hummed, whistled, and shrieked. And then came the horror of the sudden silence, silence everywhere, outside and downstairs. What was it? Was it a silence of blood? What had he done?

The children lay and breathed the darkness. And then, at last, they heard their father throw down his boots and tramp upstairs in his stockinged feet. Still they listened. Then at last, if the wind allowed, they heard the water of the tap drumming into the kettle, which their mother was filling for morning, and they could go to sleep in peace.

D H Lawrence *Sons and Lovers*

Discord in childhood

Outside the house an ash-tree hung its terrible whips,
And at night when the wind rose, the lash of the tree
Shrieked and slashed the wind, as a ship's
Weird rigging in a storm shrieks hideously.

Within the house two voices arose in anger, a slender lash
Whistling delirious rage, and the dreadful sound
Of a thick lash booming and bruising, until it had drowned
The other voice in a silence of blood, 'neath the noise of the ash.

D H Lawrence

Tree at my window

Tree at my window, window tree,
My sash is lowered when night comes on;
But let there never be curtain drawn
Between you and me.

Vague dream-head lifted out of the ground,
And thing next most diffuse to cloud,
Not all your light tongues talking aloud
Could be profound.

But, tree, I have seen you taken and tossed,
And if you have seen me when I slept,
You have seen me when I was taken and swept
And all but lost.

That day she put our heads together,
Fate had her imagination about her,
Your head so much concerned with outer,
Mine with inner, weather.

Robert Frost

New York subway

New Yorkers say some terrible things about the subway – that they hate it, or are scared stiff of it, or that it deserves to go broke. For tourists, it seems just another dangerous aspect of New York, though most don't know it exists. 'I haven't been down there in years,' is a common enough remark from a city dweller. Even people who ride it seem to agree that there is more Original Sin among subway passengers. And more desperation, too, making you think of choruses of 'O dark dark dark. They all go into the dark . . .'

'Subway' is not its name because, strictly-speaking, more than half of it is elevated. But which person who has ridden it lately is going to call it by its right name, 'The Rapid Transit'? It is also frightful-looking. It has paint and signatures all over its aged face. The graffiti is bad, violent and destructive, and is so extensive and so dreadful it is hard to believe that the perpetrators are not the recipients of some enormous foundation grant. The subway has been vandalized from end to end. It smells so hideous you want to put a clothes-pin on your nose, and it is so noisy the sound actually hurts. Is it dangerous? Ask anyone and he or she will tell you there are about two murders a day on the subway. It really is the pits, people say.

You have to ride it for a while to find out what it is and who takes it and who gets killed on it.

It is full of surprises. Three and a half million fares a day pass through it, and in the first nine months of last year the total number of murder victims on the subway amounted to six. This half-dozen does not include suicides (one a week), 'man-under' incidents (one a day), or 'spaces-cases' – people who get themselves jammed between the train and the platform. Certainly the subway is very ugly and extremely noisy, but it only *looks* like a death-trap. People ride it looking stunned and holding their breath. It's not at all like the BART system in San Francisco, where people are constantly chattering, saying, 'I'm going to my father's wedding,' or 'I'm looking after my mom's children,' or 'I've got a date with my fiancée's boyfriend.' In New York, the subway is a serious matter – the rackety train, the silent passengers, the occasional scream.

*　　　*　　　*

When people say the subway frightens them, they are not being silly or irrational. It is no good saying how cheap or how fast it is. The subway *is* frightening. It is also very easy to get lost on the subway, and the person who is lost in New York City has a serious problem. New Yorkers make it their business to avoid getting lost.

It is the stranger who gets lost. It is the stranger who follows people hurrying into the stair-well: subway entrances are just dark holes in the sidewalk – the stations are below ground. There is nearly always a bus-stop near the subway entrance. People waiting at a bus-stop have a special pitying gaze for people entering the subway. It is sometimes not pity, but fear, bewilderment, curiosity, or fatalism; often they look like miners' wives watching their menfolk going down the pit.

The stranger's sense of disorientation down below is immediate. The station is all tile and iron and dampness; it has bars and turnstiles and steel grates. It has the look of an old prison or a monkey cage.

Buying a token, the stranger may ask directions, but the token booth – reinforced, burglar-proof, bullet-proof – renders the reply incoherent. And subway directions are a special language: 'A-train . . . Downtown . . . Express to the Shuttle . . . Change at Ninety-sixth for the two . . . Uptown . . . The Lex . . . CC . . . LL . . . The Local . . .'

Most New Yorkers refer to the subway by the now-obsolete forms 'IND', 'IRT', 'BMT'. No one intentionally tries to confuse the stranger; it is just that, where the subway is concerned, precise directions are very hard to convey.

Verbal directions are incomprehensible, written ones are defaced. The signboards and subway maps are indiscernible beneath layers of graffiti.

Graffiti is destructive; it is anti-art; it is an act

of violence, and it can be deeply menacing. It has displaced the subway signs and maps, blacked-out the windows of the trains and obliterated the instructions. *In case of emergency* – is cross-hatched with a felt-tip. *These seats are for the elderly and disabled* – a yard-long signature obscures it. *The subway tracks are very dangerous: if the train should stop, do not* – the rest is black and unreadable. The stranger cannot rely on printed instructions or warnings, and there are few cars out of the six thousand on the system in which the maps have not been torn out. Assuming the stranger has boarded the train, he or she can feel only panic when, searching for a clue to his route, he sees in the map-frame the message, *Guzmán – Ladrón, Maricón y Asesino*.

Panic: and so he gets off the train, and then his troubles really begin.

He may be in the South Bronx or the upper reaches of Broadway on the Number 1 line, or on any one of a dozen lines that traverse Brooklyn. He gets off the train, which is covered in graffiti, and steps on to a station platform which is covered in graffiti. It is possible (this is true of many stations) that none of the signs will be legible. Not only will the stranger not know where he is, but the stairways will be splotched and stinking – no *Uptown*, no *Downtown*, no *Exit*. It is also possible that not a single soul will be around, and the most dangerous stations – ask any police officer – are the emptiest.

This is the story that most people tell of subways fear. In every detail it is like a nightmare, complete with rats and mice and a tunnel and a low ceiling. It is manifest suffocation, straight out of Poe. Those who tell this story seldom have a crime to report. They have experienced fear. It is completely understandable – what is worse than being trapped underground? – but it has been a private horror. In most cases, the person will have come to no harm. He will, however, remember his fear on that empty station for the rest of his life.

Paul Theroux *Subterranean Gothic*

Biocide

It took hundreds of millions of years to produce the life that now inhabits the earth – aeons of time in which that developing and evolving and diversifying life reached a state of adjustment and balance with its surroundings. The environment, rigorously shaping and directing the life it supported, contained elements that were hostile as well as supporting. Certain rocks gave out dangerous radiation; even within the light of the sun, from which all life draws its energy, there were short-wave radiations with power to injure. Given time – time not in years but in millennia – life adjusts, and a balance has been reached. For time is the essential ingredient; but in the modern world there is no time.

The rapidity of change and the speed with which new situations are created follow the impetuous and heedless pace of man rather than the deliberate pace of nature. Radiation is no longer merely the background radiation of rocks, the bombardment of cosmic rays, the ultra-violet of the sun that have existed before there was any life on earth; radiation is now the unnatural creation of man's tampering with the atom. The chemicals to which life is asked to make its adjustments are no longer merely the calcium and silica and copper and all the rest of the minerals washed out of the rocks and carried in rivers to the sea; they are the synthetic creations of man's inventive mind, brewed in his laboratories, and having no counterparts in nature.

To adjust to these chemicals would require time on a scale that is nature's; it would require not merely the years of a man's life but the life of generations. And even this, were it by some miracle possible, would be futile, for the new chemicals come from our laboratories in an endless stream; almost five hundred annually find their way into actual use in the United States alone. The figure is staggering and its implications are not easily grasped – five hundred new chemicals to which the bodies of men and animals are required somehow to adapt each year, chemicals totally outside the limits of biological experience.

Among them are many that are used in man's war against nature. Since the mid 1940s over two hundred basic chemicals have been created for use in killing insects, weeds, rodents, and other organisms described in the modern vernacular as 'pests'; and they are sold under several thousand different brand names.

These sprays, dusts, and aerosols are now applied universally to farms, gardens, forests and homes – non-selective chemicals that have the power to kill every insect, the 'good' and the 'bad', to still the song of birds and the leaping of fish in the stream, to coat the leaves with a deadly film, and to linger on in soil – all this though the intended target may be only a few weeds or insects. Can anyone believe it is possible to lay down such a barrage of poisons on the surface of the earth without making it unfit for all life? They should not be called 'insecticides', but 'biocides'.

Rachel Carson   *Silent spring*

NOW A <u>TOTAL</u> WEEDKILLER

KILLS **ALL** KNOWN WEEDS.

DeeWeed

NEW AND EASY TO USE

Will not wash out or creep sideways – beware shallow spreading shrub roots.

1

Works down through leaves.

Works up through roots.

2

Keeps ground clear for up to 3 years.

3

WARNING: NOTHING MAY GROW FOR 3 YEARS

At last an answer to cracked paving and wild unsightly weeds! New Dee-Weed's broad-spectrum, wettable powder **formula, keeps patios, drives, paths, waste ground, clear of all known weeds for up to 3 years.**

Use anytime, kills existing weeds, any height, *and* prevents re-growth.
DO NOT RE-PLANT SOIL FOR 3 YEARS.

Arable & Bulb Chemicals Ltd., Butterwick, Boston, Lincs, PE22 0JW. Tel: Boston (0205) 760479

● **Non-flammable**

● **Non-corrosive**

OFFICIALLY APPROVED *

*No need to exclude children & pets from spray area when initial application has dried.

SPECIAL READERS OFFER
100gm pack: only £3.55*
(treats 500 sq. ft.)
300gm pack: only £10.45*
500gm pack: only £16.40*
*plus 65p p&p any quantity.
Save nearly 20% on largest quantity. Control all weeds.Try Dee Weed now!

*IMPORTANT.
Dee Weed is cleared **under UK Government Pesticides Safety Precaution Scheme** for use as directed.

All orders are despatched to the Post Office within 4 days.

(i)

The sea people

The sea people is a fable in which the authors examine how men behave towards their environment and towards each other.

Once upon a time there were two islands in the sea, one bigger than the other. It was said that there had been a third island, but that this had disappeared a long time ago. At night the people of the two islands sailed out to sea in their boats to fish. In the morning they sailed back. They drew in their nets, hung them out to dry and repaired them.

However there were differences between the islanders. On the Greater Island lived tall people, some rich and some poor, some servants and some masters. Their ships were magnificent, built from the best and hardest wood. The tall people were capable and efficient. In their marketplace there was not only fish to buy, but also fruit and vegetables, birds' eggs, tools and costly materials. The nobles on the Greater Island wore necklaces of blue shells which served as money, and those who were very rich also decorated their houses with these shells.

On the Lesser Island there were small people, but none were masters so none were servants. Because nobody wanted to become rich, the small people had plenty of time to play and sing, to dance and fly their kites – to enjoy living. Sometimes they would laugh at the people on the Greater Island, for there were so many shells on the beach – beautiful pearly ones, spotted ones and striped ones. There were not very many blue ones – but why should they be worth more than all the others?

The tall people could not understand what there was to laugh about. They got up early in the morning and worked until late at night. Comfort and laziness were not tolerated under any circumstances. The farmers sowed and harvested their crops. The servants served their masters. The carpenters bent themselves busily over their planes.

One day the king decided that the Greater Island should be made even bigger and richer and more magnificent than before. To do this they would have to build embankments and dams out of stone, wood, and earth.

Soon there wasn't enough earth on the Greater Island to carry on the work. Then the king had an idea. He ordered large boats to be built which could be rowed over to the Lesser Island to collect rubble and earth.

Until now the small people had lived on their island free from worries. They had flown their kites and had listened to stories told by an old, blind man. He told tales of the wind that whispered in the trees, and of the waves that ran towards the shore.

The old man also knew something of the law, and when the small people could not agree they would come to him and let him be the judge of who was right. But now, the big people were coming across the sea every day and taking away stones and earth from the little island. The little people could see that their island was getting smaller every day, but they did not know what to do and this time the old blind man had no advice to offer.

Jörg Muller and **Jörg Steiner** *The sea people*

(ii)

The next two stages in the story

(iii)

(iv)

Assignments

Title page (60)	**Free writing** Write about the picture in any way that seems appropriate.

In the high rise Alice dreams of Wonderland (61)

1 The first section contains one main image: the parcel. Clearly it is not a real parcel. What do you think it stands for in the poem?
2 In the second section Alice is treated like someone who has received mail-order goods and then not paid for them. What do you think that this process of bill, solicitor's letter etc. is meant to stand for?
3 What is the poet saying through the use of these images?

Writing a poem
Use this poem as a pattern for a piece of writing of your own. Use this title, filling in the blank to suit your subject:
In the _____ Alice dreams of Wonderland

The ash tree (62)

Using images
Lawrence is writing about a real tree, but the ash tree is also an *image*. It reflects the emotions and voices of the parents as they row. This sort of image can be very useful to the writer: it makes it possible to express moods and feelings without having to spell them out. Choose one of the following moods/emotions and write about it in a similar way:
1 Emptiness/loneliness
2 Nervous tension
3 Boredom
4 Excited anticipation
So, for example, if you were writing about 1 you might describe a character wandering alone through a deserted place such as an abandoned factory or warehouse.

Discord in childhood/Tree at my window (63)

Both poems use a tree as an image of emotion. Which one works better for you and why?

Personal writing
Think of an occasion when a particular place, building, or natural object has been particularly important to you. Write about it.

New York subway (64)

Write a few paragraphs expressing your reactions to this piece.

Imaginative writing
Choose one of the following titles as the starting point for a piece of writing:
1 A private horror
2 The empty station
3 My nightmare
4 Space-case
5 Lost under ground

Biocide (66)

1 Explain briefly in your own words the argument that Rachel Carson is putting forward here.
2 How much of what she says do you agree with?
3 This passage was written in 1960. In what ways do you think things have changed since then?
4 What do you think should be done about this problem?

Pages 66/67

Writing an argument
Use the material on these two pages as a starting point for your own writing. Either choose your own topic or select one from this list.
1 What have they done to the land?
2 Insecticide = biocide. Biocide = suicide. So what?
3 The silent world.
4 'When our cities are full of urgent problems it's just sentimentality to fuss about pretty scenery.' Do you agree?
5 We live in a densely-populated country and we all want more of everything – roads, houses, factories. So how can we preserve our rapidly vanishing countryside?

The sea people (68)

This is not just a fantasy story. It is a fable which expresses beliefs about the real world we live in. Read it carefully and work out the answers to these questions:
1 What are the main features of the people who live on the larger island?
2 What are the main features of the people who live on the smaller island?
3 What people and attitudes in the real world do the two groups of islanders represent?

Narrative writing
Pictures (**iii**) and (**iv**) illustrate later stages in the story. The picture which illustrates the end of the story is not shown.
1 Tell the story illustrated by pictures (**iii**) and (**iv**).
2 Decide how you think the story might end.
3 Describe (or draw) the final picture, showing the two islands at the end of the story.

Baldwick Times

Tourist boost for town

Baldwick is to become a tourist attraction to rival Paris and Rome.

At least that is the aim of a group of councillors led by the Mayor, Councillor Eric Chapman. Plans are already far advanced to attract visitors to some of the town's lesser-known beauty spots. This was revealed last night in a speech to the Baldwick Chamber of Commerce by Councillor

Council to sell delights of Baldwick to foreign visitors

Chapman. 'Some people,' he said, 'think of Baldwick as a bit of a joke, but to those of us who live here, it's full of interest and character. We aim to promote the characterful aspects of the town in a bid to bring tourists in and benefit the whole community.' Among the potential tourist attractions listed by the Mayor were: the High Street, with its interesting 19th century houses, St Jude's parish church, the area of Canal Street and Bridge Street, and Maynard's Park. Photographs of these and other local 'attractions' can be seen in an exhibition entitled 'Tourists' Baldwick' at the Council Offices next week.

Tourists' Baldwick

1. St Jude's church, a fine example of mid-C19th ecclesiastical architecture.

2. The imposing buildings of the High Street.

3. Old canal with early C19th grain mill.

4. Maynard's Park in Spring.

Challenge to tourist plan

'Waste of ratepayers' money' say opponents

The opposition group on the council have tabled a censure motion for next week's meeting, criticising the Mayor's plans to promote tourism in Baldwick. Opposition leader Arthur Murray said that the plans were 'cloud cuckoo land'. 'They will add two or three pence to the rates,' he argued, 'and we shall see nothing in return. The Mayor is living in a fantasy world. This is an ordinary, hard-working town with more than its fair share of problems. No one in his right mind would pretend that Baldwick is attractive.' In support of their campaign, the opposition group are mounting an exhibition of their own, in St Jude's Parish Hall. It will be entitled 'Warts and all: the real Baldwick.'

Warts and all : the real Baldwick

1. St Jude's church from Bloxom Road.

3. The canal.

2. High Street.

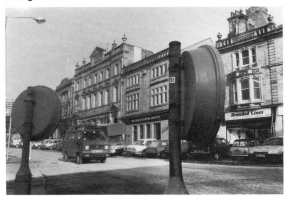

4. Maynard's Park.

BALDWICK   12,386 Gt Manchester   Ec Thurs; Md Wed; Manchester 6; Bolton 7
**Grand   High St (tel. 29816) 23rm B&B
McArthur & Sons   Bowes Rd 24hrs breakdown (tel. 39871)

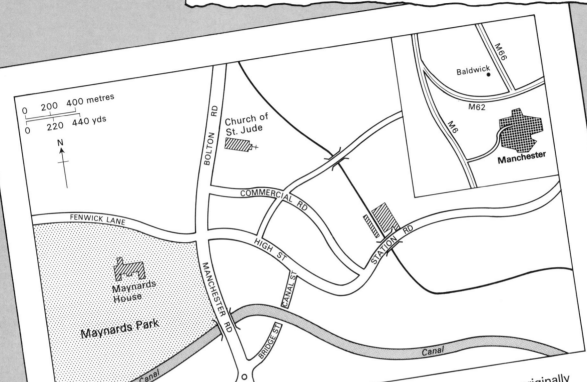

BALDWICK

The **High Street** contains an imposing row of 19th Century buildings unfortunately spoiled by a rash of 20th Century street signs and shop fronts.

Maynards House: originally an imposing Regency house in its own grounds of 5 acres, unfortunately this is now little more than a facade, having been allowed to fall into neglect by its owners, Baldwick Council.

St Jude The church was originally 14th Century, but completely rebuilt in 1846–8 by Grandison and Cater. This was at the expense of the James family. Arthur James, a cotton manufacturer who died in 1843, left £3500 for the building of a church. His descendants contributed a further £7000. James, according to the historian of Baldwick, the Revd Harold Leach, wanted the church to be seen as 'his thanks to the Almighty for his worldly prosperity'. The church itself is worthy rather than impressive, and has little to detain the visitor. Its main feature of interest is the pulpit (1879) an enormous piece of Victoriana, more typical of contemporary railway station architecture than anything more religious.

The arguments

For	Against
Will bring many more visitors to the town. Increase in trade. Increased use of facilities. Extra income for both shop owners and council. Little or no extra cost.	Not many people will be attracted. The only people who will gain will be the shopkeepers. This won't help the rest of the townspeople. It will cost a lot so the rates will go up.
Incentive to local people to improve facilities in town, keep streets etc. cleaner and more attractive.	No one will take it seriously, so it will have no effect on how people treat the town. Extra visitors will add to problems of litter etc.
Encourage young people to take interest in own town, take more care of it, know more about it.	There is nothing in it for young people, so why should they be encouraged to take an interest?
It is an interesting and unusual place – these features just need to be brought out and shown so that people can see for themselves.	Baldwick is interesting to people who live there. Nothing there for tourists, when they are so near the Lake District and Snowdonia.

Assignments

1 The Mayor's plans are due to be debated by the council. Decide which side you are on and write a speech putting your side's case.

2 The debate becomes very heated as those on each side become more and more angry with each other. Write this part of the debate as a radio script.

3 You work for the *Baldwick Times*. Write your report on the Council Debate.

4 The Council decides to go ahead with its tourism plans. As part of these it produces two pieces of publicity material:

a) a leaflet to be distributed to Tourist Information Offices. This contains a map and photographs plus a 250-word article describing the town and its attractions.

b) a leaflet describing a 'town walk'. This describes a walk round the central part of the town taking in the main places of interest.

Write the text for one of these.

Secrets

Bernard MacLaverty

He had been called to be there at the end. His Great Aunt Mary had been dying for some days now and the house was full of relatives. He had just left his girlfriend's home – they had been studying for 'A' levels together – and had come back to the house to find all the lights spilling onto the lawn and a sense of purpose which had been absent from the last few days.

He knelt at the bedroom door to join in the prayers. His knees were on the wooden threshold and he edged them forward onto the carpet. They had tried to wrap her fingers around a crucifix but they kept loosening. She lay low on the pillow and her face seemed to have shrunk by half since he had gone out earlier in the night. Her white hair was damped and pushed back from her forehead. She twisted her head from side to side, her eyes closed. The prayers chorused on, trying to cover the sound she was making deep in her throat. Someone said about her teeth and his mother leaned over her and said, 'That's the pet', and took her dentures from her mouth. The lower half of her face seemed to collapse. She half opened her eyes but could not raise her eyelids enough and showed only crescents of white.

'Hail Mary full of grace . . .' the prayers went on. He closed his hands over his face so that he would not have to look but smelt the trace of his girlfriend's handcream from his hands. The noise, deep and guttural, that his aunt was making became intolerable to him. It was as if she were drowning. She had lost all the dignity he knew her to have. He got up from the floor and stepped between the others who were kneeling and went into her sitting-room off the same landing.

He was trembling with anger or sorrow, he didn't know which. He sat in the brightness of her big sitting-room at the oval table and waited for something to happen. On the table was a cut-glass vase of irises, dying because she had been in bed for over a week. He sat staring at them. They were withering from the tips inward, scrolling themselves delicately, brown and neat. Clearing up after themselves. He stared at them for a long time until he heard the sounds of women weeping from the next room.

*   *   *

His aunt had been small – her head on a level with his when she sat at her table – and she seemed to get smaller each year. Her skin fresh, her hair white and waved and always well washed. She wore no jewelry except a cameo ring on the third finger of her right hand and, around her neck, a gold locket on a chain. The white classical profile on the ring was almost worn through and had become translucent and indistinct. The boy had noticed the ring when she had read to him as a child. In the beginning fairy tales, then as he got older extracts from famous novels, *Lorna Doone, Persuasion, Wuthering Heights* and her favourite extract, because she read it so often Pip's meeting with Miss Havisham from *Great Expectations*. She would sit with him on her knee, her arms around him and holding the page flat with her hand. When he was bored he would interrupt her and ask about the ring. He loved hearing her tell of how her grandmother had given it to her as a brooch and she had had a ring made from it. He would try to count back to see how old it was. Had her grandmother got it from *her* grandmother? And if so what had she turned it into? She would nod her head from side to side and say, 'How would I know a thing like that?' keeping her place in the closed book with her finger.

'Don't be so inquisitive,' she'd say. 'Let's see what happens next in the story.'

One day she was sitting copying figures into a long narrow book with a dip pen when he came into her room. She didn't look up but when he asked her a question she just said, 'Mm?' and went on writing. The vase of irises on the oval table vibrated slightly as she wrote.

'What is it?' She wiped the nib on blotting paper and looked up at him over her reading glasses.

'I've started collecting stamps and Mamma says you might have some.'

'Does she now –?'

She got up from the table and went to the tall walnut bureau-bookcase standing in the alcove. From a shelf of the bookcase she took a small wallet of keys and selected one for the lock. There was a harsh metal shearing sound as she pulled the desk flap down. The writing area was covered with green leather which had dog-eared at the corners. The inner part was divided into pigeon holes, all bulging with papers. Some of them, envelopes, were gathered in batches nipped at the waist with elastic bands. There were postcards and bills and cash-books. She pointed to the postcards.

'You may have the stamps on those,' she said. 'But don't tear them. Steam them off.'

She went back to the oval table and continued writing. He sat on the arm of the chair looking through the picture postcards – torchlight processions at Lourdes, brown photographs of town centres, dull black and whites of beaches backed by faded hotels. Then he turned them over and began to sort the stamps. Spanish, with a bald man, French with a rooster, German with funny jerky print, some Italian with what looked like a chimney-sweep's bundle and a hatchet.

'These are great,' he said. 'I haven't got any of them.'

'Just be careful how you take them off.'

'Can I take them downstairs?'

'Is your mother there?'

'Yes.'

'Then perhaps it's best if you bring the kettle up here.'

He went down to the kitchen. His mother was in the morning room polishing silver. He took the kettle and the flex upstairs. Except for the dipping and scratching of his aunt's pen the room was silent. It was at the back of the house overlooking the orchard and the sound of traffic from the main road was distant and muted. A tiny rattle began as the kettle warmed up, then it bubbled and steam gushed quietly from its spout. The cards began to curl slightly in the jet of steam but she didn't seem to be watching. The stamps peeled moistly off and he put them in a saucer of water to flatten them.

'Who is Brother Benignus?' he asked. She seemed not to hear. He asked again and she looked over her glasses.

'He was a friend.'

His flourishing signature appeared again and again. Sometimes Bro Benignus, sometimes Benignus and once Iggy.

'Is he alive?'

'No, he's dead now. Watch the kettle doesn't run dry.'

When he had all the stamps off he put the postcards together and replaced them in the pigeon-hole. He reached over towards the letters but before his hand touched them his aunt's voice, harsh for once, warned.

'A-A-A,' she moved her pen from side to side. 'Do-not-touch,' she said and smiled. 'Anything else, yes! That section, no!' She resumed her writing.

The boy went through some other papers and found some photographs. One was a beautiful girl. It was very old-fashioned but he could see that she was beautiful. The picture was a pale brown oval set on a white square of card. The edges of the oval were misty. The girl in the photograph was young and had dark, dark hair scraped severely back and tied like a knotted rope on the top of her head – high arched eyebrows, her nose straight and thin, her mouth slightly smiling, yet not smiling – the way a mouth is after smiling. Her eyes looked out at him dark and knowing and beautiful.

'Who is that?' he asked.

'Why? What do you think of her?'

'She's all right.'

'Do you think she is beautiful?' The boy nodded.

'That's me,' she said. The boy was glad he had pleased her in return for the stamps.

Other photographs were there, not posed ones like Aunt Mary's but Brownie snaps of laughing groups of girls in bucket hats like German helmets and coats to their ankles. They seemed tiny faces covered in clothes. There was a photograph of a young man smoking a cigarette, his hair combed one way by the wind against a background of sea.

'Who is that in the uniform?' the boy asked.

'He's a soldier,' she answered without looking up.

'Oh,' said the boy. 'But who is he?'

'He was a friend of mine before you were born,' she said. Then added, 'Do I smell something cooking? Take your stamps and off you go. That's the boy.'

The boy looked at the back of the picture of the man and saw in black spidery ink 'John, Aug '15 Ballintoye'.

'I thought maybe it was Brother Benignus,' he said. She looked at him not answering.

'Was your friend killed in the war?'

At first she said no, but then she changed her mind.

'Perhaps he was,' she said, then smiled. 'You are far too inquisitive. Put it to use and go and see what is for tea. Your mother will need the kettle.' She came over to the bureau and helped tidy the photographs away. Then she locked it and put the keys on the shelf.

'Will you bring me up my tray?'

The boy nodded and left.

*   *   *

It was a Sunday evening, bright and summery. He was doing his homework and his mother was sitting on the carpet in one of her periodic fits of tidying out the drawers of the mahogany sideboard. On one side of her was a heap

of paper scraps torn in quarters and bits of rubbish, on the other the useful items that had to be kept. The boy heard the bottom stair creak under Aunt Mary's light footstep. She knocked and put her head round the door and said that she was walking to Devotions. She was dressed in her good coat and hat and was just easing her fingers into her second glove. The boy saw her stop and pat her hair into place before the mirror in the hallway. His mother stretched over and slammed the door shut. It vibrated, then he heard the deeper sound of the outside door closing and her first few steps on the gravelled driveway. He sat for a long time wondering if he would have time or not. Devotions could take anything from twenty minutes to three quarters of an hour, depending on who was saying it.

Ten minutes must have passed, then the boy left his homework and went upstairs and into his aunt's sitting-room. He stood in front of the bureau wondering, then he reached for the keys. He tried several before he got the right one. The desk flap screeched as he pulled it down. He pretended to look at the postcards again in case there were any stamps he had missed. Then he put them away and reached for the bundle of letters. The elastic band was thick and old, brittle almost and when he took it off its track remained on the wad of letters. He carefully opened one and took out the letter and unfolded it, frail, khaki-coloured.

My dearest Mary, it began. I am so tired I can hardly write to you. I have spent what seems like all day censoring letters (there is a howitzer about 100 yds away firing every 2 minutes). The letters are heartrending in their attempt to express what they cannot. Some of the men are illiterate, others almost so. I know that they feel as much as we do, yet they do not have the words to express it. That is your job in the schoolroom to give us generations who can read and write well. They have . . .

The boy's eyes skipped down the page and over the next. He read the last paragraph.

Mary I love you as much as ever – more so that we cannot be together. I do not know which is worse, the hurt of this war or being separated from you. Give all my love to Brendan and all at home.

It was signed, scribbled with what he took to be John. He folded the paper carefully into its original creases and put it in the envelope. He opened another.

My love, it is thinking of you that keeps me sane. When I get a moment I open my memories of you as if I were reading. Your long dark hair – I always imagine you wearing the blouse with the tiny roses, the white one that opened down the back – your eyes that said so much without words, the way you lowered your head when I said anything that embarrassed you, and the clean nape of your neck.

The day I think about most was the day we climbed the head at Ballycastle. In a hollow, out of the wind, the air full of pollen and the sound of insects, the grass warm and dry and you lying beside me your hair undone, between me and the sun. You remember that that was where I first kissed you and the look of disbelief in your eyes that made me laugh afterwards.

It makes me laugh now to see myself savouring these memories standing alone up to my thighs in muck. It is everywhere, two, three feet deep. To walk ten yards leaves you quite breathless.

I haven't time to write more today so I leave you with my feet in the clay and my head in the clouds.

I love you, John.

He did not bother to put the letter back into the envelope but opened another.

My dearest, I am so cold that I find it difficult to keep my hand steady enough to write. You remember when we swam the last two fingers of your hand went the colour and texture of candles with the cold. Well that is how I am all over. It is almost four days since I had any real sensation in my feet or legs. Everything is frozen. The ground is like steel.

Forgive me telling you this but I feel I have to say it to someone. The worst thing is the dead. They sit or lie frozen in the position they died. You can distinguish them from the living because their faces are the colour of slate. God help us when the thaw comes . . . This war is beginning to have an effect on me. I have lost all sense of feeling. The only emotion I have experienced lately is one of anger. Sheer white trembling anger. I have no pity or sorrow for the dead and injured. I thank God it is not me but I am enraged that it had to be them. If I live through this experience I will be a different person.

The only thing that remains constant is my love for you.

Today a man died beside me. A piece of shrapnel had pierced his neck as we were moving under fire. I pulled him into a crater and stayed with him until he died. I watched him choke and then drown in his blood.

I am full of anger which has no direction.

He sorted through the pile and read half of some, all of others. The sun had fallen low in the sky and shone directly into the room onto the pages he was reading making the paper glare. He selected a letter from the back of the pile and shaded it with his hand as he read.

Dearest Mary, I am writing this to you from my hospital bed. I hope that you were not too worried about not hearing from me. I have been here, so they tell me, for two weeks and it took another two weeks before I could bring myself to write this letter.

I have been thinking a lot as I lie here about the war and about myself and about you. I do not know how to say this but I feel deeply that I must do something, must sacrifice something to make up for the horror of the past year. In some strange way Christ has spoken to me through the carnage . . .

Suddenly the boy heard the creak of the stair and he frantically tried to slip the letter back into its envelope but it crumpled and would not fit. He bundled them all together. He could hear his aunt's familiar puffing on the short stairs to her room. He spread the elastic band wide with his fingers. It snapped and the letters scattered. He pushed them into their pigeon hole and quickly closed the desk flap. The brass screeched loudly and clicked shut. At that moment his aunt came into the room.

'What are you doing boy?' she snapped.

'Nothing.' He stood with the keys in his hands. She walked to the bureau and opened it. The letters sprang out in an untidy heap.

'You have been reading my letters,' she said quietly. Her mouth was tight with the words and her eyes blazed. The boy could say nothing. She struck him across the side of the face.

'Get out,' she said. 'Get out of my room.'

The boy, the side of his face stinging and red, put the keys on the table on his way out. When he reached the door she called to him. He stopped, his hand on the handle.

'You are dirt,' she hissed, 'and always will be dirt. I shall remember this till the day I die.'

*   *   *

Even though it was a warm evening there was a fire in the large fireplace. His mother had asked him to light it so that she could clear out Aunt Mary's stuff. The room could then be his study, she said. She came in and seeing him at the table said, 'I hope I'm not disturbing you.'

'No.'

She took the keys from her pocket, opened the bureau and began burning papers and cards. She glanced quickly at each one before she flicked it onto the fire.

'Who was Brother Benignus?' he asked.

His mother stopped sorting and said, 'I don't know. Your aunt kept herself very much to herself. She got books from him through the post occasionally. That much I do know.'

She went on burning the cards. They built into strata, glowing red and black. Now and again she broke up the pile with the poker, sending showers of sparks up the chimney. He saw her come to the letters. She took off the elastic band and put it to one side with the useful things and began dealing the envelopes into the fire. She opened one and read quickly through it, then threw it on top of the burning pile.

'Mama,' he said.

'Yes?'

'Did Aunt Mary say anything about me?'

'What do you mean?'

'Before she died – did she say anything?'

'Not that I know of – the poor thing was too far gone to speak, God rest her.' She went on burning, lifting the corners of the letters with the poker to let the flames underneath them.

When he felt a hardness in his throat he put his head down on his books. Tears came into his eyes for the first time since she had died and he cried silently into the crook of his arm for the woman who had been his maiden aunt, his teller of tales, that she might forgive him.

Assignments

Thinking about the story

Immediate reactions

1 Write down your immediate reactions to the story. Don't bother about planning your writing – just write your thoughts and feelings as they come to you.

2 *Without reading the story again* answer these questions:
   a) What did the boy actually discover by reading the letters?
   b) Why was his aunt so angry when she caught him?
   c) How did he feel about it?
   d) How did he feel about her death and why?

3 There may be things about the story that you do not understand. If so, write down a list of questions that you would like to have answered.

Reading

Now read the story through again. As you read, answer the questions you wrote down in response to 3 above. Write answers to the following questions.

 1 How well did the young boy know his Great Aunt?
 2 What impression do you get of her at this time?
 3 Why do you think the boy decided to read the letters?
 4 Who was John?
 5 What happened to John in the war?
 6 How did it affect him?
 7 Why did he and Mary never marry?
 8 Why did Great Aunt Mary strike the boy?
 9 Was she right to be so angry with him?
10 Do you think she ever forgave him?

Expressing your response to the story

Make notes on what the story has to say about each of the following topics:

   Old age   Love   War   Forgiveness

What use does the story make of each of the following? (Write note-form answers.)

   Dialogue   Shifts of time   Letters

Use the notes you have made to write a detailed response to the story. You should conclude by explaining what you think the story is saying and stating how successful you think it is.

Your own writing

Time shifts

This story makes skilful use of dialogue, of shifts of time, and of letters. (The letters make it possible for the writer to include yet another period of time – that during the First World War when John and Mary were young.) The writing assignments on this page are intended to lead you to explore these elements in your own writing.

Dialogue

Use one of the following snippets of conversation as a starting point for writing. Develop it into a story which includes dialogue, a story that is told entirely in dialogue, or a short playscript.

1 – I told her she couldn't have done it.
  – You know what the Jamiesons are like.
  – Yes, but even so –
  – They all take after their father.
2 – . . . and I just can't bring myself to tell him.
  – I don't see why you have to.
  – He'll kill me if he finds out and I haven't told him.
  – But how's he going to find out?

Time

(If you are not sure what is meant by the use of time in narrative, look at pages 186–7, where it is explained.)
Write a story in which a change of time plays an important part. Either choose your own situation, or take one from this list:

1 Someone who has the ability to see into the future of the person(s) he is talking to.
2 A famous person who has secrets being interviewed in depth by a TV or newspaper journalist.
3 Someone facing a personal challenge or problem, who is troubled by the memory of something that he/she did years ago and still regrets doing.

Letters

Write a story which is told partly or completely through letters. Either make up your own material, or use the letter extracts printed below as a starting point.

1 . . . unless you can do something, I can't see how they can be saved. The mother is already seriously ill and is only being kept alive by continuous medical care, which they cannot really afford. Now the two small children have fallen ill as well and there seems to be little chance for any of them unless . . .

2 . . . and knowing you as I do, I am convinced that you will disapprove. I wish it was not so, but I am sure it is. Still I am not going to change my mind. I am old enough to stand on my own two feet. If you will not accept things as they are I shall manage for myself somehow . . .

5. *I'll fight you for it*

'Get off this estate.'
'What for?'
'Because it's mine.'
'Where did you get it?'
'From my father.'
'Where did he get it?'
'From his father.'
'And where did he get it?'
'He fought for it.'
'Well, I'll fight you for it.'

Carl Sandburg

The cane

At the age of eight, in 1924, I was sent away to boarding school in a town called Weston-super-Mare, on the south-west coast of England. Those were days of horror, of fierce discipline, of no talking in the dormitories, no running in the corridors, no untidiness of any sort, no this or that or the other, just rules and still more rules that had to be obeyed. And the fear of the dreaded cane hung over us like the fear of death all the time.

'The headmaster wants to see you in his study.' Words of doom. They sent shivers over the skin of your stomach! But off you went, aged perhaps nine years old, down the long black corridors and through an archway that took you into the Headmaster's private area where only horrible things happened and the smell of pipe tobacco hung in the air like incense. You stood outside the awful black door, not daring even to knock. You took deep breaths. If only your mother were here, you told yourself, she would not let this happen. She wasn't here. You were alone. You lifted a hand and knocked softly, once.

'Come in! Ah yes, It's Dahl. Well, Dahl, it's been reported to me that you were talking during prep last night.'

'Please sir, I broke my nib and I was only asking Jenkins if he had another one to lend me.'

'I will not tolerate talking in prep. You know that very well.'

Already this giant of a man was crossing to the tall corner cupboard and reaching up to the top of it where he kept his canes.

'Boys who break rules have to be punished.'

'Sir . . . I . . . I had a bust nib . . . I . . .'

'That is no excuse. I am going to teach you that it does not pay to talk during prep.'

He took a cane down that was about three feet long with a little curved handle at one end. It was thin and white and very whippy. 'Bend over and touch your toes. Over there by the window.'

'But sir . . .'

'Don't argue with me, boy. Do as you're told.'

I bent over. Then I waited. He always kept you waiting for about ten seconds, and that was when your knees began to shake.

'Bend lower, boy! Touch your toes!'

I stared at the toecaps of my black shoes and I told myself that any moment now this man was going to bash the cane into me so hard that the whole of my bottom would change colour. The welts were always very long, stretching right across both buttocks, blue-black with brilliant scarlet edges, and when you ran your fingers over them ever so gently afterwards, you could feel the corrugations.

Swish! . . . Crack!

Then came the pain. It was unbelievable, unbearable, excruciating. It was as though someone had laid a white-hot poker against your backside and pressed hard.

The second stroke would be coming soon and it was as much as you could do to stop putting your hands in the way to ward it off. It was the instinctive reaction. But if you did that, it would break your fingers.

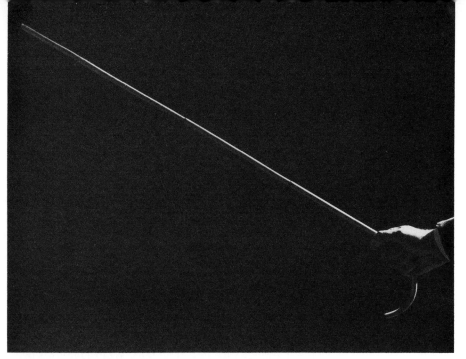

Swish! . . . Crack!

The second one landed right alongside the first and the white-hot poker was pressing deeper and deeper into the skin.

Swish! . . . Crack!

The third stroke was where the pain always reached its peak. It could go no further. There was no way it could get any worse. Any more strokes after that simply *prolonged* the agony. You tried not to cry out. Sometimes you couldn't help it. But whether you were able to or not, it was impossible to stop the tears. They poured down your cheeks in streams and dripped onto the carpet.

The important thing was never to flinch upwards or straighten up when you were hit. If you did that, you got an extra one.

Slowly, deliberately, taking plenty of time, the headmaster delivered three more strokes, making six in all.

'You may go.' The voice came from a cavern miles away, and you straightened up slowly, agonizingly, and grabbed hold of your burning buttocks with both hands and held them as tight as you could and hopped out of the room on the very tips of your toes.

That cruel cane ruled our lives. We were caned for talking in the dormitory after lights out, for talking in class, for bad work, for carving our intitials on the desk, for climbing over walls, for slovenly appearance, for flicking paper clips, for forgetting to change into house-shoes in the evenings, for not hanging up our games clothes, and above all for giving the slightest offence to any master. (They weren't called teachers in those days.) In other words, we were caned for doing everything that it was natural for small boys to do.

So we watched our words. And we watched our steps. My goodness, how we watched our steps. We became incredibly alert. Wherever we went, we walked carefully, with ears pricked for danger, like wild animals stepping softly through the woods.

Roald Dahl   *The wonderful story of Henry Sugar*

An interrogation

He was almost flat on his back, and unable to move. His body was held down at every essential point. Even the back of his head was gripped in some manner. O'Brien was looking down at him gravely and rather sadly. His face, seen from below, looked coarse and worn, with pouches under the eyes and tired lines from nose to chin. He was older than Winston had thought him: he was perhaps forty-eight or fifty. Under his hand there was a dial with a lever on top and figures running round the face.

'I told you,' said O'Brien, 'that if we met again it would be here.'

'Yes,' said Winston.

Without any warning except a slight movement of O'Brien's hand, a wave of pain flooded his body. It was a frightening pain, because he could not see what was happening, and he had the feeling that some mortal injury was being done to him. He did not know whether the thing was really happening, or whether the effect was electrically produced: but his body was being wrenched out of shape, the joints were being slowly torn apart. Although the pain had brought the sweat out on his forehead, the worst of all was the fear that his backbone was about to snap. He set his teeth and breathed hard through his nose, trying to keep silent as long as possible.

'You are afraid,' said O'Brien, watching his face, 'that in another moment something is going to break. Your especial fear is that it will be your backbone. You have a vivid mental picture of the vertebrae snapping apart and the spinal fluid dripping out of them. That is what you are thinking, is it not, Winston?'

Winston did not answer. O'Brien drew back the lever on the dial. The wave of pain receded almost as quickly as it had come.

'That was forty,' said O'Brien. 'You can see that the numbers on this dial run up to a hundred. Will you please remember, throughout our conversation, that I have it in my power to inflict pain on you at any moment and to whatever degree I choose? If you tell me any lies, or attempt to prevaricate in any way, or even fall below your usual level of intelligence, you will cry out with pain, instantly. Do you understand that?'

'Yes,' said Winston.

O'Brien's manner became less severe. He resettled his spectacles thoughtfully, and took a pace or two up and down. When he spoke his voice was gentle and patient. He had the air of a doctor, a teacher, even a priest, anxious to explain and persuade rather than to punish.

'I am taking trouble with you, Winston,' he said, 'because you are worth trouble. You know perfectly well what is the matter with you. You have known it for years, though you have fought against the knowledge. You are mentally deranged. You suffer from a defective memory.

George Orwell   *Nineteen eighty-four*

The Milgram experiment

Stanley Milgram, an American social psychologist, carried out an experiment in the United States in 1961, since repeated in many other countries with similar results.

Milgram's collaborators approached twenty- to fifty-year-old passers-by in the street completely at random and asked for their help with a series of scientific experiments supposedly designed to test the relationship between learning and punishment. When one of these volunteers arrived at the agreed time at the research department of Yale University he would always run into a young man who had supposedly come for the same purpose but who was in reality one of Milgram's assistants. Dressed in a white coat as a symbol of authority, the research director then got the two to toss a coin for which role they were to play. One of them was supposed to be the 'teacher', the other the 'pupil'. The toss was rigged so that Milgram's assistant always won the part of the 'pupil'. In the presence of the 'teacher' the assistant was then tied to a kind of electric chair and left with one hand free for working a push-button, his means of responding to questions. The pupil would give a creditable performance of anxious unease and consternation when the director explained that each wrong answer would be followed by an electric shock. The teacher had previously been given a sufficiently unpleasant trial shock of 45 volts for his own information.

Then director and teacher went into the room next door. The doors were shut; the only contact with the pupil was through a microphone and loudspeaker. The teacher was then presented with a list of words which he was to read out for the pupil to memorize and repeat by means of certain sequences of push-button signals. Then the teacher took up his position at a switchboard with thirty levers for different current strengths, ranging from 15 to 450 volts, and descriptions ranging from 'slight shock' to 'danger, severe shock'. His instructions were that the current

was to be increased with every wrong answer.

Of course the carefully tutored pupil did not really get any electric shocks but made his mistakes according to plan and worked a pre-recorded tape of his own voice. From 75 volts upwards he could be heard drawing in his breath with a hiss and stifling his groans; at 180 volts he screamed loudly, 'Stop'. After this he started to weep and to beg for mercy and eventually he howled wordlessly like an animal. From 300 volts upwards he no longer reacted at all, and the remaining questions were unanswered. But as no answer counted as a wrong answer, the teacher had to go on asking more questions and administering further shocks.

The way the experiment was set up allowed none of the volunteers to doubt its genuineness. All of them agreed on this afterwards. The real question the experiment asked was, of course: 'How far will a human being go if an anonymous authority orders him to torture or even to kill a fellow human?'

The quite appalling result was: in the United States 65 per cent of the volunteers continued to play their part of teacher right to the 450-volt limit in spite of the victim's earlier cries and his eventual silence. When this experiment was repeated at the Maxwell Planck Institute in Munich the result was 85 per cent. Since then the experiment has been repeated with a number of variations by critics and sceptics, and the statistics proved to be correct.

In other words, on an average three out of four men will be ready to torture and kill to order without questioning the reason. Not one of us should necessarily believe ourselves to be one of the rare exceptions.

Nearly all the people in the various experiments experienced an unwillingness to continue after their victim evinced his first expression of pain. But the director, leaning against the wall with his arms crossed, would not enter into any discussion and instead wearily countered every attempt at stopping with stereotyped remarks, 'Go on – it's necessary for the experiment – I can't explain it to you now – go on – you have no choice.' Most of the volunteers wriggled, sweated, groaned or laughed nervously and said more than once that they did not want to proceed. But those who were particularly vocal about the inhumanity of the experiment were those who continued to the very end.

Discussion afterwards revealed that nearly all the volunteers had thought that the victim was unconscious or perhaps even dead. Most of them were profoundly disturbed by their own behaviour and could not understand it. Trying to find reasons for it they would say things like: 'I did not want to get anything wrong, to disturb the experiment.' They told themselves that the scientists must know what they were doing.

This compulsion 'to get it right' and the inability to criticize a nameless authority is not aggression but its biologically necessary counterpart, group loyalty and subordination. These traits, too, have become pathologically overdeveloped in human society – as this experiment shows – to the point where established anonymous authorities like 'the state', 'science' or even 'the revolution' can make everything legitimate by way of a rubber stamp, white coat or armband.

The picture we generally have of the human being and human society is wrong. Before Stanley Milgram started his experiment he asked forty well-known academic psychologists and psychiatrists to predict the results. These experts predicted that the great majority of the subjects would stop the experiment at the first signs of pain in the victim. Four per cent would continue up to 200 volts (loud cries) and only 0.1 per cent would continue to the bitter end.

Something inside us refuses to replace this idealized view of mankind with a more realistic one. Anything that upsets our idealized picture we describe as 'inhuman'. Auschwitz, the Congo, Bangladesh, Vietnam – it is always 'the others' or 'the exceptions' who would do such things, never the majority. But 75 per cent of Milgram's experiment is down in black and white. And 75 per cent cannot represent exceptions; on the contrary it represents normality.

If our view of humanity is wrong then everything built on it must be wrong also, not only our educational theory, politics, peace-keeping efforts and jurisprudence but also the planning of our cities, the way we live, our scale of values, and our accepted behavioural norms. We should not base our plans for the future on idealized imaginings.

Eckehard Munck   *Biology of the future*

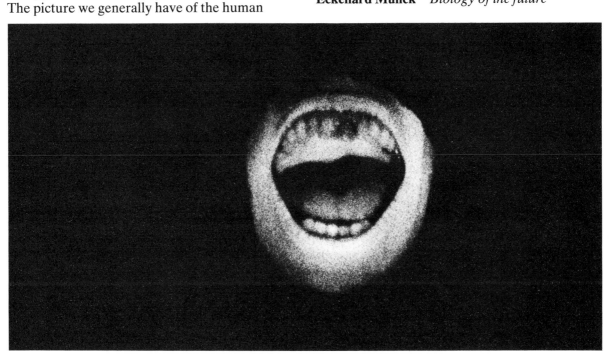

The aqueduct

It leapt over the country in great stone arches. It was empty now, with the wind blowing in its sluices; it took a year to build, from the land in the North to the land in the South.

'Soon,' said mothers to their children, 'soon now the Aqueduct will be finished. Then they will open the gates a thousand miles North and cool water will flow to us, for our crops, our flowers, our baths, and our tables.'

The children watched the Aqueduct being built stone on solid stone. It towered thirty feet in the sky, with great gargoyle spouts every hundred yards which would drop tiny streams down into yard reservoirs.

In the North there was not only one country, but two. They had rattled their sabres and clashed their shields for many years.

Now, in the Year of the Finishing of the Aqueduct, the two Northern countries shot a million arrows at each other and raised a million shields, like numerous suns, flashing. There was a cry like an ocean on a distant shore.

At the year's end the Aqueduct stood finished. The people of the Hot South, waiting, asked, 'When will the water come? With war in the North, will we starve for water, will our crops die?'

A courier came racing. 'The war is terrible,' he said. 'There is a slaughtering that is unbelievable. More than one hundred million people have been slain.'

'For what?'

'They disagreed, those two Northern countries.

'That's all we know. They disagreed.'

The people gathered all along the stone Aqueduct. Messengers ran along the empty sluiceways with yellow streamers, crying, 'Bring vases and bowls, ready your fields and ploughs, open your baths, fetch water glasses!'

A thousand miles of filling Aqueduct and the slap of naked courier feet in the channel, running ahead. The people gathered by the tens of millions from the boiling countryside, the sluiceways open, waiting, their crocks, urns, jugs, held towards the gargoyle spouts where the wind whistled emptily.

'It's coming!' The word passed from person to person down the one thousand miles.

And from a great distance, there was the sound of rushing and running, the sound that liquid makes in a stone channel. It flowed slowly at first and then faster, and then very fast down into the Southern land, under the hot sun.

'It's here! Any second now. Listen!' said the people. They raised their glasses into the air.

Liquid poured from the sluiceways down the land, out of gargoyle mouths, into the stone baths, into the glasses, into the fields. The fields were made rich for the harvest. People bathed. There was a singing you could hear from one field to one town to another.

'But, Mother!' A child held up his glass and shook it, the liquid whirled slowly. 'This isn't water!'

'Hush!' said the mother.

'It's red,' said the child. 'And it's thick.'

'Here's the soap, wash yourself, don't ask questions, shut up,' she said. 'Hurry into the field, open the sluicegates, plant the rice!'

In the fields, the father and his two sons laughed into one another's faces. 'If this keeps up, we've a great life ahead. A full silo and a clean body.'

'Don't worry,' said the two sons. 'The President is sending a representative North to make certain that the two countries there continue to disagree.'

'Who knows, it might be a fifty-year war!'

They sang and smiled.

And at night they all lay happily, listening to the good sound of the Aqueduct, full and rich, like a river, rushing through their land towards the morning.

Ray Bradbury

The soldier

If I should die, think only this of me:
    That there's some corner of a foreign field
That is for ever England. There shall be
    In that rich earth a richer dust concealed;
A dust whom England bore, shaped, made aware,
    Gave, once, her flowers to love, her ways to roam,
A body of England's, breathing English air,
    Washed by the rivers, blest by suns of home,

And think, this heart, all evil shed away,
    A pulse in the eternal mind, no less
        Gives somewhere back the thoughts by England given;
Her sights and sounds; dreams happy as her day;
    And laughter, learnt of friends; and gentleness,
        In hearts at peace, under an English heaven.

Rupert Brooke

Futility

Move him into the sun –
Gently its touch awoke him once,
At home, whispering of fields unsown.
Always it woke him, even in France,
Until this morning and this snow.
If anything might rouse him now
The kind old sun will know.

Think how it wakes the seeds, –
Woke, once, the clays of a cold star.
Are limbs, so dear-achieved, are sides,
Full-nerved – still warm – too hard to stir?
Was it for this the clay grew tall?
– O what made fatuous sunbeams toil
To break earth's sleep at all?

Wilfred Owen

Nuclear weapons

The first nuclear weapons were developed in the early 1940s and built for use against the Germans. By the time the first bombs were ready, Germany had surrendered, and instead the inhabitants of Hiroshima and Nagasaki became the first victims of nuclear attack. It was by no means an inevitable choice. Reading the minutes of the committees set up to advise the American President on the use of the bomb, and reading the accounts of the deliberations of various interested groups, I was surprised by the extent of the opposition to the use of the bomb against civilians, and by the humanity and far-sightedness of the arguments deployed. There were numerous proposals: dropping the bomb in the desert or the ocean with Japanese observers present was one line of approach, discounted for many reasons. The US Navy was convinced that a blockade would bring a Japanese surrender within months. Japan's industrial output was a fraction of its pre-war figure, and raw materials were virtually non-existent. There was one forcefully argued case for dropping the bomb on a huge forest of cryptomeria trees not far from Tokyo. The trees would be felled along the line of blast, and the power of a single bomb would be evident. Beyond all this, intercepted and deciphered radio traffic suggested that powerful figures in the Japanese military, with access to the Emperor, were convinced that Japan could not win the war and were seeking a surrender – albeit a conditional surrender that would salvage some degree of national dignity. There were those in the US administration who argued that in this instance the difference between conditional and unconditional surrender was little more than verbal, and that with some flexibility the war could be ended by diplomatic means.

However, the bomb seemed to have had its own momentum. It was a triumph of theoretical and technological daring. The scientists working on the project were so involved in solving countless problems, and so elated when they succeeded, that many of them lost touch with the ultimate goal of their labours – colossal destruction. The bomb was a pinnacle of human achievement – intellect divorced from feeling – and there appears to have been a deep, collective desire to see it used, despite all arguments. Opponents of its use were always on the defensive. Furthermore, at the beginning of the war, genocide had been the strategy of the Axis powers alone. By 1945 it had become acceptable to all combatants; fascism had to be defeated by fascism's methods, and the mass destruction at Hiroshima and Nagasaki had powerful precedents in the fire bombing of Dresden and Tokyo.

The nuclear bombing of these two cities, then, was not purely the responsibility of a handful of genocidally inclined military advisers; it was made possible by a general state of mind, by a deep fascination with technological solutions, by judgements barbarized by warfare and by nations which – rightly or wrongly – had organized themselves to inflict destruction. The public, when it heard the news of the bombing, though shocked, was by no means overwhelmingly critical. Ever since that time, attempts to prevent the proliferations of nuclear weapons have been a total failure. There are now more than sixty thousand nuclear warheads, primed and programmed for their destinations. The smaller of these are vastly more powerful than the Hiroshima bomb. If, as a species, we faced a simple test of wisdom, from the very outset we appeared to be intent on failure.

Ian McEwan

Assignments

Title page (84)	Choose one of the pictures on this page and write about it in any way that you think suitable.

The cane (85)	1 After reading this story, write down your immediate reactions to what you have read. 2 How much have things changed since Roald Dahl was at school? 3 Express your opinions in a piece of writing on the theme of 'Schools and punishment'.

An interrogation (87)	**Writing a report** At the end of the interrogation, O'Brien has to make a formal report to the Party. In this he describes what has happened and comments on Smith's reactions. Write his report.

The Milgram experiment (88)	1 Write down **your reactions** to the experiment. Comment on what you think it teaches us about human nature and also on the way in which it was carried out. 2 Write two **reports** of the experiment: a) by one of Milgram's assistants, who played the part of the 'pupil'. b) by one of the volunteers who played the part of 'teacher'. In each case describe what happened and the person's thoughts and feelings about it. 3 Write an **argument** essay commenting on this statement: 'Aggression and willingness to obey orders are both part of human nature. There's nothing we can do about that. So we have just got to learn to live with them.'

The aqueduct (90)	**Writing exposition** This short story could be described as a 'myth': a story with much deeper and wider meanings than the events it describes. 1 What would you say briefly was the meaning of this myth? 2 Study it again more closely. Look for further meanings. For example, what does it have to say about: human nature; aggressiveness; war and economics; diplomacy? 3 Write an explanation of your interpretation of the story.

The soldier (92)	1 Write down in your own words what you think this poem is saying. Write in as much detail as you can. 2 Write out any words, phrases, or sentences that you find difficult to understand. 3 Comment on a) *What* the poet says b) *How* he says it.

Futility (92)	Work on this poem in the same way as you did on *The soldier*.

Both poems	These two poems were both written during the First World War. One of the poems was written by a young man going off to join the war, the other by a young soldier who had already been involved in the war. 1 Which do you think is which? What are your reasons? 2 Do you think one is a *better* poem than the other? Why? Write a comparison of the two poems.

Nuclear weapons (93)	This short passage contains a detailed and strongly expressed argument about the dropping of the first nuclear bomb and its meaning for us today. Many people do not agree with the writer, but even if you disagree it is important to understand clearly what he is saying. 1 Read the first paragraph again carefully. Make notes on what it says about each of these topics: a) Why the first nuclear weapons were developed. b) How much opposition there was to using them against Japan. c) What alternatives were suggested to using the bomb at all. d) What alternatives were suggested to using the bomb on civilians. 2 Read the second paragraph again and make notes on these topics: a) Why many of the scientists involved in making the bomb wanted to see it used. b) Why people were, by the end of the war, prepared to accept the idea of the mass killing of civilians (genocide). 3 Read the third paragraph again and make notes on these topics: a) Why the writer thinks that the responsibility for dropping the bomb was not just the responsibility of military men. b) The conclusions the writer draws from this. **Writing an argument** Write an argument expressing your reactions to what Ian McEwan has written.

Who am I? asks mystery Mary

Crash victim suffers loss of memory

A woman who was knocked down in a road accident in the High Street last week has finally recovered consciousness — only to discover that she is suffering from total amnesia.

The woman, known to be called 'Mary' from a letter in her handbag, was knocked unconscious when run over by an Austin Metro near the junction between Back Lane and High Street. She did not regain consciousness until three days later.

When she did so she had no idea of who she was or where she was. A hospital spokesman said that such cases were not common, but there was every chance that 'Mary' would gradually recover some, if not all, of her memory. Meanwhile she has been told she must stay in bed and rest, while the injuries she suffered in the crash—none too serious, fortunately—have a chance to heal up.

The police have been making enquiries in an attempt to find out who the mystery woman is

Map from PC Matthews' notebook

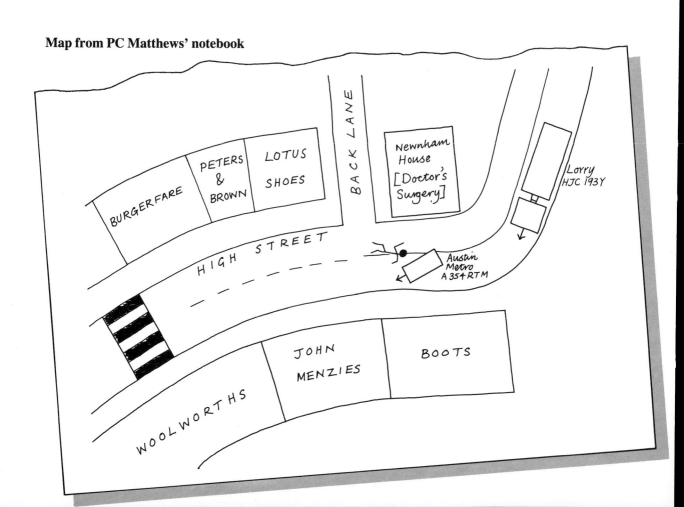

Information from PC Matthews' notebook

A. Before the accident

 1. Articulated lorry HJC 193 Y stationary just before bend in High Street by Newnham House. Driver not in cab.
 2. Austin Metro A 354 RTM proceeding west along High Street.
 3. Pedestrian crossing road from outside Lotus Shoes towards Boots.
 4. Witness Anna Morris crossing High Street by pedestrian crossing.
 5. Witness James Long standing on pavement by Lotus Shoes.

B. Apparent circumstances of accident (see witnesses' statements):

 1. Lorry parked on corner while driver asked directions.
 2. Metro pulled out to pass lorry, thus coming round bend on wrong side of road.
 3. Pedestrian in middle of road struck by Metro and knocked down.
 4. Metro brought to a halt opposite Boots.

C. Injuries / damage caused:

 1. Pedestrian struck head on road and knocked unconscious. Bruising to head and body.
 2. Driver of Metro suffering shock.
 3. Superficial damage to front offside of Metro

D. Conditions at time of accident:

   Time : 14-55   7th July
   Visibility — good.
   Weather — fine.
   Road surface — dry.

E. PC Matthews rendered first aid to injured who was then taken by ambulance to General Hospital.

The contents of the victim's handbag

Part of statement by Mr Alan Harries, driver of lorry

```
I was driving through the town, when I realized that I had missed my road.
(I wanted to get the A37 to Yeovil.)  So I stopped and left the cab.  I went
into a newsagent's shop and asked the owner about my route.  While I was doing
this, I heard the screech of brakes.  When I went outside, I saw the Metro
across the road and the woman lying on the ground.
```

Part of statement by Sheila Peters, driver of the Metro

```
I was driving along the High Street.  As I came to the corner by Newnham House
there was a lorry parked.  I pulled out to pass it.  This meant that I had to
go round the corner on the wrong side of the road.  I therefore could not see
anything in the road on the Lotus side until I was round the corner.  As I came
round it there was a woman right in front of me.  I braked and pulled the car
over to the left, but I couldn't avoid her.  There was nothing I could do.  It
was the lorry's fault.  He should never have been parked there.
```

Later statement by PC Matthews

```
There seemed to be no means of identifying the injured woman.  I therefore
examined the contents of her handbag with a view to establishing her identity.
Unfortunately it did not contain a driving licence or any other document
bearing her name and address ...
```

Assignments

1 Two witnesses, Ms Anna Morris and Mr James Long, made statements to the police about the accident. Work out what they must have seen from where they were standing. Write their statements. (Your statements should be factual and informative, but they need not agree.)
2 Write the report in the local evening newspaper dealing with the accident.
3 Decide how you think the police would have gone about discovering who 'Mary' was, based on the evidence of her handbag. Write a report of how they eventually established her identity.
4 Look at the information available about the accident victim. Decide who you think she is and how she came to be there. Make up any details that are needed to fill out your version of what happened. Now write 'Mary's story'.

6. *The way ahead*

Ten types of hospital visitor

The second appears, a melancholy splurge
Of theological colours;
Taps heavily about like a healthy vulture
Distributing deep-frozen hope.

The patients gaze at him cautiously.
Most of them, as yet uncertain of the realities
Of heaven, hell-fire, or eternal emptiness,

Play for safety
By accepting his attentions
With just-concealed apathy,
Except one old man, who cries
With newly sharpened hatred,
'Shove off! Shove off!
'Shove . . . shove . . . shove . . . shove
Off!
Just you
Shove!'

I

The first enters wearing the neon armour
Of virtue.
Ceaselessly firing all-purpose smiles
At everyone present
She destroys hope
In the breasts of the sick,
Who realize instantly
That they are incapable of surmounting
Her ferocious goodwill.

Such courage she displays
In the face of human disaster!

Fortunately, she does not stay long.
After a speedy trip round the ward
In the manner of a nineteen-thirties destroyer
Showing the flag in the Mediterranean,
She returns home for a week
– With luck, longer –
Scorched by the heat of her own worthiness.

III

The third skilfully deflates his weakly smiling
    victim
By telling him
How the lobelias are doing,
How many kittens the cat had,
How the slate came off the scullery roof,
And how no one has visited the patient for a
    fortnight
Because everybody
Had colds and feared to bring the jumpy germ
Into hospital.

The patient's eyes
Ice over. He is uninterested
In lobelias, the cat, the slate, the germ.
Flat on his back, drip-fed, his face
The shade of a newly dug-up Pharoah,
Wearing his skeleton outside his skin,
Yet his wits as bright as a lighted candle,
He is concerned only with the here, the now,
And requires to speak
Of nothing but his present predicament.

      It is not permitted.

IV

The fourth attempts to cheer
His aged mother with light jokes
Menacing as shell-splinters.
'They'll soon have you jumping round
Like a gazelle,' he says.
'Playing in the football team.'
Quite undeterred by the sight of kilos
Of plaster, chains, lifting-gear,
A pair of lethally designed crutches,
'You'll be leap-frogging soon,' he says.
'Swimming ten lengths of the baths.'

At these unlikely prophecies
The old lady stares fearfully
At her sick, sick offspring
Thinking he has lost his reason –

Which, alas seems to be the case.

V

The fifth, a giant from the fields
With suit smelling of milk and hay,
Shifts uneasily from one bullock foot
To the other, as though to avoid
Settling permanently in the antiseptic landscape.
Occasionally he looses a scared glance
Sideways, as though fearful of what intimacy
He may blunder on, or that the walls
Might suddenly close in on him.

He carries flowers, held lightly in fingers
The size and shape of plantains,

Tenderly kisses his wife's cheek
– The brush of a child's lips –
Then balances, motionless, for thirty minutes
On the thin chair.

At the end of visiting time
He emerges breathless,
Blinking with relief, into the light.

He does not appear to notice
The dusk.

VI

The sixth visitor says little,
Breathes reassurance,
Smiles securely.
Carries no black passport of grapes
And visa of chocolate. Has a clutch
Of clean washing.

Unobtrusively stows it
In the locker; searches out more.
Talks quietly to the Sister
Out of sight, out of earshot, of the patient.
Arrives punctually as a tide.
Does not stay the whole hour.

Even when she has gone
The patient seems to sense her there:
An upholding
Presence.

VII

The seventh visitor
Smells of bar-room after-shave.
Often finds his friend
Sound asleep: whether real or feigned
Is never determined.

He does not mind; prowls the ward
In search of second-class, lost-face patients
With no visitors
And who are pretending to doze
Or read paperbacks.

He probes relentlessly the nature
Of each complaint, and is swift with such
Dilutions of confidence as,
'Ah! You'll be worse
Before you're better.'

Five minutes before the bell punctuates
Visiting time, his friend opens an alarm-clock
    eye.
The visitor checks his watch.
Market day. The Duck and Pheasant will be still
    open.

Courage must be refuelled.

VIII

The eighth visitor looks infinitely
More decayed, ill and infirm than any patient.
His face is an expensive grey.
He peers about with antediluvian eyes
As though from the other end
Of time.
He appears to have risen from the grave
To make this appearance.
There is a whiff of white flowers about him;
The crumpled look of a slightly used shroud.
Slowly he passes the patient
A bag of bullet-proof
Home-made biscuits,
A strong, death-dealing cake –
'To have with your tea,'
Or a bowl of fruit so weighty
It threatens to break
His glass fingers.
The patient, encouraged beyond measure,
Thanks him with enthusiasm, not for
The oranges, the biscuits, the cake,
But for the healing sight
Of someone patently worse
Than himself. He rounds the crisis-corner;
Begins a recovery.

IX

The ninth visitor is life.

X

The tenth visitor
Is not usually named.

Charles Causley

The old man and his grandson

There was once a very old man, whose eyes had become dim, his ears dull of hearing, his knees trembled, and when he sat at table he could hardly hold the spoon, and spilt the broth upon the table cloth or let it run out of his mouth. His son and his son's wife were disgusted at this, so the old grandfather at last had to sit in the corner behind the stove, and they gave him his food in an earthenware bowl, and not even enough of it. And he used to look towards the table with his eyes full of tears. Once, too, his trembling hands could not hold the bowl and it fell to the ground and broke. The young wife scolded him, but he said nothing and only sighed. Then they bought him a wooden bowl for a few half-pence, out of which he had to eat.

They were once sitting thus when the little grandson of four years old began to gather together some bits of wood upon the ground. 'What are you doing there?' asked the father. 'I am making a little trough,' answered the child, 'for father and mother to eat out of when I am big.'

The man and his wife looked at each other for a while, and presently began to cry. Then they took the old grandfather to the table, and henceforth always let him eat with them, and likewise said nothing if he did spill a little of anything.

The Brothers Grimm

Warning

When I am an old woman I shall wear purple
With a red hat which doesn't go, and doesn't suit me,
And I shall spend my pension on brandy and summer gloves
And satin sandals, and say we've no money for butter.
I shall sit down on the pavement when I'm tired
And gobble up samples in shops and press alarm bells
And run my stick along the public railings
And make up for the sobriety of my youth.
I shall go out in my slippers in the rain
And pick the flowers in other people's gardens
And learn to spit.

You can wear terrible shirts and grow more fat
And eat three pounds of sausages at a go
Or only bread and pickle for a week
And hoard pens and pencils and beermats and things in boxes.

But now we must have clothes that keep us dry
And pay our rent and not swear in the street
And set a good example for the children.
We will have friends to dinner and read the papers.

But maybe I ought to practise a little now?
So people who know me are not too shocked and surprised
When suddenly I am old, and start to wear purple.

Jenny Joseph

The leave-taking

She was a woman with a broom or a dustpan or a washrag or a mixing spoon in her hand. You saw her cutting piecrust in the morning, humming to it, or you saw her setting out the baked pies at noon or taking them in, cool, at dusk. She rang porcelain cups like a Swiss bell ringer, to their place. She glided through the halls as steadily as a vacuum machine, seeking, finding, and setting to rights. She made mirrors of every window, to catch the sun. She strolled but twice through any garden, trowel in hand, and the flowers raised their quivering fires upon the warm air in her wake. She slept quietly and turned no more than three times in a night, as relaxed as a white glove to which, at dawn, a brisk hand will return. Waking, she touched people like pictures, to set their frames straight.

But, now . . . ?

'Grandma,' said everyone. 'Great-grandma.'

Now it was as if a huge sum in arithmetic were finally drawing to an end. She had stuffed turkeys, chickens, squabs, gentlemen, and boys. She had washed ceilings, walls, invalids, and children. She had laid linoleum, repaired bicycles, wound clocks, stoked furnaces, swabbed iodine on ten thousand grievous wounds. Her hands had flown all around about and down, gentling this, holding that, throwing baseballs, swinging bright croquet mallets, seeding black earth, or fixing covers over dumplings, ragouts, and children wildly strewn by slumber. She had pulled down shades, pinched out candles, turned switches, and – grown old. Looking back on thirty billions of things started, carried, finished and done, it all summed up, totalled out; the last decimal was placed, the final zero swung slowly into line. Now, chalk in hand, she stood back from life a silent hour before reaching for the eraser.

'Let me see now,' said Great-grandma. 'Let me see . . .'

With no fuss or further ado, she travelled the house in an ever-circling inventory, reached the stairs at last, and, making no special announcement, she took herself up three flights to her room where, silently, she laid herself out like a fossil imprint under the snowing cool sheets of her bed and began to die.

Again the voices:

'Grandma! Great-grandma!'

The rumour of what she was doing dropped down the stairwell, hit, and spread ripples through the rooms, out doors and windows and along the street of elms to the edge of the green ravine.

'Here, now, here!'

The family surrounded her bed.

'Just let me lie,' she whispered.

Her ailment could not be seen in any microscope; it was a mild but ever-deepening tiredness, a dim weighing of her sparrow body; sleepy, sleepier, sleepiest.

As for her children and her children's children – it seemed impossible that with such a simple act, the most leisurely act in the world, she could cause such apprehension.

'Great-grandma, now, listen – what you're doing is no better than breaking a lease. This house will fall down without you. You must give us at least a year's notice!'

Great-grandma opened one eye. Ninety years gazed calmly out at her physicians like a dust-ghost from a high cupola window in a fast-emptying house. 'Tom . . .?'

The boy was sent, alone, to her whispering bed.

'Tom,' she said, faintly, far away, 'in the Southern Seas there's a day in each man's life when he knows it's time to shake hands with all his friends and say good-bye and sail away, and he does, and it's natural – it's just his time. That's how it is today. I'm so like you sometimes, sitting through Saturday matinees until nine at night when we send your dad to bring you home. Tom, when the time comes that the same cowboys are shooting the same Indians on the same mountaintop, then it's best to fold back the seat and head for the door, with no regrets and no walking backward up the aisle. So, I'm leaving while I'm still happy and still entertained.'

Douglas was summoned next to her side.

'Grandma, who'll shingle the roof next spring?'

Every April for as far back as there were calendars, you thought you heard woodpeckers tapping the housetop. But no, it was Great-grandma, somehow transported, singing, pounding nails, replacing shingles, high in the sky!

'Douglas,' she whispered, 'don't ever let anyone do the shingles unless it's fun for them.'

'Yes'm.'

'Look around come April, and say, "Who'd like to fix the roof?" And whichever face lights up is the face you want, Douglas. Because up there on that roof you can see the whole town going towards the country and the country going towards the edge of the earth and the river shining, and the morning lake, and birds on the trees down under you, and the best of the wind all around above. Any one of those should be enough to make a person climb a weather vane some spring sunrise. It's a powerful hour, if you give it half a chance . . .'

Her voice sank to a soft flutter.

Douglas was crying.

She roused herself again. 'Now, why are you doing that?'

'Because,' he said, 'you won't be here tomorrow.'

She turned a small hand-mirror from herself to the boy. He looked at her face and himself in the mirror and then at her face again as she said, 'Tomorrow morning I'll get up at seven and wash behind my ears; I'll run to church with Charlie Woodman; I'll picnic at Electric Park; I'll swim, run barefoot, fall out of trees, chew spearmint gum . . . Douglas, Douglas, for shame! You cut your fingernails, don't you?'

'Yes'm.'

'And you don't yell when your body makes itself over every seven years or so, old cells dead and new ones added to your fingers and your heart. You don't mind that, do you?'

'No'm.'

'Well, consider then, boy. Any man saves fingernail clippings is a fool. You ever see a snake bother to keep his peeled skin? That's about all you got here today in this bed is fingernails and snake skin. One good breath would send me up in flakes. Important thing is not the me that's lying here, but the me that's sitting on the edge of the bed looking back at me, and the me that's downstairs cooking supper, or out in the garage under the car, or in the library reading. All the new parts, they count. I'm not really dying today. No person ever died that had a family. I'll be around a long time. A thousand years from now a whole township of my offspring will be biting sour apples in the gumwood shade. That's my answer to anyone asks big questions! Quick now, send in the rest!'

At last the entire family stood, like people seeing someone off at the rail station, waiting in the room.

'Well,' said Great-grandma, 'there I am. I'm not humble, so it's nice seeing you standing around my bed. Now next week there's late gardening and closet-cleaning and clothes-buying for the children to do. And since that part of me which is called, for convenience, Great-grandma, won't be here to step it along, those other parts of me called Uncle Bert and Leo and Tom and Douglas, and all the other names, will have to take over, each to his own.'

'Yes, Grandma.'

'I don't want any Hallowe'en parties here tomorrow. Don't want anyone saying anything sweet about me; I said it all in my time and my pride. I've tasted every victual and danced every dance; now there's one last tart I haven't bit on, one tune I haven't whistled. But I'm not afraid. I'm truly curious. Death won't get a crumb by my mouth I won't keep and savour. So don't you worry over me. Now, all of you go, and let me find my sleep . . .'

Somewhere a door closed quietly.

'That's better.' Alone, she snuggled luxuriously down through the warm snowbank of linen and wool, sheet and cover, and the colours of the patchwork quilt were bright as the circus banners of old time. Lying there, she felt as small and secret as on those mornings eighty-some-odd years ago when, wakening, she comforted her tender bones in bed.

A long time back, she thought, I dreamed a dream, and was enjoying it so much when someone wakened me, and that was the day when I was born. And now? Now, let me see . . . She cast her mind back. Where was I? she thought. Ninety years . . . how to take up the thread and the pattern of that lost dream again? She put out a small hand. *There* . . . Yes, that was it. She smiled. Deeper in the warm snow hill she turned her head upon her pillow. That was better. Now, yes, now she saw it shaping in her mind quietly, and with a serenity like a sea moving along an endless and self-refreshing shore. Now she let the old dream touch and lift her from the snow and drift her above the scarce-remembered bed.

Downstairs, she thought, they are polishing the silver, and rummaging the cellar, and dusting in the halls. She could hear them living all through the house.

'It's all right,' whispered Great-grandma, as the dream floated her. 'Like everything else in this life, it's fitting.'

And the sea moved her back down the shore.

Ray Bradbury

Looking ahead

Part of a speech which the author Kurt Vonnegut Jr gave to a group of students about to leave college.

Let us ask ourselves, 'What would be a good, new direction for the worm of civilization to take?'

Well – it should go upward, if possible. Up is certainly better than down, or is widely believed to be. And we would be a lot safer if the Government would take its money out of science and put it into astrology and the reading of palms. I used to think that science would save us, and science certainly tried. But we can't stand any more tremendous explosions, either for or against democracy. Only in superstition is there hope. If you want to become a friend of civilization, then become an enemy of truth and a fanatic for harmless balderdash.

I know that millions of dollars have been spent to produce this splendid graduating class, and that the main hope of your teachers was, once they got through with you, that you would no longer be superstitious. I'm sorry – I have to undo that now. I beg you to believe in the most ridiculous superstition of all; that humanity is at the centre of the universe, the fulfiller or the frustrator of the grandest dreams of God Almighty.

If you can believe that, and make others believe it, then there might be hope for us. Human beings might stop treating each other like garbage, might begin to treasure and protect each other instead. Then it might be all right to have babies again.

* * * *

About astrology and palmistry. They are good because they make people feel vivid and full of possibilities. They are communism at its best. Everybody has a birthday and almost everybody has a palm.

Take a seemingly drab person born on August 3, for instance. He's a Leo. He is proud, generous, trusting, energetic, domineering and authoritative! All Leos are! He is ruled by the Sun! His gems are the ruby and the diamond! His color is orange! His metal is gold! This is a *nobody*?

His harmonious signs for business, marriage, or companionship are Sagittarius and Aries. Anybody here a Sagittarius or an Aries? Watch out! Here comes destiny!

Is this lonely-looking human being really alone? Far from it! He shares the sign of Leo with T. E. Lawrence, Herbert Hoover, Alfred Hitchcock, Dorothy Parker, Jacqueline Onassis, Henry Ford, Princess Margaret, and George Bernard Shaw! You've heard of *them*.

Look at him blush with happiness! Ask him to show you his amazing palms. What a fantastic heart line he has! Be on your guard, girls. Have you ever seen a Hill of the Moon like his? Wow! This is some human being!

Which brings us to the arts, whose purpose, in common with astrology, is to use frauds in order to make human beings seem more wonderful than they really are.

*   *   *   *

The arts put man at the center of the universe, whether he belongs there or not. Military science, on the other hand, treats man as garbage – and his children, and his cities, too. Military science is probably right about the contemptibility of man in the vastness of the universe. Still – I deny that contemptibility, and I beg you to deny it, through the creation or appreciation of art.

*   *   *   *

It has been said many times that man's knowledge of himself has been left far behind by his understanding of technology, and that we can have peace and plenty and justice only when man's knowledge of himself catches up. This is not true. Some people hope for great discoveries in the social sciences, social equivalents of $F = ma$ and $E = mc^2$, and so on. Others think we have to evolve, to become better monkeys with bigger brains. We don't need more information. We don't need bigger brains. All that is required is that we become less selfish than we are.

We already have plenty of sound suggestions as to how we are to act if things are to become better on earth. For instance: Do unto others as you would have them do unto you. About seven hundred years ago, Thomas Aquinas had some other recommendations as to what people might do with their lives, and I do not find these made ridiculous by computers and trips to the moon and television sets. He praises the Seven Spiritual Works of Mercy, which are these:

To teach the ignorant, to counsel the doubtful, to console the sad, to reprove the sinner, to forgive the offender, to bear with the oppressive and troublesome, and to pray for us all.

He also admires the Seven Corporal Works of Mercy, which are these:

To feed the hungry, to give drink to the thirsty, to clothe the naked, to shelter the homeless, to visit the sick and prisoners, to ransom captives, and to bury the dead.

A great swindle of our time is the assumption that science has made religion obsolete. All science has damaged is the story of Adam and Eve and the story of Jonah and the Whale. Everything else holds up pretty well, particularly the lessons about fairness and gentleness. People who find those lessons irrelevant in the twentieth century are simply using science as an excuse for greed and harshness.

Science has nothing to do with it, friends.

Another great swindle is that people your age are supposed to save the world.

*   *   *   *

I often hear parents say to their idealistic children, 'All right, you see so much that is wrong with the world – go out and *do* something about it. We're all *for* you! Go out and *save* the world.'

*   *   *   *

. . . . It isn't up to you. You don't have the money and the power. You don't have the appearance of grave maturity – even though you may be gravely mature. You don't even know how to handle dynamite. It is up to older people to save the world. You can help them.

Do not take the entire world on your shoulders. Do a certain amount of skylarking, as befits people your age.

*   *   *   *

Many of you will undertake exceedingly serious work this summer – campaigning for humane Senators and Congressmen, helping the poor and the ignorant and the awfully old. Good. But skylark, too.

Kurt Vonnegut Jr   adapted from *Wampeters foma and granfalloons*

The way

Friend, I have lost the way.
The way leads on.
Is there another way?
The way is one.
I must retrace the track.
It's lost and gone.
Back, I must travel back!
None goes there, none.
Then I'll make here my place,
(The road runs on),
Stay here, for ever stay.
None stays here, none.
I cannot find the way.
The way leads on.
Oh places I have passed!
That journey's done.
And what will come at last?
The road leads on.

Edwin Muir

Assignments

Title page (100)	1 Which picture do you find most striking on this page? Why? 2 How would you describe the person in each portrait? 3 How else could you illustrate the theme of this unit? 4 Make up a title based on your alternative illustrations and then write expressing your thoughts and feelings about your title and pictures.
Ten types of hospital visitor (101)	1 Which of the ten sections did you find most effective? Why? 2 Make a list of four or five phrases or sentences that you found particularly striking. Say what you liked about each one. 3 List any expressions that you found puzzling or confusing and try to work out what the poet meant by each one. 4 After reading the poem did you think that the overall effect was positive, negative, optimistic, pessimistic, or what? 5 Write a few paragraphs expressing your reactions to this poem. **Narrative or descriptive writing** 1 Choose one of the people described in the poem. Think carefully about the character. Imagine him or her in a number of different situations. Now write a story or a description based on that character. 2 Following the pattern of thinking in this poem, complete this title and then write about it: Ten types of _____
The old man and his grandson (105)	Think about what this story has to say about growing old and about the way in which old people are treated. Think about the old people whom you know and have talked to. When you have thought about this, write about the subject in any way that you think is suitable.
Warning (105)	1 The speaker in the poem is looking forward to being able to do all sorts of things when she is 'an old woman'. Have they got anything in common? If so, what? 2 Which of them – if any – would you like to do when you are 'old'? 3 Is it necessary to be old before you can do these things? If so, why? 4 What kind of life do you think the speaker leads at the moment? What is there in the poem to suggest this? 5 The speaker clearly thinks that there is something liberating about being old. Do you? **Personal writing** The speaker obviously had a list of things that she would have loved to do, but felt – for some reason – she couldn't. Make a similar list of things that you would love to do but cannot do for some reason. Now base a piece of writing on this list of forbidden things. Begin with these words: 'When I am _____' (and fill in the blank yourself).

The leave-taking (106)	1 The first part of the story describes all Grandma's good qualities. Make a list of the main ones. 2 How would you describe her family? 3 How does Tom first react to the idea that his grandma is dying? 4 What argument does she use to explain it to him? 5 How does she ask the family to behave when she dies? 6 How would you describe the atmosphere at the end of the story? 7 This story, *Warning* and *The old man and his grandson* are all about growing old. How does this story differ from the other two? What in particular is the author saying to his readers?

Looking ahead (109)	**Working out the argument**
	This passage contains a number of controversial statements:
	    'Only in superstition is there hope.'
	    '. . . the arts . . . use frauds . . . to make human beings seem more wonderful than they really are . . .'
	    'We don't need more information.'
	    'A great swindle of our time is the assumption that science has made religion obsolete.'
	    'It isn't up to you' (to save the world).
	What is Vonnegut's reason for saying each of these things? Do you agree with him?
	
	Personal writing
	Think carefully about what Vonnegut has to say and then write expressing your own thoughts and feelings.

The way (111)	1 What does the poem mean by 'the way'? 2 Why can the speaker not 'retrace the track'? 3 Why can he not stay where he is? 4 Why do you think he is afraid to continue? 5 What do you think the last two lines mean? 6 What is the whole poem saying about life?

The unit as a whole	**Writing assignments** The writing topics that follow are based on the ideas in the unit as a whole. Treat them freely, using them as starting points rather than restricting 'titles'. 1 Looking after Grandma. 2 The trouble with *Homes for the Elderly* is that they aren't homes at all. 3 The will. 4 My future. 5 Lost on the way.

Population growth by major regions (millions)

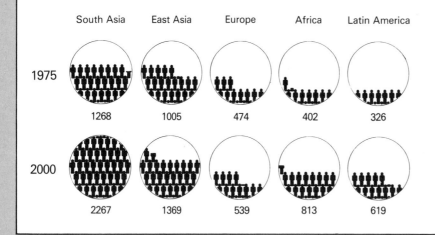

	South Asia	East Asia	Europe	Africa	Latin America
1975	1268	1005	474	402	326
2000	2267	1369	539	813	619

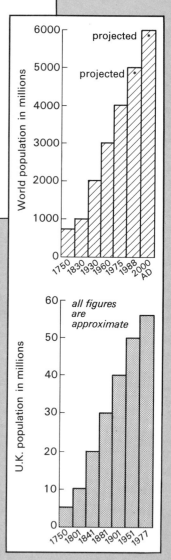

People per square kilometre of the earth's land surface

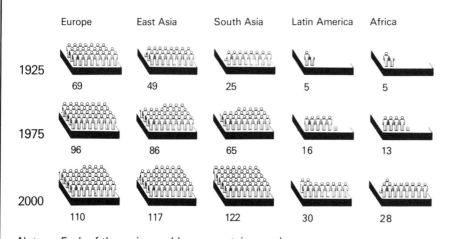

	Europe	East Asia	South Asia	Latin America	Africa
1925	69	49	25	5	5
1975	96	86	65	16	13
2000	110	117	122	30	28

Note — Each of the major world areas contains much territory of very limited use for settlement such as arctic wastes, deserts, jungles and steep mountainsides.

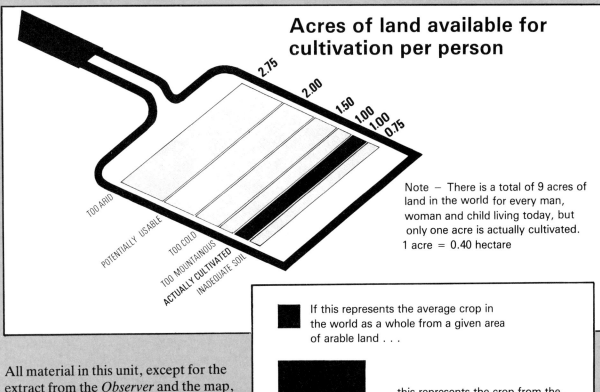

Acres of land available for cultivation per person

2.75   2.00   1.50   1.00   1.00   0.75

TOO ARID

POTENTIALLY USABLE

TOO COLD

TOO MOUNTAINOUS

ACTUALLY CULTIVATED

INADEQUATE SOIL

Note — There is a total of 9 acres of land in the world for every man, woman and child living today, but only one acre is actually cultivated.
1 acre = 0.40 hectare

All material in this unit, except for the extract from the *Observer* and the map, is taken from Eric McGraw: *Population Today* (Kaye & Ward 1979).

If this represents the average crop in the world as a whole from a given area of arable land . . .

. . . this represents the crop from the same size farm in countries where land is intensively cultivated* . . .

. . . and this represents the crop from the same size farm in countries of primitive land utilization . . .

*average of Denmark, Netherlands and Japan

1 In what part of the world is the population growth
   a) fastest?
   b) slowest?
2 In what part of the world was there in 1975
   a) the greatest
   b) the lowest population per square kilometre?
How will this have changed by the year 2000?
3 For every human being in the world there is a total of nine acres of land. Why is only one of these acres actually cultivated?
4 How much more land could actually be cultivated?
5 Look at the last diagram on this page. What further information does this provide about food production in countries where agriculture is
   a) underdeveloped
   b) intensive?

'No geological event—not the emergence of mighty mountain ranges, nor the submergence of entire sub continents—has posed a threat to terrestrial life comparable to that of human population growth.'

Professor Paul Ehrlich

'A planet cannot, any more than a country, survive half slave, half free, half engulfed in misery, half careering toward the supposed joys of almost unlimited consumption. Neither our ecology nor our morality could survive such contrasts.'

Lester Pearson

'We make so many wild claims for ourselves as human beings with superior intelligence. The least we can do is to prove our superior intelligence by controlling our numbers and standard of existence deliberately and willingly.'

H.R.H. Prince Philip

'All governments should accept the goal that within a decade no child will go to bed hungry, that no family will fear for the next day's bread, and that no human being's future and capacity will be stunted by malnutrition.'

World Food Conference, Italy, November 1974

Ethics and Ethiopia

TEN YEARS AGO next week Dr Henry Kissinger, then at the height of his powers as US Secretary of State, proclaimed 'a bold objective: that within a decade no child will go to bed the hungry'; ten years on, those words spoken at the UN World Food Conference ring hollow indeed. As we watch the horrifying footage from Ethiopia, it is clear that another, darker prophecy—by C. P. Snow in 1969—is being fulfilled. 'Many millions of people in the poor countries are going to starve to death before our eyes,' he said. 'We will see them doing so on our television sets.'

This week's film from Ethiopia is just the beginning. Most of Africa is heading into what the World Bank calls a 'nightmare' of famine and economic collapse. This year's drought, the worst for 15 years, has yet to take its full toll, and next year's harvest is expected to be even worse. Even this disaster is no more than a small downward turn in a steady decreasing trend. One-fifth less food is produced for every African now than in 1960, and if the trend continues the crop in 1988 will be no better than this year's terrible harvest, even if the weather is good.

In the world as a whole there are twice as many hungry people as when Dr Kissinger spoke. Even in years of good crops, 15 million children die of malnutrition, a figure equivalent to the casualties of two Hiroshimas a week. And more than a third of the world's land surface is being turned to desert through bad agricultural practice.

And yet, as Dr Kissinger noted in that ill-fated speech: 'For the first time we have the technical capacity to free mankind from the scourge of hunger.' More than enough is produced each year to feed everyone on earth. World food supplies are at record levels, and in Britain, as we watch Ethiopian farmers starve, our own farmers have just gathered in their biggest ever harvest to add to the grain mountains. Allowing millions of children to die while granaries overflow is a moral and social evil as foul as the slave trade—and we show as little sign of tackling it as those before Wilberforce.

Few can escape blame, either for the immediate crisis in Ethiopia, or for the greater tragedy to come. The Ethiopian Government, though more open than Haile Selassie's over a similar famine ten years ago, has been reluctant to reveal the full extent of the crisis because this would also show how much of their country is in rebel hands. Many Western governments have been slow to respond to appeals, because they do not like Ethiopia's Marxist regime. The Soviet Union has done little or nothing. The private aid agencies have not shown sufficient concern; they were about to end their appeal to combat famine in Africa this very week. And, it must be confessed, we in the media have shown indifference to the story until very late in the day.

The Observer 28.10.84

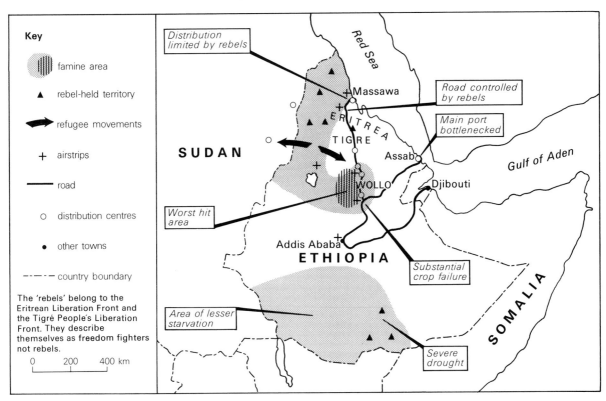

Key

 famine area

▲ rebel-held territory

➤ refugee movements

+ airstrips

— road

○ distribution centres

• other towns

--- country boundary

The 'rebels' belong to the Eritrean Liberation Front and the Tigré People's Liberation Front. They describe themselves as freedom fighters not rebels.

0   200   400 km

Distribution limited by rebels

Red Sea

Massawa

Road controlled by rebels

E R I T R E A

Main port bottlenecked

T I G R E

SUDAN

Gulf of Aden

Assab

Worst hit area

WOLLO

Djibouti

Addis Ababa

ETHIOPIA

Substantial crop failure

SOMALIA

Area of lesser starvation

Severe drought

Map of Ethiopia, Autumn 1984

Assignments

1 The poorest countries of the world are mostly situated in South and East Asia, Africa and Latin America. Look at the diagrams and charts on pages 114 and 115 and then write a paragraph explaining the information provided about these countries.

2 What solutions can be found to the problems of poverty and hunger in Asia, Africa and Latin America? (Use the information on pages 114 and 115, as well as ideas of your own to answer this question.)

3 Study the newspaper article on the opposite page; then answer this question:
Who does the writer think is to blame for the world's failure to help Ethiopia?

4 Look at the map above and then explain why it was difficult in 1984 to get aid to the famine areas.

5 Write a letter to an MP or a well-known political figure expressing your thoughts and feelings about aid to poor countries.

6 Read the quotations on this page and then write expressing your own opinions about the issues raised in this Datafile.

The white trousers

Yashar Kemal

It was hot. The boy Mustafa held the shoe listlessly and gazed out of the shop at the sun-impacted street with its uneven cobbles. He felt he would never be able to mend this shoe. It was the most tattered thing he had ever come across. He looked up tentatively, but the cobbler was bent over his work. He placed the shoe on the bench and hammered in a nail haphazardly.

'I can't do it,' he murmured at last.

'What's that, Mustafa?' said the cobbler, raising his head for a moment. 'Why, you haven't begun to try yet!'

'But, Master,' protested the boy, 'it comes apart as soon as I put in a stitch . . .'

The cobbler was silent.

Mustafa tackled the shoe again. His face was running with sweat and the sun had dropped nearer the distant hills when Hassan Bey, a well-to-do friend of the cobbler's, stepped into the shop.

'My friend,' he said, 'I need a boy to help fire my brick-kiln. Will you let me have this one? Only for three days.'

'Would you work at the brick-kiln, Mustafa?' asked the cobbler. 'It's for three days and three nights too, you know . . .'

'The pay is one and a half liras a day,' said Hassan Bey. 'All you'll have to do is give a hand to Jumali. You know Jumali who lives down by the river? He's a good man, won't let you work yourself out.'

Mustafa's black eyes shone.

'All right, Uncle Hassan,' he said. 'But I'll have to ask Mother . . .'

'Well, ask her, and be at my orange grove tomorrow. The kiln's in the field next to it. You'll start work in the afternoon. I won't be there, but you'll find Jumali.'

The cobbler paid him twenty-five kurush a week. A whole month and only one lira! It was July already, and a pair of summer shoes cost two liras, a pair of white trousers three . . . But now, four and a half liras would be his for only three days' work! What a stroke of luck! . . . First you wash your hands, but properly, with soap . . . Then you unwrap the white canvas shoes . . . Your socks must be white too. You must be careful, very careful with the white trousers. They get soiled so quickly. Your fingers should hardly touch them. And so to the bridge where the girls stroll in the cool of the evening, the breeze swelling their skirts . . . The breeze tautening the white trousers against your legs . . .

'Mother!' he cried, bursting into the house. 'I'm going to fire Hassan Bey's brick-kiln with Jumali!'

'Who says so? Certainly not!'

'But, Mother . . .'

'My child, you don't know what firing a kiln means. Can you go without sleep for three days and three nights? God knows I have trouble enough waking you up in the morning!'

'But, Mother, this is different . . .'

'You'll fall asleep, I tell you. You'll never stand it.'

'Look, Mother, you know Sami, Tewfik Bey's son Sami?' he said hopefully.

'Well?'

'Those white trousers of his and the white shoes? Snow-white! I've got a silk shirt in the trunk. I'll wear that too. Wouldn't I look well?'

Mustafa knew his mother. The tears rose to her eyes. She bowed her head.

'Wouldn't I, Mother? Now, wouldn't I?'

'My darling, you'd look well in anything . . .'

'Vayis the tailor'll do it for me. Mother dear, say I can go!'

'Well, I don't know . . .' she said doubtfully.

He saw she was giving in and flung himself on her neck.

'When I'm big . . .' he began.

'You'll work very hard.'

'And then?' he prompted.

'You'll make a beautiful orange grove of that empty field of ours near the stream. You'll have a horse of your own to ride . . . You'll order navy blue suits from tailors in Adana . . .'

'And then?'

'Then you'll tile the roof of our house so it won't let in the rain.'

'Then?'

'You'll be just like your father.'

'And if my father hadn't died?'

'You'd have gone to school and studied and become a great man . . .'

'But now?'

'If your Father had been alive . . .'

'Look,' said Mustafa, 'I'll have a gold watch when I'm big, won't I?'

The next morning he was up and away before sunrise. The dust on the road felt cool and soft under his bare feet. A flood of light was surging up behind the hill. When he came to the kiln, the sun was sitting on the crest like a great round ember. He bent over to the mouth of the kiln. It was dark inside. Around it brushwood had been heaped in little hillocks.

It was almost noon when Jumali arrived. He was a big man who walked ponderously, picking his way. Ignoring Mustafa, he stopped before the kiln and thrust his head inside. Then he turned back.

'What're you doing around here, hey?' he barked.

The boy was struck with fear. He felt like taking to his heels.

'What're you standing there stuck for, hey?' shouted Jumali.

'Hassan Bey sent me,' stammered Mustafa. 'To help you . . .'

With surprising agility Jumali swung his heavy frame impatiently back to the kiln.

'Now that's fine!' he growled. 'What does Hassan Bey think he's doing, sending along a child not bigger than the palm of your hand?' He flung his hand out. 'Not bigger than this hand! You go right back and tell him to find someone else.'

Mustafa was dumb with dismay. He took a few wavering steps towards the town. Then he stopped. The white trousers danced before his eyes. He wanted to cry.

'Uncle Jumali,' he begged weakly. 'I'll work harder than a grown man . . .'

'Listen to the pup! Do you know what it means to fire a kiln?'

'Oh yes . . .'

'Why, you little bastard, three days, three nights of feeding wood into this hole you see here, taking it in turns, you and I . . .'

'I know, I know!'

'Listen to the little bastard! Did you learn all this in your mother's womb? Now push off and stop pestering me.'

Mustafa had a flash of inspiration.

'I can't go back,' he said. 'Hassan Bey paid me in advance and I've already spent the money.'

'Go away!' shouted Jumali. 'You'll get me into trouble.'

Mustafa rebelled.

'But why? Why d'you want to take the bread out of my mouth? Just because I'm a child . . . I can work as hard as anyone.' Suddenly he ran up to Jumali and grasped his hand. 'I swear it, Uncle Jumali! You'll see how I'll feed that kiln. Anyway, I've spent the pay . . .'

'Well, all right,' Jumali said at last. 'We'll see . . .'

He lit a stick of pinewood and thrust it in. The wood crackled and a long tongue of flame spurted out.

'Damn!' he cursed. 'Filled it up to bursting, they have, the bastards! Everything they do is wrong.'

Still cursing, he gave Mustafa a few instructions. Then he lit a cigarette and moved off into the shade of a fig-tree.

When the flames that were lapping the mouth of the kiln had receded, Mustafa picked up an armful of brushwood and threw it in. Then another . . . And another . . .

The dusty road, the thick-spreading fig-trees, the stream that flowed like molten tin, the ashen sky, the lone bird flapping by, the scorched grass, the small wilting yellow flowers, the whole world drooped wearily under the impact of the noonday heat. Mustafa's face was as red as the flames, his shirt dripping, as he ran carrying the brushwood from the heat of the sun to the heat of the kiln.

At the close of the sizzling afternoon, little white clouds rise up in clusters far off in the south over the Mediterranean, heralding the cool moist breeze that will soon enwrap the heat-baked creatures as in a wet soothing towel. As the first fresh puff of wind stirred up the dust on the road, Jumali called to Mustafa from where he lay supine in the heavy shade of the fig-tree.

'Hey, boy, come along and let's eat!'

Mustafa was quivering with exhaustion and hunger.

Hassan Bey had provided Jumali with a bundle of food. There was white cheese, green onions and wafer-bread. They fell to without a word. The sun sank down behind the poplar trees that stood out like a dark curtain against the glow. Mustafa picked up the jug and went to the stream. The water tasted like warm blood. They drank it thirstily. Jumali wiped his long moustache with the back of his hand.

'I'm going to sleep a while, Mustafa,' he said. 'Wake me up when you're tired, eh?'

It was long past midnight. The moon had dropped behind the wall of poplars. Mustafa's thin sweating face shone red in the blaze. He threw in an armful of wood and watched the wild onrush of flames swallow it up. There was a loud crackling at first, then a long, long moaning sound that was almost human.

Like a baby crying its heart out, he thought.

'Are you tired? D'you want me?' came Jumali's sleepy voice.

A tremor shook his body. He felt a cold sweat breaking out all over him.

'Oh no, Uncle Jumali!' he cried. 'I never get tired. You go on sleeping.'

He could not bear to go near the kiln any more. Now he heaped as much wood as possible close to the opening and shoved it in with the long wooden fork. Then, backing before the sudden surge of heat, he scrambled on to a mound near by and stood awhile against the night breeze. But the air bore down, heavy and stifling, drowning him.

There is a bird that sings just before the break of dawn. A very tiny bird. Its call is long-drawn and piercing. He heard the bird's call and saw a widening ribbon of light brighten up the sky behind the hill.

Just then Jumali woke up.

'Are you tired?' he asked.

'No . . . No . . . I'm not tired . . .' But his voice broke, strangling with tears.

Jumali rose and stretched himself.

'Go and sleep a little now,' he said.

He was asleep when Hassan Bey arrived.

'How's the boy doing?' he asked. 'Working all right?'

Jumali's lips curled.

'A chit of a child . . .' he said.

'Well, you'll have to shift along as best you can. I'll make it worth your while,' said Hassan Bey as he left.

When Mustafa awoke the sun was heaving down upon him and the earth was like red-hot iron. His bones ached as though they had been pounded in a mortar. Setting his teeth, he struggled up and ran to the kiln.

'Uncle Jumali,' he faltered, 'I'm sorry I slept so long . . .'

'I told you you'd never make it,' said Jumali sourly.

Mustafa did not answer. He scraped up some brushwood and began feeding the kiln. After a while he felt a little better.

Hurray! he thought. We've weathered the first day.

But the two huge searing days loomed before him and the stifling clamminess of the infernal nights. He chased the thought away and conjured up the image of the white trousers . . .

The last night . . . The moon bright over the poplar trees . . .

'Wake me up if you get tired,' says Jumali . . .

The fire has to be kept up at the same level or the bricks will not bake and a whole two days' work will have been in vain. The flames must flare out greedily licking at the night. The hated flames . . . He has not the strength to reach the refreshing mound any longer. He can only throw himself on the ground and let the moist coolness of the earth seep into his body. But always the fear in his heart that sleep will overcome him . . .

His eyes were clinging to the east, groping for the ribbon of light. But it was pitch dark and Jumali snored on loudly.

Damn you, Uncle Jumali! Damn you . . .

Suddenly, the whole world started trembling. The dark curtain of poplars, the hills, the flames, the kiln were turning round and round. He was going to vomit.

'Jumali! Uncle Jumali . . .'

He had fainted.

It was a good while before Jumali called again in his drowsy voice.

'Are you tired, Mustafa?'

There was no answer. Then he caught sight of the darkened kiln. He rushed up and fetched the child a furious kick.

'You've done for me, you little bastard! They'll make me pay for the bricks now . . .'

He peered into the opening and took hope. A few small flames were still wavering against the inner wall.

Mustafa came to as the dawn was breaking. His heart quaked at the sight of Jumali, his hairy chest bared, stoking the kiln.

'Uncle Jumali,' he faltered, 'really, I never meant to . . .'

Jumali cast an angry glance over his shoulder.

'Shut up, damn you! Go to hell!'

Mustafa hung his head and sat there motionless until the sun rose over the hill. Then he fell asleep in the same position.

A brick kiln is large and spacious, rather like a well that has been capped with a dome. When it is first set alight the bricks take on a leaden hue. The second day, they turn a dull black. But on the morning of the third day, they are a fiery red . . .

Mustafa awoke with fear in his heart. The sun was quarter high and Hassan Bey was standing near the kiln. The bricks were sparkling like red crystal.

'Well, my boy?' Hassan Bey laughed. 'So we came here to sleep, did we?'

'Uncle, I swear that every night . . .'

Jumali threw him a dour look. He dared not go on.

They sealed up the mouth of the kiln.

The cobbler had shaggy eyebrows and a beard. His back was slightly hunched. The shop, dusty and cobwebby, smelled of leather and rawhide.

A week had gone by and still no sign of Hassan Bey. Mustafa was eating his heart out with anxiety, but he said nothing. Then one day Hassan Bey happened to pass before the shop.

'Hey, Hassan!' the cobbler called. 'When are you going to pay the lad here?'

Hassan Bey hesitated. Then he took a one-lira note and two twenty-five kurush coins and placed them on the bench.

'Here you are,' he said.

The cobbler stared at the money.

'But that's only a lira and a half. The child worked three days . . .'

'Well, he slept all the time, so I paid his share to Jumali. This, I'm giving him simply out of consideration for you,' said Hassan Bey, turning to leave.

'Uncle, I swear that every night . . .' began Mustafa, but his voice stuck in his throat. He lowered his head.

There was a long, painful silence.

'Look, Mustafa,' said the cobbler at last, 'you're more than an apprentice now. You patch soles really well. From now on you'll get a lira a week for your work.'

Mustafa raised his head slowly. His eyes were shining through the tears.

'Take these five liras,' said the cobbler, 'and give them to the tailor Vayis with my compliments. Tell him to cut your white trousers out of the best material he's got. With the rest of the money you can buy your shoes. I'm taking this fellow's money, so you owe me only three and a half weeks' pay . . .'

Mustafa laughed with glee.

In those days the blue five-lira note carried the picture of a wolf, its tongue hanging out as it galloped swift as the wind.

Assignments

Thinking about the story

Immediate reactions

1 Write down your immediate reactions to the story. Don't bother about planning your writing – just write down your thoughts and feelings as they come to you.

2 *Without reading the story again* answer these questions:

a) Why was it so important to Mustafa to earn the money by firing the brick kiln?

b) What were your first impressions of Jumali?

c) How did you feel at the end of the story?

3 Is there anything about the story that you do not understand? If so, write down a list of questions that you would like to have answered.

Reading in more detail

Now read the story through again. As you read, answer these questions (and, of course, try to answer any questions you have written down yourself).

1 What do you think of the work Mustafa does and the amount he gets paid for it?

2 What is his mother's initial reaction to the idea and why does she change her mind?

3 What do you think the emotional relationship is between mother and son? What is your evidence for this?

4 Explain in your own words how the brick kiln worked and why the job was likely to be difficult for Mustafa.

5 How does Jumali react when he sees Mustafa? Why do you think this is?

6 What is the reader's first impression of Jumali? To what extent does it change as the story proceeds?

7 Did you find any parts of the description of the firing particularly vivid or striking and if so, which and why?

8 What do you think of the way that Hassan Bey, who actually *owned* the kiln, behaved during the firing?

9 What is your impression of the character of Hassan Bey from the whole story?

10 What do you think is the significance of the final sentence of the story?

Thinking about the story as a whole

What is the *point* of this story? Does it have a moral or message? Or is it a straightforward account of life in another country?

Short story writing

Write a short story based on one of the two pictures above, or one of these themes:

1 Slave labour
2 Disappointment
3 Empty victory
4 Ambition
5 Vision

PART B

The craft of writing

1. *Your writing*

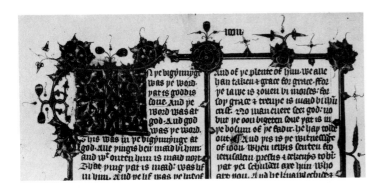

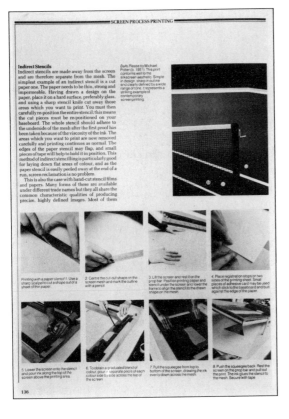

1 What have all these illustrations got in common?

2 In what ways do these forms of communication differ from the ones opposite?

3 Compared with the methods of communication shown on the opposite page, these are fairly recent. Does this mean that writing and printing will eventually disappear?

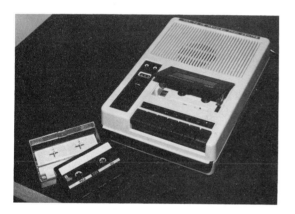

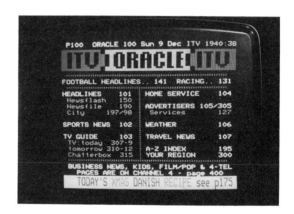

4 What uses can you see for writing in the age of the computer and video?

5 In school, students spend a lot of time writing. They will probably spend very little of their adult lives writing. So why do so much in school?

6 What are the commonest uses you make of writing outside school?

7 In what ways do you expect to use writing after you have left school?

Writing in school

In your last twelve months at school you probably have to do more writing than you ever will again. It certainly feels like it at the time. Different teachers set students to write for different reasons and expect different kinds of writing.

1 Copy up this table and fill it in for all the subjects you study, *except English*.

Subject	number of lessons per week	number of homeworks per week	average time per lesson spent writing	average time per homework spent writing	total time per week spent writing

Now answer these questions:

a) Which subjects demand the greatest **amount** of writing?
b) For each subject what is the **purpose** of the writing?
c) Would it be possible to learn as much and do less writing?
d) Are there any subjects where it would be useful to do *more* writing? (If so, why?)

Different teachers use different words to describe the **form** of writing they want done. Sometimes different teachers use the same word to mean different things. For example: essay, writing, composition, report, notes.

2 Copy the list of subjects from Exercise 1. Against each one write down the name the teacher normally gives to the type of writing you are asked to do (eg 'essay'). If different words are used, put them all down. Against each one write your own explanation of what it means. Now answer these questions:

a) Do you find that two teachers use the same word to mean different things?

b) Do you ever find that two teachers use different words to mean much the same thing?

c) Are there occasions when you need more guidance about what you are expected to write?

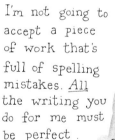

3 Look at the list of subjects you made for Exercise 1. Think about the ways in which different subject teachers comment on what you have written. Now answer these questions:

a) Can you think of two subjects which have different ideas about what is 'good' writing? How are they different?

b) Can you think of two subject teachers who have different ideas about the meaning of 'rough' and 'best'?

c) Why do you think there are these differences?

Writing for English

The previous two pages were about subjects other than English. They asked you to think about the **amount**, **purpose**, and **form** of the writing which different subjects require. They also asked about how the teachers of different subjects **comment** on the language you use in your writing. This page is about the writing you do for English.

4 Think about the writing you have done recently for English. Answer these questions:

  a) How does the amount compare with other subjects?
  b) What different types (or 'forms') of writing are you asked to do?
  c) What do you think are the purposes of the writing you do in English lessons?
  d) In what other ways is writing done in English different from that done for other subjects?

Writing done in English lessons can be for a number of different audiences:

  a) Yourself
  b) A friend in the class (if books are exchanged)
  c) The rest of the class (if books are passed round, or work is read out or displayed)
  d) The rest of the school (if your writing is put in a magazine)
  e) Your teacher.

Writing done for the English examination can be assessed in two ways:

  a) As part of a folder of course work
  b) In a formal examination.

5 a) Suppose you were asked to write your own thoughts and feelings about a topic and were told what the audience would be. In what ways would each of the five audiences listed above affect what you wrote?
  b) Would there be certain things which you would be prepared to write for one audience and not for another? If so, what?
  c) How would you feel if you thought you were writing just for your teacher and then found that your writing had been printed in a magazine for anyone to read? Why?
  d) Which do you think is the better test of a person's ability as a writer: course work or an examination? Why?
  e) Suppose your own teacher, who marks course work, and an examiner, who is a complete stranger, sit down to mark the same piece of your work. How do you think their attitudes would differ? Whose marking would you prefer, and why?
  f) Suppose you were given a fairly personal topic to write about: by your English teacher; by an unknown examiner.
  Would you write differently in each case, or the same?

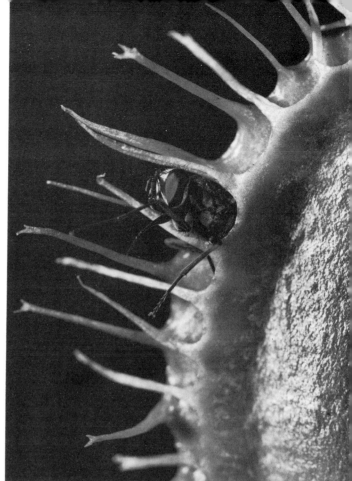

6 Choose one of these photographs. Do two short pieces of writing about the one you have chosen:

a) As you might for an English lesson

b) As you might for a different school subject (eg for the left-hand picture it might be Geography).

Links

Look at the advertisements on pages 47 and 53. These were obviously written for different audiences. Look at them carefully. Now write a detailed description of the audience for each advertisement. Explain your reasons for thinking this.

Summary

1 Different school subjects require you to write in different ways.
2 Writing is used for different purposes.
3 The form of writing required can differ.
4 The writing you do may be judged differently.
5 When you write for English lessons you may have a number of different audiences.
6 The audience you write for may affect what you include in your writing.
7 It may also affect the way in which you write.

Audience and purpose

In everyday life, when you write something, it usually has:

an **audience**: the person or people whom you want to read it

a **purpose**: the reason you wrote it and the effect you want to have on your audience.

1

2

3

DON'T HOOT
I'm going as fast as I can

4

and I didn't want it to end like that. All right, so we both said things we didn't mean, and I'm sorry for what I said – but there's no need to end it all just because we've had one row. Please, please

1 Copy and complete the following table:

Message Number	Audience for message	Purpose of message
1.	general public, especially shoppers	to give information to persuade people to buy things

Now make up similar short messages to illustrate this table:

Message Number	Audience for message	Purpose of message
1.	school pupils	to control behaviour
2.	car drivers	to give information
3.	general public	to persuade

Your audience can affect your message in these ways:

Knowledge

Relationship

Expectations

2 For each pair of pictures explain in your own words how and why the message is different.

3 Each of these messages is aimed at the same kind of audience. Both are about the same subject. They are different because they have different purposes. Explain clearly what the purpose of each message is.

a

b

4

a

b

Write two short conversations:

a) Between an inexperienced female cyclist who wants to get her bike repaired and a 'macho-minded bike shop mechanic'

b) Between the same cyclist and one of the workers at Lunar Cycles.

On your bike

Lunar Cycles of 3 London Road, London SE1 take the strain out of bicycle repairs by doing them for you. On top of that, since they're a co-operative of women workers you don't have to face the sometimes off-putting attitudes of the more macho-minded bike-shop mechanics. To find out more . . .
(Guardian)

5 Use the information below to write three short messages:

   a) To advertise an electric drill (eg in a magazine)

   b) To inform someone who has bought one of what it will do

   c) To warn of the dangers involved in using one and advise the user of precautions to be taken.

Electric drills

Universal chuck.

Will drill holes up to 6 mm.

Hammer drilling operation for drilling into brick and concrete.

Drills holes in wood, metal, plastic, ceramics.

Can have variable speeds.

Many different attachments: circular saw, sander, lathe.

Speeds up to 3000 rpm.

Easy to catch long hair, loose clothing in drill.

Drilling can throw up sharp fragments of metal, stone or wood, which damage the eyes.

Links

Describe the audience and purpose of each of these pieces of writing:

It happened like this (28)

Hertz advertisement (47)

Advertisement (67)

Summary

1 In everyday life the writer of any message usually has in mind an audience and a purpose.

2 The audience for a message can affect it in a number of different ways.

3 The amount of knowledge that the audience has about the subject of the message will affect what the writer includes and how it is expressed.

4 The writer will also be affected by how well he or she knows the audience.

5 The writer must also take into account what the audience expects from him or her in that situation.

6 You may wish to write about the same subject matter for the same audience, but have a different purpose. The purpose – for example to inform, or to persuade, or to warn, or to control – will affect the message.

Preparing to write

There are four stages in almost every piece of writing:

1 **Thinking about what to write: generating ideas**
2 **Deciding how to write it: planning and drafting**
3 **Writing it**
4 **Checking it through.**

Sometimes this is all very simple and stages 1 and 2 are done very quickly, in your head, almost without you realizing it. At other times it is necessary to spend a lot of time preparing your work very carefully. When you are writing for English you may have to go through this process:

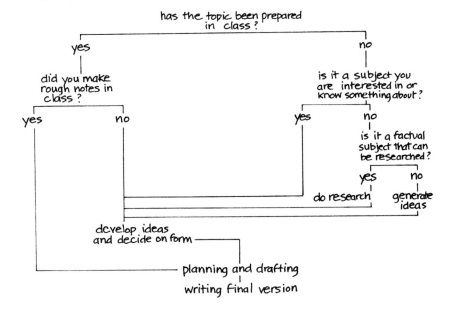

Generating ideas: Method 1

1 Topic: *Marathon*
Write down all the words and ideas that the title suggests to you:

fun run · jogging · crowds · Olympic Games · a long way · exhaustion

2 Choose a word from the list and write it at the head of a column. Beneath it write whatever word that first word suggests to you. Now write whatever word the second word suggests to you, and so on:

jogging
training shoes
keeping fit
squash
injury
unconscious
hospital

3 Do the same with other words from your original list:

fun run · jogging · crowds · Olympic Games · a long way · exhaustion

jogging	crowds	Olympic Games	a long way
training shoes	football	drugs	isolation
keeping fit	violence	disqualification	loneliness
squash	vandalism	disgrace	desolate
injury	prison	shame	weeping
unconscious		outcast	
hospital			

4 Take a pencil and link up any words that you think could have something in common, or could be useful as the start for a piece of writing:

fun run
jogging
training shoes
keeping fit
unconscious
hospital

a long way
isolation
loneliness
desolate
weeping

5 Do the same again, using a different coloured pen or pencil:

crowds
football
violence
vandalism
prison

Olympic Games
drugs
disqualification
disgrace
shame
outcast

6 By now you should begin to know what you are going to write about. It may come from a single word: exhaustion.

It may come from one of the lists: jogging
training shoes
keeping fit
squash
etc.

It may come from one of your sets of links:

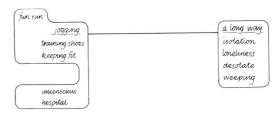

fun run
jogging
training shoes
keeping fit
unconscious
hospital

a long way
isolation
loneliness
desolate
weeping

Generating ideas: Method 2

7 Topic: *What should be done about football hooligans?*
Take a full page and write a short version of the topic in the centre. Draw a line out from it and write the first idea you have about the topic. Draw other lines out for other main ideas you have:

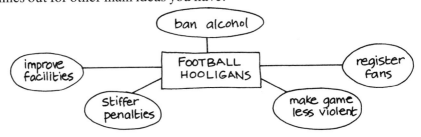

8 Now gradually add further ideas:

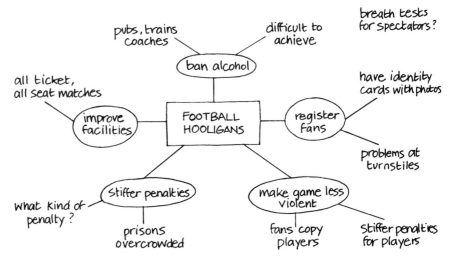

Developing your ideas

Having a string of ideas is not the same as being ready to start writing. This

crowds	Olympic Games
football	drugs
violence	disqualification
vandalism	disgrace
prison	shame
	outcast

is not a plan for a piece of writing. Before writing you need to think more about *what* you are going to write and *how* you are going to write.

9 Add to your notes:

a) Jot down any further ideas you have had.
b) Make a list of things you still need to think about.
c) Make a note of anything you need to find out.
d) Jot down any important words, phrases and sentences you think of.

10 Think about *how* you are going to write:
   Mode: description – narrative – exposition – argument – mixture
   Form: report – letter – newspaper story – interview

11 Write down all your ideas as you think of them:

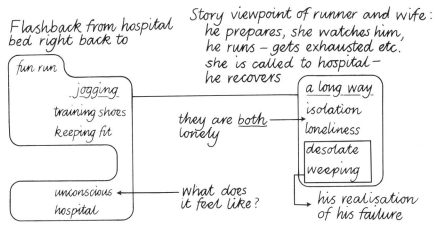

Assignments

1 Use the flowchart on page 138 to help you decide how you should set about each of these writing topics:

   2082   Stony faces   Power   The black rainbow

Use **Method 1** to help you to generate ideas about one of the topics.

2 *Should corporal punishment be used in schools?*
Develop your ideas on this essay title by adding to the diagram:

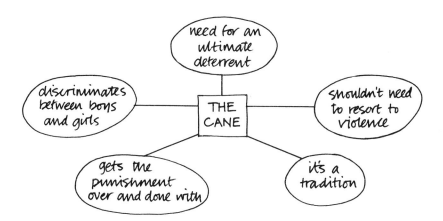

Summary

1 It is an essential part of writing to develop and organize your ideas.
2 By taking a positive attitude it is possible to generate ideas for starting writing.
3 When you have a set of starting ideas, you need to spend further time thinking carefully about the subject.
4 You also need to make decisions about the form your writing will take.

Planning and drafting

The previous section suggested ways of generating and developing ideas. It showed how to move from a title to a set of notes:

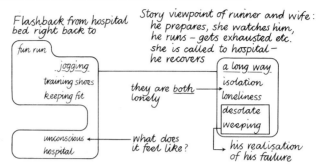

This is not yet a plan. If you tried to write directly from it you would probably find that your story did not run smoothly but got tangled up as you wrote it. There is one more stage before you actually get down to writing: you need to make a plan. Planning can take a number of forms. You can:

1 **Think the topic out and get it clear in your head.**
2 **Make a written plan in note form.**
3 **Write a rough draft.**

Thinking it out in your head

If the subject is complicated, then you may find this difficult. (More people claim to be able to plan in their heads than can do it successfully.) If the topic is simple, however, there is no reason why it should not work successfully.

Making a plan in note form

If you cannot carry all the ideas in your head, then you need to jot them down in note form. Notes do not have to make sense to anyone but you. They simply remind you of the main points and the order in which they come:

1   In hospital – waking up – remembering
2   How it all began – jogging – kit etc
3   Marathon is announced – discussion with wife etc
4   Preparations – wife's viewpoint
5   The big day
6   Start – both viewpoints
7   The race – his thoughts as he gets going
8   Increasing tiredness – loneliness – isolation
9   Exhaustion – collapse
10 Back to present – meeting with wife.

1 Make a similar note-form plan for one of the topics in the assignments on page 141.

Writing a rough draft

What most successful writers do is write a rough draft. They write the whole thing out in rough. Then they read it through, cross things out, alter words and sentences, and add new material. This is an example from the work of the author John le Carré. When he was writing *Smiley's People*, he began one section like this:

> 'Isadora,' he said and pointed at a jetty further down the shore.
> The planks of the jetty yielded alarmingly to Smiley's tread. The *Isadora* was a forty-foot motor-launch down on her luck, a Grand Hotel awaiting demolition. The port-holes were curtained, one of them was smashed, another was repaired with Scotch tape. As he reached the end of the jetty, he realized she was also adrift: the *Isadora* had slipped her moorings at the stern and shifted twelve feet out to sea, which was probably the longest journey she would ever make. The cabin doors were closed, their windows also curtained. There was no small boat.

Then John le Carré worked on his first draft:

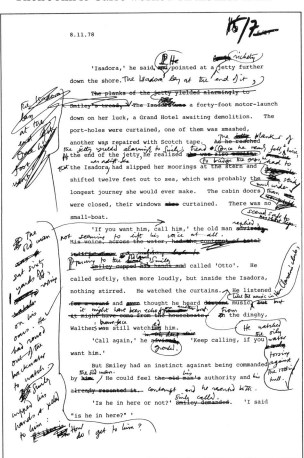

The final version was:

> 'Isadora,' he said.
> He pointed at a rickety jetty further down the shore. The *Isadora* lay at the end of it, a forty-foot motor launch down on her luck, a Grand Hotel awaiting demolition. The portholes were curtained, one of them was smashed, another was repaired with Scotch tape. The planks of the jetty yielded alarmingly to Smiley's tread. Once he nearly fell, and twice, to bridge the gaps, he had to stride much wider than seemed safe to his short legs. At the end of the jetty, he realized that the *Isadora* was adrift. She had slipped her moorings at the stern and shifted twelve feet out to sea, which was probably the longest journey she would ever make. The cabin doors were closed, their windows curtained. There was no small boat.

2 **a)** In what ways has John le Carré changed this passage?

b) Is the second version an improvement? What are your reasons for thinking so?

c) Give an example of a change that you think is an improvement and explain why.

Improving a draft

3 This is the opening paragraph of a short story by a fourth year writer. She is setting the scene for a story in which the most savage lion attacks the lion tamer during his act and escapes. It terrorizes a nearby village until it is finally captured by the lion-tamer's son.

> It was the night before the circus was opening and the atmosphere was of great excitement. The preparation was going smoothly and according to plan and acts were being practised to perfection. Final adjustments were made to the tightropes, trapezes, and lights. The animals were receiving their last training for their acts and the clowns continued to throw custard pies at each other. The elephants were excellent in the ring and all the performers were quite content with their performances. Then the lions came on and Ted Brown excelled himself while taming them. He was admired by all the members of the circus for his bravery and perseverance with his animals. They could guarantee a wonderful reception from any crowd when his act came on.

a) Think about whether this is the best way to introduce the story: would it be possible to give the reader the same background information in a better way?

b) Look at her use of words – are there any that could be replaced by more appropriate words?

c) Look at the way she has constructed her sentences – could improvements be made here?

d) Copy the paragraph out, writing on every other line.

e) Make alterations to it, improving it as John le Carré worked on *Smiley's People*.

f) When you are satisfied with it, copy out your new version.

4 Choose the opening paragraph from a piece of your own writing and redraft it in the same way.

5 Write a set of instructions explaining how to put up a tent. Use the drafting method described in this unit to enable you to produce instructions that are clear and unambiguous.

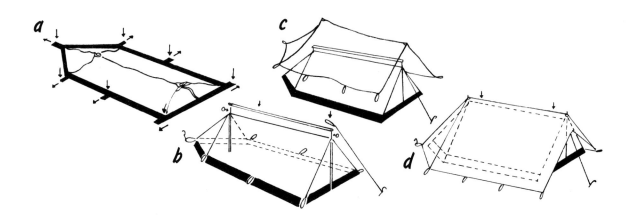

6 Look at the picture and choose one of these titles to work on:

> It's a bargain!
> The big disappointment
> 'We spend Christmas eating and drinking more than we ought to, and then straight afterwards we go out and spend more than we can afford at the sales.' What is your opinion?

a) Generate ideas for a piece of writing on your chosen topic. Use one of the methods described in *Preparing to write* (138–141).

b) Make a plan for the whole essay.

c) Write a first draft of your opening paragraph, writing on every other line.

d) Alter and improve your first paragraph.

e) Write a final version of your opening paragraph.

Summary

1 When you have decided **what** you want to write and **how** you want to write it, you still need to make a plan. This is when you decide on the **order** in which you want to write things.

2 Your plan may be made in your head, or it may take the form of written notes.

3 You may also write a rough draft, or first version, which you can then alter and improve.

4 Writing and altering a rough draft is an effective way of producing good writing.

2. *Aspects of writing*

When we write about a subject our own thoughts, feelings and attitudes have an important effect on the way we set about it. The first three units in this chapter look at how this works:

Points of view (148)

Tone (152)

Speaking figuratively (156)

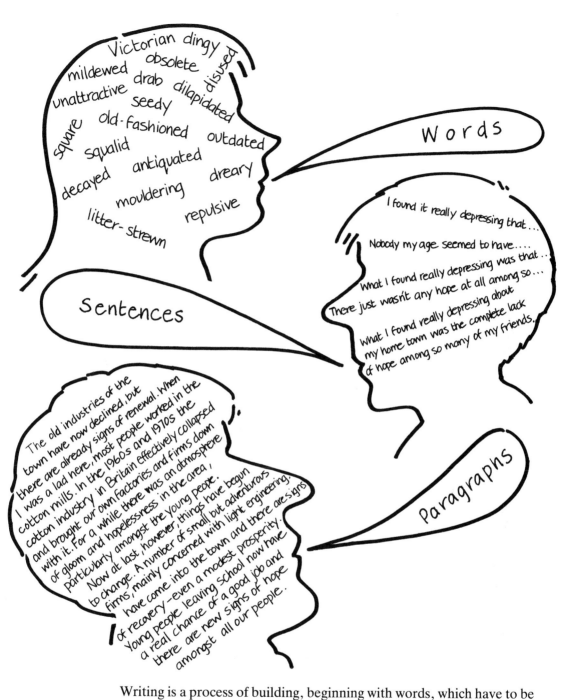

Writing is a process of building, beginning with words, which have to be chosen with care. Sentences, too, have to be constructed with thought and care. The combination of sentences into paragraphs completes the building process.

Words (160)

Sentences (166)

Paragraphs (170)

Points of view

Hartland House

A Desirable country residence set in its own grounds. An imposing 18th century dwelling with ample accommodation, comprising, on the ground floor 3 reception rooms, dining room, breakfast room, kitchen, utility room, study, cloakroom, shower room . . .

B The suspect was interviewed at his home, Hartland House, Northam, North Devon. At the time of the interview he was sitting in a deckchair on the terrace at the back of the house, apparently reading a book. When I addressed him, he jumped up in a most suspicious manner and moved towards the French windows . . .

C As the sun set and the clouds began to roll in from the sea, Hartland House took on a sinister air. Maria had been sitting on the terrace, but now a chill wind sprang up and drove her indoors. The sombre sky and the sound of the wind in the trees made her nervous: was it her imagination, or could she hear voices outside? . . .

1 Each of these three pieces of writing is about the same house, but they all look at it from different points of view. Explain in your own words what the three points of view are.

2 Write three short descriptions of a place you know well:

a) As written in a guide book
b) As written in a crime story or ghost story set there
c) As written by an old woman who has lived there all her life.

Personal and impersonal: two descriptions of Savoy

A For half the year, snow covers the ground and the night temperatures are well below zero. In the old days, families would gather in the evenings on the ground floor of their house, among the animals for warmth, shelling nuts, spinning hemp which made them famous for their sacks and rope, and telling stories to the children. Towards the end of the last century these *veillées* passed out of fashion, partly because the Church – a powerful force in this region – declared it improper for humans to bed down with animals!

In early summer, the women of the family left for the high pastures, where the cattle were put to graze on the rich young grass. They took with them their small children, their bedding, pots and pans, and bees. During the summer they lived in simple shelters built from stone gathered from the mountain streams, milking the cows, making butter and cheese, collecting and bottling honey and tending to the children. Below in the valley, the men sowed wheat and rye, tended the tobacco and vines and visited their womenfolk each Sunday, taking provisions and no doubt news.

John Ardagh (ed) *Rural France*

B One morning in the alpage*, years ago, I woke up to find all the pastures white. One cannot really talk of the first snow of the year at an altitude of 1600 metres, because often it snows every month, but this was the first snow which was not going to disappear until the following year, and it was falling in large flakes.

Towards midday there was a knock on the door. I opened it. Beyond, almost indistinguishable from the snow, were thirty sheep, silent, snow on their necks. In the doorway stood Boris.

He came in and went over to the stove to thaw out. It was one of those tall stoves for wood, standing free in the centre of the room like a post of warmth. The jacket over his gigantic shoulders was white as a mountain.

For a quarter of an hour he stood there silent, drinking from the glass of gnole*, holding his huge hands over the stove. The damp patch on the floorboards around him was growing larger.

In the night, he said, I saw it was snowing. And I knew my sheep were up by the peak. The less there is to eat, the higher they climb. I drove up here before it was light and I set out. It was crazy to climb by myself. Yet who could come with me? I couldn't see the path for the snow. If I'd lost my foothold, there was nothing, nothing at all, to stop me till I reached the church-yard below. For five hours since daybreak I have been playing against death.

alpage: Alpine pasturage
gnole: brandy

John Berger *Boris* (slightly cut)

3 **a)** One of these passages can be described as **personal** writing, while the other is **impersonal**. Which is which and why?

b) They are both about the same place, but the effect of each is different. How would you describe the effect that each one has on you?

Viewpoints

ENGLISH	A–	Her work is imaginative and original. She has really begun to think for herself and this is showing both in her writing and in her comments on the books she reads. *CS*
FRENCH	C⁺	Her translations are always well-written, but often have little to do with the original text. She must learn that accuracy is more important than imagination. *RN.*
PHYSICS	D	She seems to live in a world of her own. She <u>must</u> learn to stick to the facts. *JWW*

4 What does this group of comments tell us about:

a) The girl whose report it is

b) The three teachers who wrote the comments?

These comments are examples of personal writing in which the different viewpoints of the writers lead them to write in very different ways.

5 Choose two of the people in the pictures below. Write about the scene on the opposite page from the viewpoint of each of the people you have chosen. You can write a description, or a story, or an account of their thoughts.

Links

1 Read *Love is a many-splendoured thing* on page 24.
   a) From whose viewpoint do we see this part of the play?
   b) How do you think Grandad and Janet would have described the two conversations to other people?
   c) Write a short account of the conversation they had with Grandad, as Grandad might have told it, or an account of the one they had with Janet as she might have told it.

2 Read *Breakfast time* on page 30. Write a short account of that conversation from either Mrs Pugh's or Mr Pugh's viewpoint.

Summary

1 The same writing topic can be approached from different viewpoints.
2 The viewpoint may be just a matter of **purpose**.
3 Writing can be personal or impersonal.
4 Viewpoint may also be a matter of personal feelings and attitudes.
5 The viewpoint of a particular piece of writing affects the reader's understanding.

Tone

Tone of voice

When we are speaking we can use the same words to mean different things. We convey our meaning by the tone of voice we use:

A

Girl: Is this your book?
Boy: Yes it is.
Girl: Here you are.
Boy: Thanks very much.

B

1 With a partner practise saying this short conversation twice:

a) In a way suitable for drawing A
b) In a way suitable for drawing B.

When the boy says, 'Thanks very much', it clearly has a different meaning in the two conversations.
What is the difference of meaning?
How is it expressed?

Tone in writing

We can express our attitudes and feelings by using **tone** when we write as well as when we speak. In speech we do it by the way we say things. In writing we do it by the words we choose and the way we arrange them into sentences.

2 Applying for a job

A Dear Personnel Manager,

I saw an ad in the paper this week that you were looking for trainees. Well I'm going to leave school soon and I reckon that that's the sort of job I'd like, so . . .

B Dear Sir,

I wish to apply for a traineeship, as advertised in yesterday's 'Letchworth Gazette'.

I am sixteen years old and shall be leaving school at the end of this term. I have taken four subjects at . . .

a) How would you describe the tone of letter A?
b) How would you describe the tone of letter B?
c) Which letter stands a better chance of success and why?

Writing can range between **formal** and **informal**.

VERY	often a	usually	VERY
←— larger		a smaller	—→
FORMAL	audience	audience	INFORMAL
As you know your audience less your writing becomes more formal.			As you know your audience better your writing becomes less formal.

3 Imagine that you are the man in the pictures. Write two accounts of what happened to you:

a) To be read by your employer
b) To be read by a close friend or relative.

Tone of newspaper reports

a

Congratulations to battling headmistress Isobel Hayward (report and picture page 3) in her fight against the rowdy rebels of Holmethorpe High. Her punk fifth formers want to put silly teenage fashion before the normal decencies of school behaviour. And now because they can't get their own way. they've gone on strike! How stupid can you get? Can't these adolescent idiots see that the only people they are hurting are themselves – and their long-suffering parents?

b

At Holmethorpe Lea High School yesterday senior pupils disrupted lessons and then walked out. The trouble arose because of conflict between the Headmistress, Mrs Isobel Hayward, and members of the fifth year. Mrs Hayward has insisted that fifth formers at the school, an 11–18 comprehensive, should wear regulation school uniform. In recent weeks some of them have been adapting the official uniform in a variety of unorthodox ways. Yesterday the trouble came to a head when twelve pupils were sent home.

c

It's a sad day when students facing examinations have to put their future careers at risk in the defence of freedom. Yet that's just what the gutsy fifteen-year-olds of Holmethorpe Lea have done. A series of pettifogging and small-minded attacks on them and their way of life left them with no choice but to respond in this way. Their headmistress Mrs Isobel Hayward (56) took the predictably reactionary stance of insisting that school uniform regulations should be obeyed to the letter. Rules brought in twenty years before these young people were even born! FUNNY PLACES, SCHOOLS

4 **a)** Describe the **tone** of each account.
  b) Explain exactly what it is in each passage that makes you think this.
  c) The stories are printed as if they came from newspapers. Which paper do you think each might have come from and why?

5 Write two contrasting newspaper accounts of this event. Use a clearly different tone in each.

Links

1 Study *Breakfast time* (30). How would you describe the tone used by Mrs Pugh in this scene?

2 Read the scene from *Roots* (48–49). Describe the tone you think Mrs Bryant uses on these pages.

3 How would you describe the contrasting tones of the two pieces on page 47?

4 Compare *The soldier* and *Futility* (92). How would you describe the main tone of each of these poems?

Summary

1 When two people speak to each other they very often express part of their meaning by the tone of voice each uses.

2 It is possible to use different tones in writing, too.

3 Writing may have a formal or informal tone.

4 It is important to use the appropriate tone, according to the situation.

5 Apart from degrees of formality, writing can have a very wide range of tone, according to the writer's audience and intentions.

Speaking figuratively

Often when we speak and write we do not use words literally. We speak or write figuratively, using **figures of speech**.

Irony

Simile

Metaphor

1 For each figure of speech:

   a) Explain the literal meaning of the words spoken.
   b) Explain what the speaker really means.
   c) Explain the point of using that figure of speech.

When we use **irony** we say something that is more or less the opposite of what we mean, usually in order to amuse, mock or hurt.

When we use **similes** we aim to make our meaning clearer by using some kind of comparison. We make this clear to the reader by using words such as *like* or *as*.

A **metaphor** also works by comparing two different things, but it does not use the signal *like* or *as*. Metaphors work much more directly.

Metaphors and similes are **images**. They work by building up a picture in the reader's mind in order to help him or her to understand more clearly and vividly what the author is writing about.

Images

Many writers use images as a kind of short cut in their journey to communicate with the reader.

If you were asked to write a description of this man, you could begin by describing the overall impression that his face makes on you.
On the other hand you could begin by jotting down images. You could focus on his eye:

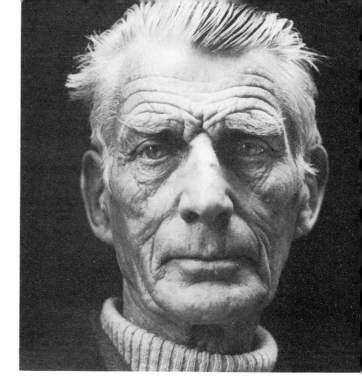

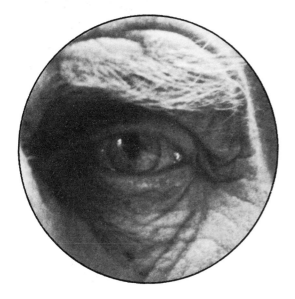

It might suggest this to you:

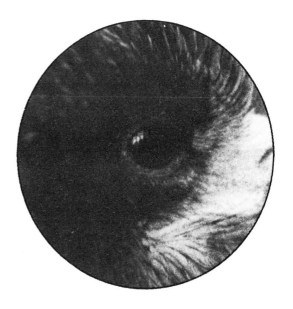

Which comes from this:

This was the comparison that Dickens used in this description:

> He was a hook-nosed man, and with that and his bright eyes and his ruffled head, bore a certain likeness to a roused bird of prey.

Charles Dickens *Our mutual friend*

How images work

2 For each of the following passages, answer these questions:
  a) What subject is the author writing about?
  b) What image does he use to describe it?
  c) Why do you think he uses that particular image?
  d) Does the image work for you? Does it make the writing clearer or more vivid?

  A . . . suddenly the night turned white, black, white, black, white. A great hammer banged on the tin tray of the sky crushing their ear-drums again and again. Anti-aircraft guns.
  B Pigs must have hot blood, they feel like ovens.
  C She had never spoken to him, yet his face was already familiar to her: so big, so uncertain, so sweaty. She had seen it yesterday, she had seen it the day before, and for all she knew, the day before that as well – my Lord she was not a walking diary!
  D Look at this village boy, his head is stuffed
  With all the nests he knows . . .

3 Write an imaginative description based on this picture:

You may find it helpful to concentrate on some of these extracts from the picture, as was done on page 157:

4 Invent images to describe the following:

toothache   thirst   panic   exhaustion

Choose one of your images and build it into a piece of descriptive writing.

Links

1 Read the poem *In the high rise Alice dreams of Wonderland* (63).
The parcel she receives is an image. What do you think the writer means us to understand by it? What are the main images in the second section and what do you understand by them?
2 What are the main images in *Sometimes it happens* (29)?
What do they mean to you?
3 Read *Ten types of hospital visitor* (101). Find examples of metaphors and similes in the poem. Write them down. Then explain what they mean to you.

Summary

1 Often when we write we do not use language in its literal sense.
2 We may write the opposite of the truth in order to make a joke, to criticize, or to hurt a person's feelings.
3 We may use an image in order to make the meaning clearer.
4 A common form of image is the simile, in which the writer compares his subject to something else, in order to make his meaning clearer. This comparison is signalled to the reader by the use of *like* or *as*.
5 Another common form of image is the metaphor. This again uses comparison, but does not signal it to the reader. The comparison is direct.

Words

Vague or precise?

Often the difference between good and bad writing is the difference between the use of vague and precise words.

1 Which of the following sets of instructions is better and why?

Mending a puncture

A

First of all you pull the tyre off one side of the wheel using one of those special bendy tools – know what I mean? Then you undo the thing that holds the air thing that pokes out of the inside of the wheel. Right? Push it through the little hole and then get the tube off . . .

B

First lever the tyre off one side of the wheel, using tyre levers. Then unscrew the ring holding the valve in place. Push the valve through the hole in the rim so as to free the inner tube . . .

2 Explain clearly and accurately how to wire up a 13 amp plug, using the information provided in the diagrams. Make your writing clear enough to be understood without reference to the drawings.

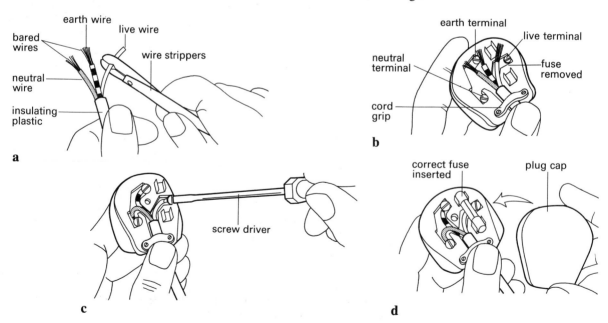

3 Write clear instructions on how to do one of the following:

    a) Cook scrambled egg

    b) Mend a piece of broken china

    c) Sew on a button.

Emotional bias   Words may be neutral, or they can be favourable or hostile to the person, place or thing being described.

 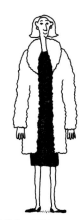 

A   Mabel Hammerton is long-legged and slim and dresses beautifully. She lives in a first floor apartment near fashionable Camden Lock . . .

B   Mabel Hammerton is tall and thin and wears expensive clothes. She lives in a first floor flat in Camden . . .

C   Mabel Hammerton is lanky and skinny and wears fancy gear. She lives in a maisonette in Gutteridge Road, London NW1 . . .

4   Compare the three descriptions of Mabel Hammerton:
  a)   In what ways, if any, are the facts in each different?
  b)   In what ways are the words used different?
  c)   What does this tell us about the attitudes of the writers to Mabel Hammerton?

5   Draw three columns headed: **Favourable**, **Neutral**, **Hostile**. Put the words in the appropriate column.

large	thin	clever
bulky	lean	intelligent
stout	slender	sharp
obese	slim	bright
ample	twiggy	witty
plump	cadaverous	crafty
dumpy	spindly	shrewd
well-covered	emaciated	cunning
podgy	scrawny	brilliant
tubby	spare	brainy

6   Choose one of the following subjects. Write two descriptions of it, one from a favourable point of view, the other from a hostile point of view:

  a)   A seaside resort   **c)**   A school
  b)   An old building   **d)**   A pop star

Make sure that you keep the facts of your description the same, and alter only the words.

Newspeak

It is sometimes tempting to imitate the language used in newspapers. Here is a warning from a writer who has studied the press for many years.

Words, phrases, whole sentences even, appear to be mass-produced like plastic kitchen-utensils, each one identical to the next. It is a language of its own, never encountered in real life. Even the most hardened news reporter abandons it as he leaves the office. If he did not, here is how he might converse with his wife at the breakfast table.

– That was postman Fred Rigg riding high on his bike, peddling his mailbag. He brought a letter from Mum, shapely blonde vivacious divorcee, mother of six, Rita Grunge (58), which has just landed on the doormat with a sickening thud. It's ages since she's been to see us. Says she wants to take a stroll down memory lane. I can see from your face that you're pleased. The smile that says it all.

So a visit from battling granny is looming, is it? I suppose she's adamant. Fancy dropping that bombshell on us at this moment in time.

Yes, and I'm afraid there's more shock horror in store. She wants to bring boyfriend, portly bowlerhatted bespectacled retired bricklayer Ron Glubb (72). He still seems to be a reluctant groom, unwilling to pop the question. I have a gut reaction feeling he doesn't want to wed her. At first her hopes rose, then they faded and now seem dashed. He's probably thinking in terms of remaining an office romeo.

Fritz Spiegl
Keep taking the tabloids!

---

7 Explain in your own words the meaning of each of the following newspaper extracts:

   a) GAS RIG MEN GRILLED BY VILLAGERS
   b) 8 HELD OVER LEAK
   c) HOSPITAL AXE HITS PATIENTS – DOCTOR
   d) The newspaper found itself crucified under a flood of letters from irate readers.

The best words   Good writing consists of the best words in the best order.

A   Mum and dad wouldn't let me play with bullies
Who used rude words and who wore torn clothes.
They had holes in their trousers. They ran in the street
And climbed cliffs and bathed in the nude.

I was more scared than anything of their strong muscles
Their strong hands and their legs pinning my arms.
I was afraid of the rude way those boys pointed
And imitated my accent behind me in the street.

B   My parents kept me from children who were rough
Who threw words like stones and who wore torn clothes.
Their thighs showed through rags. They ran in the street
And climbed cliffs and stripped by the country streams.

I feared more than tigers their muscles like iron
Their jerking hands and their knees tight on my arms.
I feared the salt coarse pointing of those boys
Who copied my lisp behind me on the road.

8   Compare the two poems:

a)   Make a list of places where whole sentences have been rewritten.
b)   Make a list of changes in individual words.
c)   State in each case which version you think is better and why.
d)   Decide which version is better overall and why.

9   The third verse of the original poem goes like this:

They were ___ **1** ___ , they ___ **2** ___ out behind hedges
Like ___ **3** ___ to ___ **4** ___ at my world. They threw mud
While I looked the other way, pretending to ___ **5** ___ .
I ___ **6** ___ to forgive them, but they never ___ **5** ___ ed.

Choose the best words from these lists to fill the spaces:
1 quick/crafty/lithe/strong   **4** moo/bark/bleat/roar
2 sprang/jumped/leaped   **5** grin/laugh/sneer/smile
3 cows/dogs/sheep/lions   **6** wanted/wished/longed

In each case explain **why** you chose the word you did.

tough
heavy
gutsy
strong
macho
savage
cruel
aggressive
daring

attack
brawl
rumble
punch-up
fray
scrap
roughhouse
scuffle
fracas

cut and run
panic
have no guts
cold feet

chicken
coward
sissy
baby
hide
slink
cringe

the lads
the gang
the boys

evade
funk
cop out
dodge
duck
skulk
flee
flit
fly
bolt
cut and run
skedaddle

outface
stand up to
confront
make a stand
hold out
hold off
resist
show spirit
show a brave face
look in the eyes

shake
tremble
shiver
cower
get the wind up
flap
panic
take fright
shaking
nerves
butterflies

10 Use the material and ideas on this page as the starting point for a piece of writing. You can use words from the lists, but you will probably want to make your own lists of words and ideas before you start to write. As far as possible, base your own writing on personal experience. Write about thoughts and feelings as well as 'what happened'.

11 Write a brief account of your thoughts and feelings as you experience one of the situations below. Concentrate on choosing words that convey precisely how you thought and felt.

  a) Being driven in a car by a driver whose driving you do not trust and nearly having an accident.

  b) Being alone at night, when it is dark and windy. You hear a noise and have to decide whether to go and investigate or not.

  c) Attending an interview which you have been dreading.

12 Write a short description based on this picture. Try to choose words that capture the mood and atmosphere of the occasion.

Links

1 Further examples of newspaper and magazine language will be found on pages 7 and 28.

2 The language of advertising is illustrated on page 47. (And it is interesting to read what Shakespeare thought of inflated language in his sonnet on page 23.)

3 There is contrasting vocabulary within one short passage in *The mask* on page 52: see how the language changes as the mood of the boys changes.

4 The comments of Beatie Bryant (and her boyfriend) on the importance of words are worth reading, too. (48)

Summary

1 Good choice of words is a very important part of effective writing.

2 It is often important to look for precision in writing, especially in technical or explanatory writing.

3 A writer's attitude towards the subject may be shown by the words s/he uses, since many words have a built-in emotional bias.

4 Newspapers often use language in a sloppy or garbled way. This is to be avoided.

5 Good writing consists of the best words in the best order, and this requires care and patience on the part of the writer.

Sentences

Sentences can be short or long. Effective writing usually contains a mixture of short and long sentences; the writer matches the length of sentences to what is being said. If you use only long or only short sentences you may find that you have unexpected effects on your audience.

1 I like fishing. I like coarse fishing best. I started fishing at seven years old. My Dad took me. My Dad is a keen angler. He belongs to the Birmingham A.C. He fishes for them in matches. It was a match he took me to. Now I go fishing on my own. I like fishing for carp and pike. I have got three rods. One is a match rod. One is a carp rod. One is a pike rod.

   a) What is wrong with this piece of writing?
   b) Rewrite it in a more suitable style.

Short sentences can be built up into longer sentences by using the conjunction *and*. If this is the only word you use as a link, however, you may find that your longer sentences become even more boring than the short ones were.

2 Last term we did a musical and it was about the life of Al Capone, and it was very enjoyable and I played the part of his girl-friend Mae and we all had to be able to dance and sing and I had a big song called 'Never Till Now' and it was all about my love for Al Capone and the audience always liked my song particularly.

   a) Write this passage out as a series of separate sentences.
   b) Decide which of these short sentences should be combined into longer sentences.
   c) Think of ways of combining them without using 'and'.
   d) Rewrite the passage making these alterations.

All **and** does in a sentence is to act like a plus sign:

I had a big song called 'Never Till Now'	+	It was all about my love for Al Capone	+	The audience always liked my song particularly.

It doesn't say which of these three pieces of information is the most important. If we rewrite the sentence, we can make one of these three elements more important than the others:

A The song the audience liked particularly was one I had about my love for Al Capone, called 'Never Till Now'.

B The big song I had, called 'Never Till Now', which the audience liked particularly, was about my love for Al Capone.

C The big song I had about my love for Al Capone, which the audience liked particularly, was called 'Never Till Now'.

3 Each version has a particular emphasis. How would you describe that emphasis in each case?

Linking words

Constructing longer sentences that mean exactly what you want them to is a matter of two things:

a) Putting the elements in the best order

b) Using the right linking words.

Linking words have a number of different purposes. The commonest, apart from *and* and *but* are:

when	who	because	if	so that	although
before	which	as	unless	in order that	even if
after	that	since			
until	whom				
while	whose				

4 Write a total of six sentences illustrating the use of linking words. Choose one word from each of the six columns and use it as a link between two shorter sentences. For example: *so that*

I got home early so that there would be time to take the dog for a walk.

5 The words above are grouped according to meaning. How would you describe the meaning and purpose of each group?

6 These three sentences can be linked in more than one way according to the sense that you want to make. Write three long sentences, each of which combines them in a different way and so gives a different emphasis.

Hamish Lock is in our form at school.
He is always talking about motorbikes.
A lot of the girls try to avoid him.

Style

There is a link between the length of sentences and the kind of thing the writer is trying to say in them. Short sentences are usually clear and have a strong impact – *in the right situation*. If you have something more extended or complicated to say, then you will probably need longer sentences.

7 **a)** What is wrong with this set of instructions?
b) Rewrite the instructions in a more suitable style.

> **Making a cup of tea**
>
> If you wish to make a cup of tea it is necessary to begin by boiling some water. In order to do this, start by filling the kettle and then plug it into the socket and switch it on. While the water is heating, you will be able to make preparations for the next stage by getting out cups, saucers, teaspoons, milk, sugar and the teapot. It is necessary for the tea to be kept as hot as possible and one way of contributing to this aim is to make sure that the teapot is warmed before the tea is actually made. When the kettle is nearly boiling, therefore, you should . . .

Sometimes it is very effective to write a number of short simple sentences. If a writer wants to convey the idea of a simple-minded man thinking a number of plain, uncomplicated thoughts, then it is better to write a number of short, uncomplicated sentences like this: ▬ ▬ ▬ ▬
than one long complicated sentence like this: ▬▬▬▬▬▬▬

8 These are two versions of the beginning of a novel about a terrorist assassin. Compare them:

A Murder didn't mean much to Raven. It was just a new job. You had to use your brains. It was not a question of hatred.
B Murder wasn't a question of hatred and it didn't mean much to Raven, to whom it was just a new job in which you had to use your brains.

a) Are there any differences in the information contained in each one?
b) How many sentences are there in each?
c) What is the average number of words per sentence in each?
d) Which one is more effective as the beginning of a novel and why?

9 Compare these two versions of a description in a similar way:

A

The beach was like a diamond haze. Something dark was fumbling along it. Ralph saw it first. He watched it intently. His gaze drew all eyes that way. The creature stepped from mirage on to clear sand. They saw that the darkness was not all shadow. It was mostly clothing. The creature was a party of boys. They were marching approximately in step in two parallel lines. They were dressed in strangely eccentric clothing.

B

Within the diamond haze of the beach something dark was fumbling along. Ralph saw it first, and watched till the intentness of his gaze drew all eyes that way. Then the creature stepped from mirage onto clear sand, and they saw that the darkness was not all shadow but mostly clothing. The creature was a party of boys, marching approximately in step in two parallel lines and dressed in strangely eccentric clothing.

a) What are the most important things that the writer wants to convey?

b) Which version achieves this better?

c) Does the length of the sentences help? If so, how?

10 Sometimes it is not the **subject** of a piece of writing that decides how long sentences should be, but the **audience**.

A **How bread is made** **B**

Bread is usually made in a warm, moist, draught-free atmosphere so the yeast will grow quickly . . . Kneading spreads the yeast and, at the second kneading, air evenly through the dough. Quite good bread can be made without two kneadings, but is likely to be of less even texture as a result. Baking takes place at a very high temperature to kill the yeast, and so stop the bread rising more than is required, and to make it light and crisp.

Flour is mixed with yeast and water to form a soft dough. The dough is then put into a warm place to rise (proving). During this time the dough expands to twice its original size. This is called risen dough. The risen dough is then baked at high temperature in an oven. After this the bread is ready to eat.

a) What is the difference between the audiences for the two passages?

b) How much difference is there in the choice of words between A and B?

c) How much difference is there in the length of sentences?

11 Write two short descriptions of your school:

a) For an uncle who works abroad as a headmaster

b) For a younger brother or sister who is six years old.

Summary

1 If you use short sentences all the time, your writing will become monotonous, or may irritate your audience.

2 Short simple sentences can be linked together using *and* or *but*.

3 If this is done too frequently, it can become tiresome.

4 Other linking words can introduce the ideas of **time** (when), **cause** (because), **result** (so that), **condition** (if), **concession** (although), **qualification** (which).

5 By changing the order of elements in a sentence, and using different linking words, the whole meaning of the sentence can be altered.

6 Sometimes short sentences are very effective, while at other times it is better to use long sentences.

7 What you do depends on the meaning you want to convey and the audience for whom you are writing.

Paragraphs

The reader

Writing is usually divided into paragraphs. The use of paragraphing is a help to the reader. Read the passage below. It is divided into six paragraphs. Except for the first, the beginning of each paragraph is marked by indenting:

The watch belonged to my grandfather and it hung on a hook by the head of his bed where he had lain for many long weeks. The face was marked off in Roman numerals, the most elegant figures I had ever seen. The case was of gold, heavy and beautifully chased; and the chain was of gold too, and wonderfully rich and smooth in the hand. The mechanism, when you held the watch to your ear, gave such a deep, steady ticking that you could not imagine its ever going wrong. It was altogether a most magnificent watch and when I sat with my grandfather in the late afternoon, after school, I could not keep my eyes away from it, dreaming that someday I too might own such a watch.

It was almost a ritual for me to sit with my grandfather for a little while after tea. My mother said he was old and drawing near his time, and it seemed to me that he must be an incredible age. He liked me to read to him from the evening paper while he lay there, his long hands, soft and white now from disuse and fined down to skin and bone by illness and age, fluttered restlessly about over the sheets, like a blind man reading braille. He had never been much of a reader himself and it was too much of an effort for him now. Possibly because he had had so little education, no one believed in it more, and he was always eager for news of my progress at school. The day I brought home the news of my success in the County Minor Scholarship examination he sent out for half an ounce of twist and found the strength to sit up in bed for a smoke.

'Grammar School next, then Will?' he said, pleased as Punch.

'Then college,' I said, seeing the path straight before me. 'Then I shall be a doctor.'

'Aye, that he will, I've no doubt,' my grandfather said. 'But he'll need plenty o' patience afore that day. Patience an' hard work, Will lad.'

Though, as I have said, he had little book learning, I thought sometimes as I sat with my grandfather that he must be one of the wisest men in Yorkshire; and these two qualities – patience and the ability to work hard – were the cornerstones of his philosophy of life.

Stan Barstow *One of the virtues*

The main purpose of paragraphs is to **divide the thought** of the writing into shorter, manageable sections. The first part of the story is about the narrator's feelings about the watch. This is given a separate paragraph by the writer to mark it off from the rest.

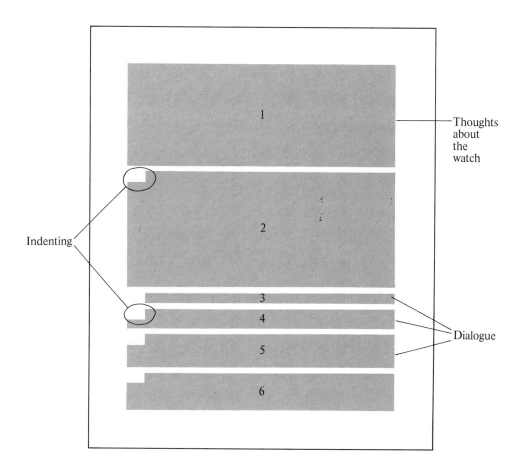

1 Read the rest of the passage again. Make up suitable titles for paragraphs 2 and 6.

There is no standard length for a paragraph. If there is a lot of information to be included about a particular aspect of the subject, then that paragraph will be long. If the point can be made briefly, then the paragraph should be short. There are, however, two rules that can be made:

a) A paragraph should not be so long that the reader loses track of the thought being expressed. If in doubt, divide a long paragraph into two shorter ones.

b) It is confusing for the reader if a piece of writing consists only or mainly of many very short paragraphs. The exception to this is speech.

In a story that contains **dialogue**, it is normal to use a new paragraph each time a new person speaks.

2 Make a similar paragraph plan for this examination essay topic: *'Paying college students or sixth formers wages to study would be as foolish as paying mothers wages to do housework.' Discuss.*

The writer   Thinking in paragraphs can help the writer to plan a piece of writing. Suppose you were writing a short answer to this examination question:

How could we lessen the risk of accidents in the home, bearing in mind, particularly, the dangers to the very young and to the old?

You might begin by jotting down ideas as they occur to you:

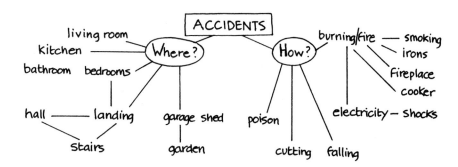

These ideas could be organized in two ways:

a)   Types of accident **or**
b)   Places where accidents occur.

Suppose you decide to work on **b)**; your notes list ten places. If you give each one a paragraph to itself, this may make too many short paragraphs. The places must therefore be grouped in some way:

> **Downstairs**: kitchen, living room, hall
> **Upstairs**: stairs, landing, bedrooms, bathroom
> **Outside**: garden, garage, shed

It is, however, confusing to the reader if you jump straight in to 'Accidents downstairs'. Similarly to stop writing leaving your reader in 'The shed' would not be very helpful. Your essay needs a beginning and an end. These can be two shorter paragraphs, giving a total of five:

1   Introduction
2   Downstairs
3   Upstairs
4   Outside
5   Conclusion

Each paragraph title can now be used as a 'hook' on which to hang your ideas:

Introduction   many serious accidents in home – especially for old – and very young – need to take precautions
Downstairs   kitchen – cooker/iron – fire
            – sharp knives – cutting
            – bleach – poison   and so on.

Planning the paragraph

Like any piece of writing a paragraph should have a beginning, a middle and an end.

1. It should begin by introducing the topic.
2. It should then develop and explore the topic.
3. It should round off the topic and lead to the next paragraph.

The paragraph that follows is based on the introduction to the 'Accidents in the home' essay.

> The modern home can be a very dangerous place. Every day we hear of people being burned to death while they sleep, children being accidentally poisoned and pensioners falling and injuring themselves badly. Yet with a little careful thought it is possible to avoid most, if not all, of these accidents. An examination of each part of the house will show how this can be done.

3
  a) What is the paragraph about?
  b) Which sentence introduces the paragraph?
  c) What is the purpose of the last sentence?

4 Each of the following exam topics is intended to be completed in an hour. For each one:

Decide what the essay should contain.
Decide how many paragraphs there should be.
Decide what each paragraph should be about.
Write an essay plan containing your ideas.

  a) Describe a place that a casual visitor might consider unattractive but that you have become fond of over a period of time.
  b) Sometimes offers of help go disastrously wrong. Describe an occasion when your attempt to help somebody did not turn out as you expected.
  c) Write a leaflet which will be given to all families coming to live in your area. Explain life in your community, giving interesting information.

Summary

1. Writing is normally divided into paragraphs.
2. The beginning of a new paragraph is shown by indenting.
3. Each paragraph covers a different aspect of the subject.
4. A new paragraph is also used to indicate a change of speaker in dialogue.
5. The writer should use paragraphing as an aid to planning.
6. A paragraph should usually consist of three parts: an introduction, the development, and a conclusion.

3. *Ways of writing*

Description

Miriam Thompson was 15 years old, attractive, and a natural rebel. You only had to see the look in her eyes and the jut of her chin to know that she was both independent and determined. When you got to know her better, you soon found out that she usually got her own way, even when that way led her into conflict with the authorities.

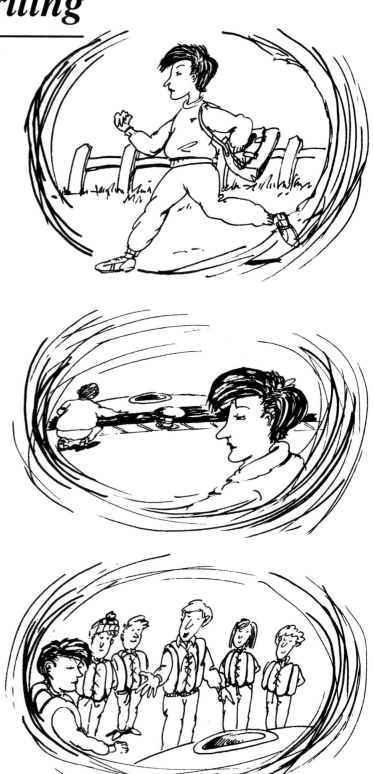

Narrative

That day Miriam arrived at school early. The Duke of Edinburgh Award Silver group were going on a canoe trip to the Wye. The canoes were soon loaded onto the trailer. The ten members of the group boarded the minibus, and they were off. Miriam had never been canoeing before and she wasn't sure whether she would enjoy it or not.

It wasn't long before they were at Haggers Bridge and offloading the canoes . . .

Exposition

The first thing you've got to learn is how to get into the canoe. Now that may sound stupid – it's pretty easy to get into a canoe. But you'd be surprised how many people make a mess of it. Now what you have to do is this . . .

Argument

'Look at the notice. We mustn't go any further.'

'I think it's just a lot of fuss about nothing. They just put those notices up to scare you.'

'I still think we ought to stop.'

'Rubbish. It's just getting interesting. I'm not scared. I'm going to have a look at this weir. You coming or not?'

Letters

. . . and they look after you very well here. My broken arm is mending very well and the bruises and cuts are beginning to heal up. Sister says that I should be out in a day or two. Give my love to Dan and Pippa . . .

Reports

ACCIDENT REPORT

Date: 15th June 1985

Subject: Accident at Haggers Weir involving Miriam Thompson. All the students had the rules of the water explained to them very clearly. In particular the danger of approaching Haggers Weir was stressed. Before the students were allowed to go on the water they were questioned about the safety rules that had just been explained. I was satisfied that all of them had heard and understood the rules . . .

The four modes of writing

Most writing belongs to one of four types or **modes**:

Description
Narrative
Exposition
Argument

Description

Descriptive writing gives an idea of what a person, place or thing is like, or used to be like:

> It was a narrow winding street with open booths on both sides – booths selling embroidered slippers, booths selling cheap cotton cloth, booths selling vegetables or fruits or sweetmeats or chunks of meat hung up on hooks. Over the shops were wooden verandahs and arched windows set in thin crumbling walls.

Narrative

Narrative writing tells a story. It may be true or made up:

> Prem and Indu, escorted by the troupe of triumphant children, walked down the street with the measured dignity of invited wedding guests.
> 'Up here!' cried the children. They stood aside, grinning, while Prem and Indu walked into a dark doorway by the side of a booth selling coloured drinks in bottles. The stairs too were very dark. Upstairs Sohan Lal met them . . .

Exposition

Exposition is writing that explains something – for example how a thing works, or what a particular situation is:

> It was a pity the students had nowhere to go before and after classes except out in the street; but the college was only an ordinary residential house in the middle of a street consisting of other ordinary residential houses, so there was no question of grounds. Between classes the students had either the corridor or the street, and most of them preferred the street. Consequently the College had a bad name in the neighbourhood.

> All from **Ruth Prawer Jhabvala**   *The householder*

Argument

Argument is writing that puts across an opinion or point of view:

> One trouble, it sees to me, is that the majority of the people who rule us, who have our money and power, are lawyers and military men. The lawyers want to talk our problems out of existence. The military men want us to find the bad guys and put bullets through their brains. These are not always the best solutions – particularly in the fields of sewage disposal and birth control.
> **Kurt Vonnegut Jr**   *Wampeters, foma and granfalloons*

Which mode?

1 To which of the four modes does each of these passages belong?

A I remember him as a tall, barely articulate source of smells. The principle smells were of mouldy cloth, mothballs, seaweed, powerful tobacco and the tars that collect in the stem of a very old pipe.
Clive James *Unreliable memoirs*

B The important thing about making an omelette is to make sure that the pan is really hot before you put the egg in. To do this satisfactorily you need a very heavy iron pan. When you have beaten the eggs, heat the pan up until the oil begins to smoke.

C I can't stand pop music! It's noisy, tuneless and silly.

D Oilcan Harry, feeling bored,
Tied his sister to a Ford.
Harry chuckled at the gag.
Sister found it quite a drag.
Dennis Lee *Gangsters, ghosts and dragonflies*

2 When you are given a topic for writing, it is sometimes fairly clear which mode of writing is most suitable. For each of the following topics, which mode would you choose?

a) You are a passenger in a train. Suddenly the old man opposite lurches forward and collapses. Tell the story.

b) Giving your reasons, say whether you agree or disagree with the saying, 'A woman's place is in the home.'

c) Imagine that you are a visitor from a country overseas. Give an account of the differences you would find in this country, compared to what you are used to, in the following respects: dress; food; religion; shopping.

d) Down our street:
Think of the street in which you live and write about the people who live there.
All from *EMREB 1981*

3 Sometimes you are given a writing topic which allows you to choose which mode you will write in. Think of two different modes in which you could write about each of these topics and explain briefly how you would go about each one.

a) Disaster Area. *SWEB 1982*
b) Friends. *LREB 1983*
c) The lift. *WJEC 1983*
d) The fight for survival. *WJEC 1983*

4 Choose one of the writing topics from the previous exercise. Think of two completely different approaches to the topic. Write detailed plans for each approach.

Combined modes   When you write at any length, you will often find that you need to combine two or more modes. A narrative, for example, often has to include some description. Many arguments contain exposition.

5 Which two modes are combined in each of the following passages?

A You can't teach people to write well. Writing well is something God lets you do or declines to let you do. Most bright people know that but writers' conferences continue to multiply in the good old American summertime. Sixty-eight of them are listed in April's issue of *The Writer*. Next year there will be more. They are harmless. They are schmoos.

Kurt Vonnegut Jr   *Wampeters, foma and granfalloons*

B The old man walked through the town, now and again drawing his tattered cloak tighter to shield his body from the cold and biting wind. On one side of the road was a row of trees, on the other the town's public garden. The night was darker now and the cold more intense, for the wind was blowing straight along the road.

C 'Police Superintendent,' a voice inside called sharply. The old man started at the sound, but composed himself again to wait. Name after name rang out from within as the clerk read out the English addresses on the letters and flung them to the waiting postmen. From long practice he had acquired great speed in reading out the titles – Commissioner, Superintendent, Diwan Sahib, Librarian – and in flinging out the letters.

Both from **Dhumektu**   *The letter*

6 Each of the writing topics that follows can be written about in a number of different ways. Choose one topic and work on it in detail:

a) Think of as many different ways as you can of writing about it. Make rough notes on all of them.
b) Choose **two**, which seem to you to be the most promising.
c) Make a detailed plan for each of the two approaches, showing clearly in which mode(s) you intend to write.
d) Choose one of the two and write about it in full.

Topic **A**   Write in any way you please about **one** of the following:
a) In that world there is a ruler
And that ruler is without mercy –
Hunger is what they call him.

b) I'm walking about the streets with my hands in my pockets.
Nobody really cares about me.

c) I slowly bent my head
Intently to the ground.
I listened again.
SCE 1982

Topic **B**   Write a composition suggested by this picture.   *LREB 1984*

Links

1   *Leaving home* (10) is mainly narrative. What other modes does it use and how does it use them?
2   What is the main mode in the *Strip-cartoon romances* (26)?
3   Read the story *Trust* on pages 38–43. Look particularly at the ways in which the author uses description in her story. How does this add to the effectiveness of the story as a whole?
4   What modes are present in *New York subway* (64)? Which is the most important?

Summary

1   There are four main modes of writing: description, narrative, exposition and argument.
2   Descriptive writing gives an idea of what a person, place or thing is like or used to be like.
3   Narrative writing tells a true or fictional story.
4   Exposition is writing that explains something.
5   Argument is writing that puts across an opinion or point of view.
6   Writing often contains a combination of two or more modes.
7   Sometimes topics set for writing may make it clear which is the most suitable mode of writing to use.
8   At other times the writer has a choice of mode.

Description

1 These two pieces of writing are both about the same scene. Which do you think is better and why?

A As it got hotter the people on the beach got busier. The children were running everywhere and getting in the way. The men pulled on the ropes and dragged the boat towards the sea. Two men shouted instructions to them as they pulled. It was exciting and noisy.

B The sun grew hotter and the scene on the beach more animated. The children were bundles of concentrated energy, little parcels of explosive bursting into the sea. The seawater and sweat ran lines along the bare skins of the men who worked in the rising heat, pulling at the ropes, drawing the boat inch by inch down the slope of the beach. The big carpenter and a thin man who seemed to know all about it shouted orders, 'Heave now, ease now,' and the boat crept or stayed. Sometimes the figures of the men guiding its passage were caught in a stark dramatic stance as they steadied it from going off course. There was something almost cinematic about the mixture of shouts and the heat and the merriment and the sweat and the steaming breath rising from under the pot lids and the male smell of rum and the streaks of white salt staining the faces and backs of men and the sand crushed by heavy feet into hollows and the children squirting their joy upon the sea – and the boat resisting.

A. N. Forde *Sunday with a difference*

To write a good description, you need to **observe**, using all five senses. You also need to be able to **remember** what you have observed. In passage B the writer is describing something he had remembered since he was a very small child.

2 Imagine that you are in the scene shown in this photograph. Imagine what you can see, hear, smell, taste and feel. Write a description based on your observations.

Focus

When you have observed the subject which you wish to describe, you still need to decide how to organize your writing. In what order should you write about it? Sometimes it is useful to focus on one aspect of the subject which you think is the most important, revealing, or interesting:

Miss Plimsoll's nose was sharp and pointed, like that of Voltaire. It was also extremely sensitive to cold. When the thermometer fell below 60 degrees it turned scarlet; below 50 degrees it seemed a blue tinge with a little white morbid circle at the end; and at 40 degrees it became sniffly and bore a permanent though precarious drop below its pointed tip. I remember with what interest I watched that drop as we drove from the station at Sofia. My parents went in front in the first carriage and Miss Plimsoll and I followed in the brougham. The night was cold and we drove along an endless wind-swept boulevard punctuated by street lamps. With the approach of each successive lamp Miss Plimsoll's little face beside me would first be illuminated frontways and then as we came opposite the lamp, spring into a sharp little silhouette, at the point of which the drop flashed and trembled like a diamond.
Peter Ustinov   *Dear me*

3   What impression do you get of Miss Plimsoll as a person? How does the writer achieve that impression?

4   Write a description of a person. Focus on the most important feature of that person. Use your focal point to organize and give sense to your writing. Choose a person you know, or an invented character, or use the photograph below.

Selection

Two people can look at the same subject and see very different things in it.

In the same way a writer selects details in order to create the impression he wants the reader to have of the subject he is describing:

The waters are out in Lincolnshire. An arch of the bridge in the park has been sapped and sopped away. The adjacent low-lying ground, for half a mile in breadth, is a stagnant river, with melancholy trees for islands in it, and a surface punctured all over, all day long, with falling rain. My Lady Dedlock's 'place' has been extremely dreary. The weather, for many a day and night, has been so wet that the trees seem wet through, and the soft loppings and prunings of the woodman's axe can make no crack or crackle as they fall. The deer, looking soaked, leave quagmires where they pass. The shot of a rifle loses its sharpness in the moist air . . .
Charles Dickens   *Bleak House*

5 What kind of details is the writer selecting in this passage? What impression does he create?

6 Write two short descriptions based on the photograph at the top of the facing page. In the first concentrate on the kind of details represented by pictures **a**, **b** and **c**. In the second emphasize the details represented by pictures **d** and **e**.

7 Write two contrasting descriptions based on this photograph. (Remember that it is a description and not a story that you are writing.)

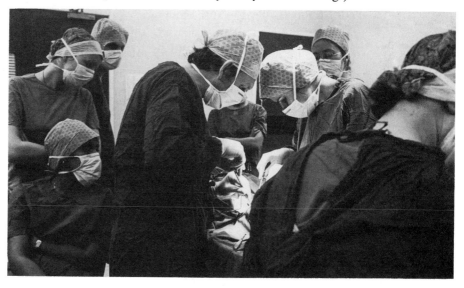

Summary

1 In order to write a good description you have to **observe** carefully.
2 You then need to **organize** your writing.
3 This can be done by providing a particular **focus**.
4 The writer can control the effect of his description by **selecting** the right details.

Narrative

When you write a story, you have first to decide who the narrator is.

A

Coughing and half-blinded by smoke, I made my way slowly up the ladder . . .

B

Terrified, I stared out of the window. Then to my surprise and delight I saw a fireman climbing up a ladder towards me . . .

1 a) Who is the narrator in passage A?
   b) Who is the narrator in passage B?
   c) Write the first 100 words of the story based on the picture. Begin by writing out passage A and continue with the same narrator.
   d) Now do the same, beginning with passage B.

Stories like these are sometimes called 'I' stories' or, more properly, **first person narration**. The narrator is one of the characters in the story. There are both advantages and disadvantages in this form of narrative.

2 a) List any books you remember reading that have used first person narration.
   b) List all the advantages you can think of for this type of narration.
   c) List any disadvantages you can think of.

More often stories are told as if the narrator was someone standing outside the events he/she is describing:

C
The fire had now caught hold. Dense black smoke streaked with orange flame billowed upwards.

Viewpoint

If you use this type of third person narration there is another choice to make: **viewpoint**.

D

It was the first time that Gerry had been sent up on his own. As he clambered up the ladder, slowly and cautiously, he could just make out the faces of the two girls, through the swirling smoke . . .

E

Clinging to her sister in terror, Marie gazed helplessly down through the choking smoke. Suddenly she gave a gasp of excitement and relief. She had just spotted the shining helmet . . .

F

Mr Murray continued to stare upwards. The fireman was moving so slowly and when he reached the point where the smoke was thickest he seemed to stop altogether . . .

3 **a)** Explain the viewpoint of each of these versions.

b) Copy passage **D** and write the next 100 words of the story using this viewpoint.

Do the same for either **E** or **F**.

Time   Any story tells the reader about a number of events that happened in a certain order:

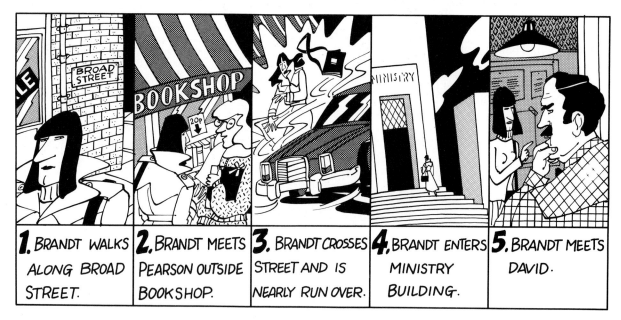

1. BRANDT WALKS ALONG BROAD STREET.
2. BRANDT MEETS PEARSON OUTSIDE BOOKSHOP.
3. BRANDT CROSSES STREET AND IS NEARLY RUN OVER.
4. BRANDT ENTERS MINISTRY BUILDING.
5. BRANDT MEETS DAVID.

You can tell the story in the order in which it happened:

A Brandt walked briskly along Broad Street, only pausing occasionally to look back in the direction from which she had come. Nothing. At the appointed place, outside a small bookshop, she stopped and waited. At 10 o'clock precisely, Pearson arrived . . .

On the other hand, you can change the order and the emphasis:

B Brandt moved slowly along the gloomy corridor of the Ministry building. Suddenly she heard a slight sound behind her. She swung round and saw a man framed in the doorway. It was David. Then it all became clear to her. She hadn't seen anyone following her along Broad Street because they were already in the building. Pearson had been unwilling to talk when they met because . . .

C Brandt walked up Broad Street and had a few words with Pearson at her usual place outside the bookshop. Then she turned to cross the road. Just as she was about to step off the kerb, her attention was drawn to a young child playing with an enormous pink and yellow balloon on the far pavement. As she watched, the child let go of the balloon and it started to drift up and out of her reach. Brandt started forward into the road to try to help, without looking to right or left. There was a screech of brakes and an angry hooting as a large Mercedes swerved to avoid her...

4 **a)** Versions A and B tell the story in a different order. What is the order for each? How does the change of order change the effect that the story has when you read it?

b) Version C doesn't change the order, but it is still different from A. How is it different? What is the effect of this?

c) Write a conclusion to version B.

5 Write two different versions of this story:
a) Describing the events in the order in which they are shown
b) With a different order and/or emphasis.

Dialogue

A story may rely very heavily on dialogue:

When I returned to the spot where I had left Ramesh, he was lying flat on the ground with his right ear pressed tightly to it. I rested my cage on the ground and stooped very close to him.

'Is something wrong?' I whispered. 'Why are you doing that?'

'I'm checking for something. I think we made too much noise.'

'Do you think somebody is around?'

'I don't know.'

'Ramesh are you afraid?' I was becoming a little afraid too, for no reason I could think of.

'A little bit,' Ramesh said. 'You see, if anybody is around, we might have to explain why we are here.'

'Ramesh, who is the owner of this place?' I asked him directly. Ramesh did not answer my question.

He said, 'Look, I'm going to climb up that big saaman tree to see if anybody's coming. Stay here and wait.'

'Look a watchman coming.'

'Where?'

'Not too far. Shh hide quick!'

'You going to leave your cage?'

'Forget the cage. Just hide.'

V. Ramsamooj Gosine   *The bird catchers*

At the other extreme, a story can be told without the use of any direct speech at all. Any conversations that have taken place are simply reported:

Captain Wiles let his eyes scan the tops of the bracken and he nodded, satisfied that he had that part of the heath to himself.

The captain had not forgotten the first time he went shooting. That had been a few days after he had moved in. He had come up here and shot at what he supposed to be a walking pheasant. But it had turned out to be a crawling Freddy Grayson. Mr Grayson had come to him that evening with a holed cap in his hand and wrath in his eye. He had told Captain Wiles a few things about dangerous shooting that he didn't know. He had told Captain Wiles a great many things blunt and to the point, finishing with some advice about sticking to a pair of oars. The captain had vowed that never again would he go shooting amongst small boys. And so he was glad that, on this afternoon, the heath was deserted.

Jack Trevor Story   *The trouble with Harry*

6 a) In the first passage we are told little about the characters' thoughts and feelings and not much about their actions. Most of it is conversation. What do we learn about the characters' thoughts, feelings, and actions, from the words that they speak?

b) How effective is this heavy use of dialogue?

c) In the second passage we read no direct speech at all. We are left to work out for ourselves what was said in the conversations that are remembered by Captain Wiles. What is the effect of this?

d) Rewrite the first narrative, using no direct speech.

e) Write a detailed account of the conversation between Captain Wiles and Mr Grayson, using direct speech.

7 Use some of the techniques you have learned about in this unit to answer one of the following examination writing topics:

a) Write a story in which the problems or pleasures of baby-sitting play an important part. *NWREB 1983*

b) Childhood memories. *WJEC 1984*

c) Write a story called 'The Burglar'. *NREB 1983*

d) 'Clang! In an instant I realised the keeper of the old castle had thought all visitors had gone and I was locked in alone'. Continue this story. Try to create a feeling of fear and tension. *Northern 1982*

e) Imagine that you are one of the people in the photograph below and write your conversation.

Links

You will find many examples of narrative writing in Part A. Use them as a resource. Study the ways in which the writers of these pieces have used the techniques described in this unit, and others, to achieve their effects.

Summary

1 The writer of a narrative has to decide on who the narrator is to be.

2 A story may be told using a first person narrator ('I').

3 If a third person narrator is used, then the author can choose from which character's viewpoint he will describe part or all of what happens.

4 A story describes a sequence of events. The narrator may follow this sequence and describe things in the order in which they happened.

5 The author may prefer to change the order or emphasize one part of the sequence, in order to achieve a particular effect.

6 Stories often contain dialogue. The author has a choice about the amount of dialogue she/he uses and how it is used.

7 It can be effective to make up a story which consists of almost nothing but dialogue.

8 On the other hand it can sometimes be better not to use dialogue directly at all, but to rely on reported speech.

Exposition

Exposition is writing which sets out to answer questions like these:

Writing an exposition consists of these stages:

1 Asking the right questions
2 Collecting and organizing the information
3 Making a plan
4 Deciding how to tell it
5 Writing and checking.

Asking the right questions

Sometimes the topic you are writing about will suggest the questions you ought to be asking:

(a) The 1988 Ideal Homes Exhibition offers a competition for the design of an ideal kitchen or workroom.

Write an entry for the competition describing the lay-out and equipment of EITHER the kitchen OR the workroom. (Do not draw diagrams.)

London 1984

At other times this decision is left to you:

Keeping fit. *AEB 1980*
Repairs. *SREB 1981*

1 For each of the topics above make a list of the questions you would need to ask in order to write about it effectively.

Collecting and organizing

How you collect and organize the information depends of course on the situation in which you are writing.

Sometimes – in an examination, for example – the necessary information is provided. You ask yourself questions in order to sort it out.

Sometimes you already have all the necessary information in your head. You use the questions to organize your own knowledge.

Sometimes you will need to do research in the school or public library. Asking the right questions will shorten your job considerably.

At other times you will have to find out for yourself and ask people questions.

2 Suppose you were set each of the following topics for homework, how would you set about collecting the information needed?

a) Assume that your family has arranged a fortnight's exchange of homes with members of a family from another area or country. The other family will need to know details about local shopping, travel and leisure facilities. Draw up a concise report, outlining the information you think they will need.   *London 1984*

b) Write clear instructions on how to do a simple repair job. Restrict yourself to the repair of something usually in regular use.   *SEREB 1983*

Making a plan

When you have collected the necessary information, you need to decide on the most effective order in which to present it.

Choose one of the following and explain how it works, and the purpose for which it is used: a thermos flask, a refrigerator, a milking machine, a tape recorder, the ten-speed gear on a bicycle, a camera.   *N.I. GCE 1983*

This is an examination question and so you have to rely on knowledge you already have. Begin by jotting down what you know:

> used to keep hot things hot and cold things cold – inner part of flask made of glass – two walls with vacuum between – heat conducted by air, but not by vacuum – heat can radiate through vacuum, so glass silvered to reflect heat back – glass very thin – easily broken – contained in strong metal or plastic case – set on rubber mounts to absorb bangs and reduce shock waves

Examine what you have jotted down and read the question again. The question asks for two types of information: **how it works** and **the purpose for which it is used**. After looking at your notes you can see that this gives the following main headings:

1 Purpose for which it is used   3 Construction of flask
2 Scientific principles behind it   4 Construction of container.

3 Choose one of the questions in Exercise 2 and go through all the stages of preparing and writing an answer.

Deciding how to tell it

Even when you have collected all your information, there is more than one way in which you can present it:

A	B
George is 1.52 metres tall and weighs 78 kilograms. His hair is between mid-brown and fair in colour and is cut to just below his collar.	George is short and fat and has long mousy hair.

The information in A is not a matter of opinion. We can, for example put George on the scales and check that he does in fact weigh 78 kilograms. The information in B is a matter of opinion: what one person thinks of as 'fat' another does not. A is an example of **objective** writing. B is an example of **subjective** writing.

The way in which a piece of exposition presents information can vary in another way:

C	D
Muslims were part of the small Indian community of Trinidad, which was the community into which I was born; and it could be said that I had known Muslims all my life. But I knew little of their religion. My own background was Hindu . . . **V.S. Naipaul** *Among the believers*	The estimated population of Trinidad and Tobago in 1942 was 522,168, and of the island of Trinidad 490,094, of whom nearly one third were locally born of East Indian extraction . . . *Encyclopaedia Britannica*

Passage C is **personal**: the author 'takes part' in what is being described. Passage D is **impersonal**: the author does not appear but 'stands back' and observes the subject matter.

4 Write two short descriptions of the seaside resort shown in the illustration. The first should be subjective and personal; the second should be objective and impersonal.

Fuenterila

On Mediterranean coast
Population 27,000
has 163,000 visitors in June–September
average August midday temperature is
   28 degrees C
average hours of sunshine per day in
   August : 10.37
flying time from Luton : 4 hours 20 minutes
        Manchester : 5 hours 10 minutes

5 These photographs show the same city area. There is a gap of several years between the two. Write an account of the ways in which the area has changed and the effects this may have had on the inhabitants.

Summary

1 An exposition is written to answer questions about the nature, working, origins, or purpose of something.
2 The writer needs to begin by asking the right questions.
3 It is then necessary to assemble information. This may be readily available, or it may be necessary to do research in the library or elsewhere.
4 Then the writer has to decide how best to arrange and organize the material.
5 When this has been done a detailed plan may be made and then writing can begin.
6 Exposition may be objective or subjective.
7 It may also be personal or impersonal.

Argument

What is an argument?

wrangle	disagreement		belief	
bickering	dispute	debate	opinion	
set-to	quarrel	discussion	conviction	bias
abuse	clash	controversy	stand	prejudice
tiff	altercation	argument	position	
jangle	squabble			
barney	slanging match			

ARGUMENT: 1 a quarrel; altercation
2 a discussion in which reasons are put forward in support of and against a proposition, proposal, or case; a debate
3 a point or series of reasons present to support or oppose a proposition
4 a summary of the plot or subject of a book

Collins English Dictionary

An argument is different from an **opinion**:

I DON'T THINK THE GOVERNMENT OUGHT TO BE ALLOWED TO RIDE ROUGH-SHOD OVER THE UNIONS. IT'S NOT RIGHT...

An argument is different from a **prejudice**:

THESE TEENAGERS TODAY THINK THEY'RE IT. THEY'RE ALL THE SAME. NO-GOOD LAYABOUTS WANTING SOMETHING FOR NOTHING. NOW IN MY YOUNG DAY...

An argument is different from a **squabble**:

IT'S MINE! GIVE IT BACK! GIVE IT **BACK** I SAID! IF YOU DON'T GIVE IT BACK, I'LL ...

None of these does what an argument does, which is to answer the question: **WHY?**

The reasons why

If you are writing an argument, you must at least present the **reasons why** on one side in full:

> One of the biggest mistakes that the present government has made is to put its faith for the future in nuclear power. Over the past twenty years there has been a string of accidents at nuclear power stations both in Britain and throughout the world. The various responsible authorities try to hush up these 'minor incidents' but enough is known about them for us to realize that they are an inevitable part of the process of generating electricity at nuclear power stations. In addition to this there are the hazards of disposing of nuclear waste. Various solutions have been suggested but none of them overcomes the objection that we really do not know what will happen when this highly dangerous material is buried deep in the ground or dumped on the ocean bed.

1 Make a list of the reasons the writer gives for believing that it is a mistake to rely on nuclear power.

Listing your reasons

2 Choose one of the following unfinished statements and complete it so that it is true of you:
   a) The ideal school would . . .
   b) If there's one thing I can't stand it's . . .
   c) The most important thing for our country today is . . .
   d) If I had the power, I'd ban . . .
   Now make a list of your reasons for believing this.

Developing a line of reasoning

At this stage you may have a good range of reasons for believing what you do:

> If there's one thing I can't stand it's being forced to do things in school I don't want to.

> Useless subjects   Uniform   Homework   Games   Assembly

Each of these ideas needs to be developed before it can be used as part of a full written argument:

> Useless subjects — Geography/RE.
>
>   — only doing them because I had to choose something on that option
>
> What would I do with the time?
>
>   — more useful subjects – e.g. electronics
>   — more time for important subjects
>
> Uniform – not practical and unattractive
>
>   — pupils not consulted
>   — rules for the sake of rules
>   — we need to learn to make our own decisions about clothes

3 Take the subject you started working on in Exercise 2 and develop your reasons in the same way.

Organizing your argument

When you have developed your reasons fully, you then have to arrange them into an ordered way, so that a person who reads your argument will follow what you are trying to say. Try to find one or more main lines running through your argument, to which the other points can be linked. In the example on the previous page there seem to be two:

Time   Making our own decisions

The other reasons and ideas can be arranged under these two main headings:

Time
Pointless subjects – R.E. and geography
                   – waste time when they won't be useful later
                   – have to do homework on them
                   – time better spent on subjects that really need it
                     (e.g. maths)
Morning assembly – not religious
                 – never enough time for discussions - assembly
                   time could be spent on that

Making our own decisions
Uniform – forced to wear clothes that are unfashionable and
          unsuitable
        – leads to a lot of silly rules (e.g. shoes)
        – we ought to be learning to make our own decisions
Games   – forced to play games we don't like (hockey)
        – many of us like games but aren't consulted (e.g. what
          about badminton, yoga)
        – never discuss reasons behind these and other rules

4 Make a plan based on the notes you have made so far. Then use it to help you write up your argument in full.

Looking at both sides

You often hear people repeat the old saying: 'There are two sides to every argument'. If we take the argument above, about school, it is not difficult to think of opposing arguments:

FOR

Pointless subjects – R.E. and
geography waste time when
they won't be useful later

have to do homework on them
could use time for maths

AGAINST

not pointless for everybody
some people want them for
careers

everyone has different needs
school can't please everyone -
impossible to have completely
individual system

5 Look at the plan you made for Exercise 4. Divide a page into two columns FOR and AGAINST. Write all your original ideas in the FOR column. Then fill in the AGAINST column with the opposing arguments.

Types of argument essay

The first part of this unit (pages 194–196) examined one type of argument essay: in which you take one side of the argument and develop it as strongly as you can. If we bring in the arguments on the opposing side, then there are two other types of essay:

The balanced argument

The argument that deals with the opposition

6 For each of the following examination questions, decide which type of essay you would write, and make brief notes on how you would go about it.

a) What are your reactions to the following remarks made by a teenager? 'It's all very well for grown-ups to criticize young people, but they have made a mess of their own lives. They have set a bad example with their wars, unemployment, heavy drinking and broken marriages. Why don't they listen to us for a change?' *Welsh GCE 1983*

b) These brief statements have all been used in instant judgment of the increasing electronic gadgets we can buy in the shops: watches, TV games, calculators, mini-computers, etc.

'They're more efficient' – 'They'll turn us into robots' – 'They make life easier' – 'They destroy self-reliance' – 'They're more accurate' – 'There's no craftsmanship in them' – 'They'll revolutionize the world' – 'They are only a passing novelty' – 'They are fun' – 'They're boring and monotonous' – 'They educate you' – 'They stop you thinking for yourself'

Write an essay in which you attempt a **fair** assessment of the benefits and/or the disadvantages of 'the electronic revolution in the home'. When possible, refer to your own experience of these devices.

NWREB 1983

c) Explain as clearly as you are able, why you do or do not believe in **one** of the following: (i) Life after death
(ii) Ghosts
(iii) Fortune telling. *EAEB 1983*

7 Choose one of the titles above. Make a full plan and then write the essay.

This question is taken from *JMB Joint 16+ 1978*.

8   What sort of wedding?

Read the following article carefully and then write about what you think is important in a wedding. You may agree or disagree with the views expressed below, but you must include some ideas of your own. The photograph (of an Indian wedding procession) may help you think of other points.

There seems to be an increasing feeling against the formality of a traditional wedding – a desire to depart from the set pattern, whether the ceremony is in a church or a register office. Many young people think that whether you believe in God or not is beside the point. They feel a wedding can be a great occasion and memorable without all that absurd dressing up and extravagant festivities. One girl recently walked up the aisle to 'The Entrance of the Queen of Sheba' and down it with her husband to Stevie Wonder singing 'You Are the Sunshine of My Life'.

My own wedding was a very private occasion. We did not invite our families or our friends. Since we needed two witnesses, my husband asked a colleague from work even though he didn't know him very well. I asked the man who introduced us. He came on his motor-bike. We drove to the ceremony in my old Land-Rover sporting L-plates. I wore a dark green tunic-style trouser suit, which was not new, but which I felt good in. I had a lace stole, which I'd crocheted myself, around my shoulders. The men wore casual clothes. We had no flowers. I do not like to see flowers pushed uncomfortably into a button-hole or twisted into bouquets. My husband sent me red roses but they were at home in a vase. We had no ring, no cake and no photographs.

The wedding ceremony lasted ten minutes. Afterwards my husband and I went to a local hotel for a meal. The man who introduced us followed on his motor bike.

Adapted from *Observer* article 21 November 1976

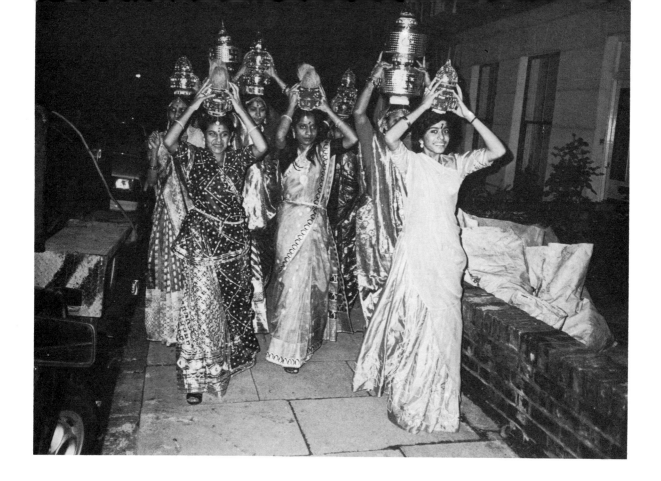

Links

Examples of writing in the argument mode will be found in Part A especially:

Looking ahead (109)

Nuclear weapons (93).

There is substantial material for arguments in the datafile pages and in many cases there are specific writing assignments which ask for this mode of writing.

Summary

1 Arguments are distinguished from opinions, prejudices and squabbles by the fact that they are supported by reasoning and evidence.

2 When you are presenting an argument you should begin by developing your line of reasoning in as much depth as possible.

3 You should then decide on the best pattern for your argument before beginning to write.

4 As well as a one-sided argument, it is also possible to present opposing views in your writing.

5 This can be done in order to disprove them and to strengthen your own case.

6 It is also possible to present a balanced argument. In this both sides are presented evenly and then a conclusion is drawn.

Letters

Letters are a special form of communication between people and they have their own rules. If these rules are not followed, then communication becomes difficult or even impossible.

COMPUTER COMPLAINT

Helen recently bought a home computer by mail order, from a company that manufactures them and sells direct. The machine went wrong very soon after she had bought it. She wrote to the company to complain. This is what happened to her letter.

1 It arrived at the company's offices.

2 Eventually it reached the right department.

3 At last it reached the right person.

1 At each stage in its journey, Helen's letter failed to communicate properly with the person who was reading it. For each of the three sets of pictures work out what was missing from her letter, or wrong with the way it was written.

Mistakes in layout and content

The things that Helen did wrong fall into two main categories:

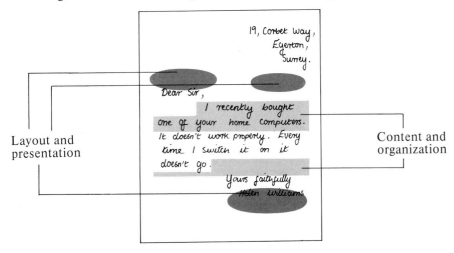

Layout and presentation

Content and organization

Layout and presentation

A letter to someone whom you do not know should be set out like this:

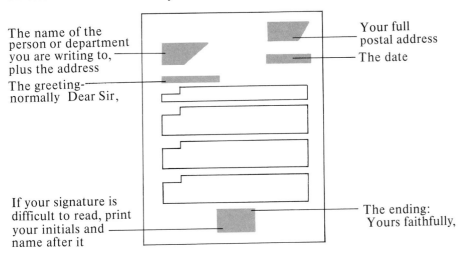

The name of the person or department you are writing to, plus the address

The greeting— normally Dear Sir,

If your signature is difficult to read, print your initials and name after it

Your full postal address

The date

The ending: Yours faithfully,

2 Why do you think you need to put:
  a) your own address
  b) the date
  c) the name of the person or department you are writing to?

Less formal letters

If you are writing to someone whom you have met, spoken to on the phone, or written to before, you may prefer to use:

Dear Mr/Mrs/Miss/Ms_____
and
Yours sincerely,

In this case you can sign either using initials plus surname, or first name plus surname.

Content and organization

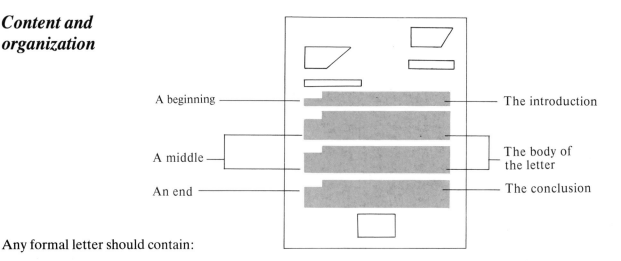

A beginning — The introduction

A middle — The body of the letter

An end — The conclusion

Any formal letter should contain:

The introduction

The person who receives your letter is probably busy. She or he likes to be able to plan the day's work. It is very helpful to be able to look quickly through the day's letters and sort them into groups. Then problems can be dealt with one at a time in a systematic way. You can make this possible by using the first paragraph of your letter to indicate what the letter will be about:

> I wish to complain about a computer bought from you, which has proved to be faulty.

The reader knows at once that this is a complaint about a faulty computer and not an enquiry about software or some other problem.

The body of the letter

The main information, ideas, and other material should be divided into paragraphs. These should be as concise and clear as you can make them:

Details about the machine

> I bought the machine, a 48K model 280, serial number 4357291C by mail order. Your invoice number was 7519/F/3C, dated 11th July 1984.
>   Following the instructions in the manual I plugged the computer into the mains. I connected it to our portable colour TV set. Although I followed the Manual carefully, I was unable to get any picture at all on the TV.

Description of what went wrong

The conclusion

Formal letters are nearly always written to achieve some purpose – to get things done. It is useful to finish the letter with a short paragraph telling (or reminding) the reader briefly what the letter has been about:

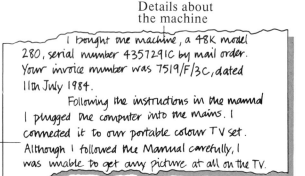

> This fault has occurred well within the 12-month guarantee period. I should be grateful, therefore, if you would arrange to have the machine repaired or replaced.

3 The following extract is from a letter to a newspaper:

'Is it not high time that something was done to control the overindulged and pampered louts, both male and female who roam the streets of our towns making the air hideous with their so-called music blaring from transistor radios, daubing the walls with their moronic slogans and vandalizing street lights and telephone boxes?

Since they have, apparently, no experience of discipline either at home or at school, and no sense of purpose in their lives, the law must have a hand and punish them . . .'.

Write a letter to the Editor of the newpaper in reply, expressing your reactions.

London 1984

4 A proposal to build a hypermarket on the outskirts of a local town has caused much bad feeling between its supporters and its opponents. In a letter to the Editor of your local newspaper, state your own views on the proposal and attempt to reduce the bad feeling.   *AEB 1981*

5 You have been on a week's work experience from your school. Write a letter of thanks to the person whose job it was to supervise you at your place of work, who taught you a lot, and who was friendly and helpful even when you made a serious mistake. Your letter should bring out these points.

NREB 1983

Summary

1 There are certain rules about writing letters, which help to ensure that they communicate effectively. If these rules are ignored, communication breaks down.
2 Formal letters should be set out in a certain style to assist their readers.
3 The content of formal letters is also important. If it is organized in the proper way, communication will be made much easier.
4 The letter should begin with an introductory paragraph explaining the general subject matter of the letter.
5 The main body of the letter then sets out its subject matter clearly and concisely.
6 The last paragraph should be a conclusion summarizing the main purpose of the letter.

Reports

> His written work is scrappy and disorganised
> Oral work is promising, however. — French — GRC

> I then followed the suspect along the Embankment and into Embankment Gardens. He stopped for a while and then sat on a bench near the entrance. He stayed there until 21.06 hours. At this point a man wearing

> The Photographic society has had another good year. The highlight of the winter season was the Christmas Exhibition. This attracted a very high standard of entries.

> 50 cc of liquid A was poured into a beaker. 10 cc of liquid B was then added. The liquid turned a cloudy white. It was tested for

1 These extracts are all examples of **reports**.
   a) Can you see what they have in common?
   b) Are they like any of the four modes described earlier in this chapter: description, narrative, exposition, argument? If so, how?

Telling the story   A report is partly narrative. It tells the story of something that happened in the past. Therefore, when you write a report you normally:
   a) Use the past tense
   b) Describe the events in the order in which they happened.

2

> I was walking Benjie, my spaniel, along the cliff path – you know, my usual when I suddenly sort of slipped. I don't know how it happened. One minute I was walking along enjoying the view and the sun and the next I was lying at the bottom with this terrible pain in my leg. I tried to get up but I couldn't. Of course I shouted and shouted for help, but nobody came. I think I must have passed out, because

> **CLIFF FALL SURVIVOR**
> A woman who fell down a 50-foot cliff in Dorset and lay at the bottom for 10 hours was winched to safety yesterday. Mrs Coral Hatton, aged 52, who suffered a broken leg, was spotted by a late evening jogger. Portland Coastguard said that Mrs Hatton, of St George's Road, Portland, had been walking her dog when she somehow slipped and fell down the cliff. Her dog stayed with her. A hospital spokesman said today that her condition was quite comfortable.

   a) Write down the main events of the story in the order in which they happened and number them.
   b) In what order does the first report present the events? Write the numbers only in that order. Now do the same for the second report.
   c) Which of the two reports is easier to follow?
   d) Why do you think the second report presents events in the order it does?

Explaining the facts

A report is partly exposition. The writer has to set out and explain a number of facts to the reader. When you write, you have to decide:
a) Which facts are important
b) How to arrange the information.

3 You are the secretary of the school Historical Society. The Society recently went on a trip to Dunstanburgh Castle. These are some of the notes you made:

1. weather fine but a bit cold
2. coach along A1 to Alnwick
3. Jim Easton sick - had to stop
4. country lanes to Craster
5. Craster - fishing village, famous for kippers
6. coach parked near souvenir shop and toilets
7. bought postcard and chewing gum
8. walked along coast for about a mile
9. Helen Smithson lost her anorak
10. saw a seal down on the beach
11. reached castle - 50p to go in
12. castle nearly all in ruins, built by Simon de Montfort in 1313
13. keep was originally meant as gatehouse - two huge towers
14. built right on edge of cliffs
15. covers ten acres

You are going to write a short report for the school magazine. You have space for only about half the information in your notes.
a) Which points would you include and why?
b) Which points would you exclude and why?
c) In what order would you put the points you included?

Personal or impersonal?

Like other writing of this kind, a report can be presented personally or impersonally, subjectively or objectively. (These terms are explained on page 192.)

4 Study the four extracts at the top of the facing page. For each one state whether it is personal or impersonal, objective or subjective, and why.

5 a) Write a report on one of the following:
  (i) A School Outing
  (ii) A School Community Service Project
  (iii) The Activities of a School Society.   *SEREB 1981*
b) You are the supervisor in a supermarket. You have reason to suspect a customer of shoplifting and demanded a search. This was at first refused, but the customer has given way. The search has revealed the customer to be innocent. However a complaint has been made against you for rudeness and officiousness. Write a *factual and unemotional* report on the incident for the manager.   *LREB 1983*

Reporting speech

Reports do not usually contain direct speech, although there are some exceptions to this, particularly newspaper reports. Speech is usually

either **a)** presented as reported or indirect speech
or **b)** summarized.

Direct The Headmaster said, 'It has been a very successful year on the sports field. In particular the first eleven has won all but two of its fixtures.'

Indirect The Headmaster said that it had been a very successful year on the sports field. In particular the first eleven had won all but two of its fixtures.

The rules for writing indirect speech are given on page 213.

Summary The Headmaster praised the sporting achievements of the school.

When you are writing a report you have to decide how important the details of a piece of speech are. Then you can make up your mind whether to report it in full or summarize it. Sometimes you may wish to combine the two.

6 Read the following information and then write a report according to the instructions at the end of it.

There has been a raid on Waterman's the Jeweller's shop in Mansfield Road, Stowmarket. As the first policeman to arrive on the scene, after it was all over, you take the following statements from three witnesses:

Mr Sid Collins (the shop manager)

'It must have been about eleven o'clock, because I remember glancing at the clock as I was serving the previous customer and it was then ten to eleven. I suddenly heard this enormous crash. It sounded as if the room was falling down around us, but we all automatically looked towards the window. The funny thing was that the first thought that crossed my mind was that a car had actually crashed into the window. The burglar alarm didn't go off, because it is switched off during the day. If it wasn't, it would go off every time someone opened the door. I couldn't see much straight away because the hardboard doors at the back of the display window were shut. So, when I had collected my wits, I ran to the door. There is a button at the back of the counter that we can press to make the alarm go in the daytime, but in the heat of the moment I forgot to press it. Anyway, when I got to the door, there was a man standing in the little passageway that leads from the door to the street with the windows either side of it. As soon as he saw me, he raised a great big stick above his head. It was a pick-axe handle. Then he shouted, "Get back in. Get back in." I didn't have anything to defend myself with and I wasn't going to argue with a pick-axe handle, so I just shouted "You get out" and ran back into the shop. I closed the door and there were two or three customers and my assistant standing still near the counter and staring at me. Then I heard the alarm bell go. My assistant had pressed it. I didn't see what the man looked like because he had a stocking pulled over his face. Six of the display trays with the most expensive jewellery have gone. They didn't touch any of the cheaper stuff.'

Mrs Rita Cross

'I was looking in the window of the clothes shop next door when a loud screech of brakes made me look round, and there was this black van just skidding to a halt – one of those where the side doors slide back. A huge man carrying a stick and something heavy in a little sack jumped out and went towards Waterman's. He swung this little sack round in a circle two or three times to get a good speed up, and then let it go straight at the middle of Waterman's window. There was a terrific crash. Then suddenly there were two more men there and they had an enormous sack each. They started picking great trays of things out of the window and putting them into their sacks. The man with the stick bashed a few big lumps out of the window to help the other two and then went and stood in the shop entrance. He had a stocking on his face. The other two didn't. They were shorter than the other man. One was young and thin. The other one was getting on a bit, about in his fifties I would say because his hair was grey. Then they dashed back and got in the back of the van while the one with the stick got in the side and the van roared off. I just stood there. I couldn't move. I didn't try to shout out. It was ever so quick and everywhere seemed so quiet. Then the alarm bell started ringing. No, I didn't take the number of the van.'

Mr Carl Steadman

I was sitting in the car opposite the clothing shop waiting for my wife to do a bit of shopping. I was the next vehicle behind where the van stopped, but I was doing something with the radio and the first thing I heard was the crash. Someone screamed. There were three men all at Waterman's window, pulling glass out and stuffing things from the window into sacks. They must all have been youngsters by the speed they did the job and then scampered back to the van. They were not very tall, but the man with the stick and stocking, he was huge and didn't seem to hurry as much as the others. Once he had got in, they were off. The van was a black Transit, but I didn't think of taking the number. I looked as it went off, though, and I think it was a 'T' registration and I'm pretty sure the letters HE were in front of the numbers.'

WHAT YOU HAVE TO DO:

From these three accounts, you have the information about what occurred. Before detectives and forensic scientists start work, you have to present the officer in charge of this case with a report which simply describes the facts of what happened. You do this by combining the three accounts you have into a report. The witnesses say many things that the officer will not want to know, but they do give at various points the important facts and it is these you must concentrate upon.

Write the report in about 150–200 words.

EMREB 1983

Links

The *Datafiles* on pages 21, 37, 75 and 99, provide practice in this type of writing.

Summary

1 Reports are partly narrative.
2 Events are normally narrated in chronological order, using the past tense, although there are exceptions to this.
3 Reports are partly exposition.
4 It is important to select and present facts intelligently.
5 Reports may be personal or impersonal, subjective or objective.
6 Reports normally present speech in a summarized or indirect form.

4. *The technicalities*

Punctuation

The purpose of all punctuation is to help the reader to understand more easily what is being read.

The full stop
main uses

1 To mark the end of a sentence
2 Sometimes, but not always, to show that a word has been abbreviated.

The rule here is that two groups of abbreviations do not need full stops:

a) Those that are made up entirely of capital letters: *NATO*   *USA*
b) Those which end with the last letter of the word being abbreviated:
   Mr   *Dr*

All other abbreviations need full stops: *I.o.W.*   *Thur.*   *etc.*

Exclamation mark
main uses

1 To show that something is entertaining or amusing
2 To mark shouts, cries and exclamations
   Then I turned round and fell right into the middle of the canal!
   'Look out!' shouted the policeman.

The exclamation mark should be used sparingly.

Question mark

The main use of the question mark is to show questions in normal prose writing and in direct speech. It is not normally used in reported speech:

'Where are you going?' she asked.
She asked him where he was going.

Capital letters
main uses

1 The beginning of a sentence
2 Personal names
3 Names of countries, towns, and other geographical names
4 People's titles: *Mr   Sir*
5 Main words in book titles: *The Return of the Native*
6 Days of the week and months of the year
7 Names of organizations, societies, movements etc.: *Ecology Party*
8 Periods of history and events in history: *Crimean War*
9 Names of ships, cars etc.: *Ford Sierra*
10 Abbreviations (see above).

Comma

main uses

Like all punctuation marks, the comma is used to aid the reader's eye as it passes over the text. It is not easy to use well, because its use is partly a matter of style. There are a number of rules, however.

1 Commas separate parts of a sentence to avoid confusion.
   Each of the following lacks a comma, and as a result is confusing to the reader:
   > POLICE USE DOGS AND HORSES AS MISSILES
   > RAIN DOWN ON THEM
   > *I fell to the ground and when I got up my nose was still hurting.*

2 Commas mark off words in parentheses and can act like brackets in a sentence:
   > *Uncle George, the well-known radio personality, has finally retired.*

3 Commas separate the items in a list:
   > *He is the most stupid, idle, incompetent, unentertaining circus performer I have ever seen.*

4 Commas mark off the spoken words in direct speech: (See page 212.)

5 Commas are used between the clauses in a sentence.
   (Clauses are explained on pages 216 and 217).
   > *That morning, when I got up, the mountain was hidden from view, which was a disappointment, as I had set my heart on climbing it.*

Beyond these basic rules, using commas well is a matter of practice, and of observing what experienced writers do.

exceptions

a) Sometimes when the meaning of a sentence is clear without a comma, modern writers leave it out. The previous example could be written:
    > *That morning when I got up, the mountain was hidden from view, which was a disappointment as I had set my heart on climbing it.*

b) There is one situation when using commas or missing them out actually affects the meaning of the sentence. Compare these two versions of the same sentence:
    (i) *Yesterday three students* whom I sponsored *successfully climbed Snowdon.*
    (ii) *Yesterday three students,* whom I sponsored, *successfully climbed Snowdon.*

In (i) the words 'whom I sponsored' mark off the students from all the other students who may have climbed Snowdon that day. They **define** the students I am talking about. Sentence (ii) is different: yesterday only three students climbed Snowdon. The words enclosed by commas simply provide some additional information about them. The fact that I sponsored them doesn't define or mark them off.

Colon

main uses

1 To introduce a list:
He decided to take a small repair kit: pliers, screwdriver, adhesive tape, thin wire, and a tube of superglue.

2 To introduce a lengthy piece of direct speech:
When they had calmed down she said: 'I can understand why you are angry. I would be angry myself. But there is nothing anyone can do about it, so you might as well face up to the facts.'

3 To introduce an idea for which the first part of the sentence has prepared the reader:
He was a boring little man with only one real belief: that punctuality is the greatest virtue.

Semi-colon

main uses

1 To separate items in a list, when the items are too long to be separated by commas:
She has a wide range of interests: going for long and energetic walks alone in the mountains; performing unusually intricate and little-known national dances in traditional costume in the small hours of the morning; inventing and then preparing exotic and highly-spiced vegetarian dishes.

2 To stand between parts of a sentence which could stand as separate sentences, but which are closely linked in meaning:
She was a talented musician and could play the sitar and the tabla; her brother was equally talented as a sportsman and played hockey for the county.
Here a full stop would separate the two parts too much. A comma would be wrong.

Apostrophe

main uses

1 To show where one or more letters have been missed out:

we've (= we have) *he'll* (= he will)
who's (= who is) *they'll* (= they will)
you'd've (= you would have) *I'm* (= I am)
Mike's going (= Mike is going) *she's* (= she is)

It is important to note that:
whose means 'belonging to whom' *its* means 'belonging to it'
who's means 'who is' *it's* means 'it is'

2 To show possession. The way to get this right is to ask yourself: *'To whom does it belong?'* When you have answered that question then add either **'** or **'s** according to this rule:

a) We add **'s** to words that do not end in s.
   Mike's bike (= the bike belonging to Mike).

b) If a word already ends in **s** we just add **'**.
   the girls' mother (= the mother belonging to the girls).

3 The possession rule is also used to cover phrases like:
a month's holiday *five minutes' delay*
This is because the meaning is similar. 'A month's holiday' means the same as a holiday *of* a month.

wrong uses

The apostrophe is often used wrongly by sign-writers, advertisers, newspapers, books and many people who should know better. Therefore you should ignore how other people use it and follow the rules.

Writing speech

Speech can be written down in three different ways: **script**, **direct speech**, **reported speech**.

Script

Script is the method normally used for writing plays and transcribing conversations. It is not normally used when writing a prose narrative. The main features of script are shown in this example:

Scene 2   The Body and Soul Disco.
 (Loud disco music. **Miss M** *and* **Disco Dancers** *enter.* **John** *is at the door. A* **Doorman** *approaches him.)*[3]
JOHN:[1]   [2]Er, excuse me. This is the Body and Soul Disco, isn't it?
DOORMAN: [2]Are you Mr Faust? We've been expecting you. Go straight in.
                          (Music quietens as **John** *enters the Disco.)*[3]

[1]   The speaker's name is in capitals. The name of any character in stage directions should stand out. The speaker's name is followed by a colon.
[2]   The words spoken begin at the same point on the line.
[3]   Any instructions for the actors or the stagecrew are put in brackets and underlined (or, in a book, printed in *italics*).

Direct speech

In direct speech the actual words spoken are still used, but they are included in a narrative, or story. This means that the words 'she said', 'he replied' etc., have to be used to make clear what is going on:

As Miss M and the Disco Dancers went into the disco a blast of sound hit them. As John approached the door he saw a Doorman, who came up to him.
    'Er, excuse me,' John asked, 'this is the Body and Soul Disco, isn't it?'
    'Are you Mr Faust?' asked the doorman. 'We've been expecting you. Go straight in.'

1   The spoken words are contained within double "_____" or single '_____' inverted commas.
2   Each new piece of speech begins with a capital letter.
3   At the end of each piece of speech, before the inverted commas, there must be one of these punctuation marks , . ! ?
4   If you put the *he said* words before the speech, put a comma before the inverted commas:
    He said, '_____.'

5   If you put the *he said* words in the middle of a piece of speech, follow them with a comma or a full stop:

'_____,' he said, '_____.'

or

'_____,' he said. '_____.'

6   If you follow the *he said* words with a full stop the next piece of speech must begin with a capital letter:

'Are you Mr Faust?' asked the doorman. 'We've been expecting you.'

7   Otherwise a capital letter is not needed:

'Er, excuse me,' John asked, 'this is the Body and Soul Disco, isn't it?'

8   Every time there is a new speaker, start a new line and begin writing about 1cm in from the margin.

Reported speech

As its name suggests, reported, or indirect, speech is used in reports and in certain kinds of narrative. In some reports it is only necessary to give a summary of what has been said. At other times a full and detailed record is needed. This is when reported speech is used. (This is explained in more detail on page 206.)

Reported speech gives as much information as direct speech, but it does it in a different way.

Direct speech: *'I am very pleased to be here now,' she said.*

Reported speech: *She said that she was very pleased to be there then.*

As the example shows, reported speech requires a number of changes from direct speech.

1 **Pronouns**	I	becomes	he/she	etc.
2 **Verb tense**	is will have walked		was would had had walked	
3 **Time/place words**	now here		then there	
4 **Other changes**	Common phrases of greeting, apology etc. are summarized. *'Good morning,' she said. 'I'm sorry I'm late.'* becomes *She greeted them and apologized for being late.*			

Sentence grammar

There are three types of sentence:

Statement: *He wants stew.*
Question: *Where is he?*
Command: *Come here!*

Parts of a sentence

Sentences normally have a **subject** and a **verb**.

SUBJECT	VERB	REST OF SENTENCE
He	wants	stew
he	is	Where

In a command the subject is 'you'. It is often left out:

(you)	Go	home

Verbs

The verb in a sentence must be complete (the technical term is finite). If it is not, then the sentence is not complete.

Correct: *My two friends Tab and Prem were walking across the field.*
My bedroom has just been painted white all over.

Incorrect: *Walking across the field, my two friends Tab and Prem.*
My bedroom painted white all over.

Singluar and plural

The subject of a sentence can be *singular* (one) or *plural* (more than one). Some verbs change according to whether the subject is singular or plural:
Tab was walking across the field.
Tab and Prem were walking across the field.

Single words

It is useful to be able to classify words according to the ways in which they are used. The commonest way of doing this is to divide them into the following parts of speech:

PART OF SPEECH	EXAMPLE			
Nouns	assistant	heap	island	peace
Adjectives	purple	big	lengthy	beautiful
Verbs	is	have	hit	run	become
Adverbs	very	slowly	gradually	
Pronouns	it	he	you	them
Conjunctions	and	but	because	although
Prepositions	under	beside	up	into

These terms describe the jobs that different types of words do in a sentence. Some of them can also be used to describe the job done in a sentence by a group of words working together.

Nouns   Nouns are words used to name **people**:   woman   doctor
                                        places: town   valley
                                        things: trousers   record
                                        ideas: hope   happiness

*At the **time** I was living in **Australia**. It was towards the **end** of the **war**,*
*and I was almost fifteen – an uncomfortable **mixture** of **child** and **woman**,*
Australian and English.

Pronouns   **Pronouns** stand in the place of nouns. They are often used to avoid repetition.

*Peter Britton is married to Carla Thomas. When **he** first met **her she** was*
*working in London and **he** was a long distance lorry driver.*

Adjectives   **Adjectives** are words that work with nouns. They help to make the meaning
of a noun more precise. We say that adjectives **qualify** nouns.

*Jack planned his **new** face. He made **one** cheek and **one** eye-socket **white**,*
*then he rubbed red over the **other** half of his face and slashed a **black** bar*
*of charcoal across from **right** ear to **left** jaw.*

(Notice that 'red' in the second line is not being used as an adjective here,
but as a noun: it could be replaced, for example, by 'paint'.)

Adjectives do not have to stand next to the noun they qualify. They can be
separated from it in the sentence:
*His tie is **red**.*
*He made the children very **unhappy**.*

Verbs   **Verbs** are words used to describe   **actions**:   run   hit
                                                          states: seem   appear
                                                           changes: become   grow

*Jack **planned** his new face. He **made** one cheek and one eye-socket white,*
*then he **rubbed** red over the other half of his face and **slashed** a black bar*
of charcoal across from right ear to left jaw.

*There are also **auxiliary verbs**.* These work with other verbs. The main ones
are: be   am   is   was   were   being   been   has   had
have   having   may   might   can   could   must   ought
will   shall   would   should   do   did

Adverbs   **Adverbs** work to make the meanings of verbs more precise. (They 'add' to
the meaning of a verb.) They also add to the meaning of adjectives and other
adverbs. We say that adverbs **modify** verbs, adjectives and adverbs. Adverbs
generally answer these questions:
      when?   where?   how?   how much?

*He ran **heavily** across the field. His legs felt **increasingly** tired and his*
*speed **gradually** decreased until he was not **even** walking, but stumbling*
***very slowly** in a kind of dream.*

Word groups

Phrases The job done in a sentence by nouns, adjectives, verbs, and adverbs can be done by a single word or by a group of words, a phrase.

Noun	single word	I bought a **hat**.
	phrase	I bought **a yachting cap**.
Adjective	single word	It was a **blue** cap.
	phrase	It was a cap **with a peak**.
Verb	single word	I **bought** a hat.
	phrase	I **have been buying** a hat.
Adverb	single word	I bought it **there**.
	phrase	I bought it **in that shop**.

Clauses The job done in a sentence by nouns, adjectives and adverbs can also be done by a clause. A clause is like a phrase, but it contains a finite verb. (See page 218.)

Noun	single word	My best hat is a **cap**.
	clause	**What I am wearing** is my best hat.
Adjective	single word	It is a **blue** cap.
	clause	It is a cap **that I like very much**.
Adverb	single word	I bought it **there**.
	clause	I bought it **where I always buy my hats**.

Types of sentence

Sentences can be of three types:
Simple
Compound
Complex

Simple sentences A **simple** sentence consists of one clause. It contains one finite verb.
a) *He is unhappy.*
b) *My cousin Peter is at the moment feeling very sorry for himself.*
Notice that although (**b**) is a much longer sentence than (**a**) it is still only a simple sentence because it contains the same basic parts:

SUBJECT	VERB	REST OF SENTENCE
He	is	unhappy
My cousin Peter	is . . . feeling	at the moment . . . very sorry for himself.

Compound sentences A compound sentence is made up of two (or more) clauses joined by *and* or *but*.

> *He is unhappy and I am furious.*

Here there are two of everything.

SUBJECT	VERB	REST OF SENTENCE
He	is	unhappy
I	am	furious

A compound sentence may be quite short, like the one above, or it may be very long:

One day last week my very close friend the leader of the Three Daggers Rock Group was driving his white Rolls Royce along the M4 on his way home and I was pushing my rusty Raleigh 3-speed roadster along the cycle track after a hard day's work at the Tech.

This example still has only two subjects:

a) *my very close friend the leader of the Three Daggers Rock Group*
b) *I*

It has only two verbs:

a) *was driving*
b) *was pushing*

The two clauses are joined by *and*.

Complex sentences A complex sentence is made up of two or more clauses. One of the clauses is the most important (the **main** clause) and the others are less important (the subordinate clauses). Subordinate clauses are clauses that do the jobs of nouns, adjectives and adverbs. In the example that follows, the main clause is in **bold** type.

*When I got back to the classroom **I met Margaret**, who had been looking for me since break.*

Usually the main clause of a sentence makes sense on its own:

. . . I met Margaret . . .

The subordinate clauses do not make complete sense on their own:

When I got back to the classroom . . .
. . . who had been looking for me since break . . .

Common errors

Punctuation

Apostrophe

There are two very common errors involving the use of the apostrophe:

1   Adding **'s** to make a plural. This is always wrong. **'s** can only mean either 'belonging to' (as in 'John's book') or 'is' (as in 'John's late').

2   **its/it's**
its = of it
it's = it is
(See page 211.)

Linking sentences with commas

I walked round the corner, I was just in time to see him go.
This must be:

(a)   I walked round the corner. I was just in time to see him go.
or (b)   I walked round the corner; I was just in time to see him go.
or (c)   I walked round the corner and I was just in time to see him go.

The use of the semi-colon is explained on page 210.

The dash

It is a common feature of sloppy or hurried writing that the dash is used frequently and thoughtlessly:

Peter dialled Mary's number – she wasn't in again – so he decided to go round.

It is nearly always better to do without it:

Peter dialled Mary's number, but she wasn't in again, so he decided to go round.

Sentence construction

Subject/verb agreement

In a long sentence it is easy to forget the number of the subject and so fail to write the correct form of the verb:

Wayne and Carole, who used to live near George, was going to a disco.

If you ignore the adjective clause and just read the main clause, you can see that this is wrong:

SUBJECT	VERB	REST OF CLAUSE
Wayne and Carol (= they)	was going	to a disco

If in doubt ask yourself: 'What is the subject of this clause/sentence? Is it singular or plural? Is the verb correct?'

Sentence without a finite verb

Normally a sentence should contain a finite verb. The following forms of the verb are not finite:

infinite: to write
present participle: writing
past participle: written

So these sentences are not complete:

Italic pens to write important letters
Writing out your name in full
Anything not written in blue or black ink

Hanging participle   the **-ing** form of the verb can work as a noun or as an adjective:

Walking is fun. (noun)
He is a walking example of the effects of laziness. (adjective)

Sometimes the -ing form can work as part of an adjective phrase:

Walking along the promenade I caught sight of the Punch-and-Judy man.

Here 'walking' refers to 'I' and is being used correctly. (You can check this, by asking yourself, 'Who was walking?' The answer to this question must appear in the sentence.) It is in this third use that mistakes can happen, especially if the -ing verb and the noun/pronoun it refers to become separated in your mind:

Walking along the promenade the sea seemed very blue and calm.

'Who was walking?' 'The sea.' The sentence clearly has to be rewritten:

As I walked along the promenade, the sea seemed very blue and calm.

No main clause   Sometimes when you are writing a complex sentence, especially one with a number of subordinate clauses, it is possible to forget that you haven't put in a main clause:

When the Carnival day finally arrived, Binny, who had been looking forward to wearing the dress that Maria had made specially for her.

If you look carefully at this sentence you can see that there are four subjects and three verbs:

SUBJECT	VERB	REST OF CLAUSE
a) the Carnival day	arrived	When . . . finally . . .
b) who	had been looking forward	to wearing the dress
c) Maria	had made	that . . . specially for her
d) Binny	?	

(a), **(b)**, and **(c)** are all subordinate clauses. **(a)** is an adverb and **(b)** and **(c)** are adjectives. **(b)** tells us about Binny and **(c)** tells us about the dress. We are left with 'Binny' as a subject followed by no verb. 'Binny . . . what?' we want to know.

who/whom/ whose/who's	These words can all be used to introduce an adjective clause. Each has a different purpose. **who** acts as the subject of the clause: *That woman who is standing over there by the piano is a famous athlete.* **whom** acts as the object of the clause: *That woman whom you have just criticized is a famous athlete.* **whose** means 'belonging to whom': *That woman whose drink you have just spilt is a famous athlete.* **who's** means 'who is': *That woman who's talking to Adam is a famous athlete.*
Split infinitive	The infinitive is the **to** _____ form of the verb. If possible you should avoid putting anything between the 'to' and the verb: *He failed to completely polish the car.* is clumsy and should be rewritten *He failed to polish the car completely.* It is, however, important to make sure that you do not alter the meaning: *He completely failed to polish the car.* means something else.
one/you/I	When you are writing about your own thoughts and experience, especially in lengthy sentences, it is easy to swap pronouns part-way through: *When one has had some experience of underwater swimming, you can get down quite deep without breathing apparatus and I have often done this.* This needs rewriting as, for example, *When one has had some experience of underwater swimming, it is possible to get down quite deep without breathing apparatus. I have often done this.*

anyone/someone/no one These three are all singular, and therefore need the singular form of the verb. Also they cannot be followed later in the sentence by the pronouns **they** or **their**:

Anyone who wants to go to Italy this summer must make sure that they are on the list I have put up on the notice board.

'. . . they are' must become 'he is' or 'she is' or – to be fair and logical – 'he or she is'. This is clumsy. It is better to rephrase the start of the sentence:

All those who want to go to Italy this summer must make sure that they are on the list . . .

Collective nouns Collective nouns are singular nouns that refer to groups of people: team, government, school etc. Since they are singular they should logically be followed by a singular verb. This practice is dying out and sometimes the 'correct' form seems strange:

As the team came out onto the field it was wearing its normal strip of red shirts and white shorts.

Nowadays we would expect 'they were wearing their . . .'
The solution here is to ask yourself whether the sentence is looking at the group of people as one unit or as a set of individuals. If they are a unit, then the noun is best treated as a singular:

The government has decided.

If they are being thought of as individuals, then the collective noun is best treated as a plural:

The first team are now going on their holidays.

Whichever you do, you should be consistent throughout. You must not start in the singular and end in the plural, or vice versa.

less/fewer Nouns can be either countable or uncountable. Countable nouns can have a plural, usually formed by adding s at the end:

tree/trees   girl/girls etc.

You should not use **less** with countable nouns. You should use **fewer**:

There are fewer butterflies in the countryside nowadays.

Uncountable nouns do not have a plural (because they refer to things that cannot be counted, like 'milk' or 'happiness'). With them you should use less:

There is less milk in my glass than there is in yours.

Mistakes with words

have/ve The word **have** is shortened in speech to **'ve**. When we say it quickly, it sounds like 'of'. This is no reason for writing it down as 'of'. As a reminder, here are the main occasions when the mistake can be made:

SHORT FORM	LONG FORM
would've	would have
should've	should have
might've	might have
could've	could have

lie/lay The verb 'to lay' must be followed by an object: to lay something. Its other forms are: he laid, they have laid:
Our hens all lay good eggs and they laid a lot yesterday.

The verb 'to lie' is never followed by an object: you can not 'lie something'. Its other forms are: he lay, they have lain.
He is lying on the grass where he lay yesterday. He has lain there for a week. I think he's dead.

Past tense forms In the past tense   **lay** becomes **laid**
        say becomes **said**
        pay becomes **paid**
In any verb that ends in a consonant+y the **y** changes to **i** when **-ed** is added.

        fry becomes **fried**
        try becomes **tried**

wrote/written Some 'strong' verbs have both a past tense form and a past participle. It is important to use the correct form. An example of this is the verb *to write*.
Yesterday I wrote a letter to Uncle George. I have written to him every Christmas since I was seven.

PRESENT TENSE	PAST TENSE	PAST PARTICIPLE
I write	I wrote	I have written
I drink	I drank	I have drunk
I speak	I spoke	I have spoken
I give	I gave	I have given

sat/sitting
stood/standing The correct forms are:
I was sitting *looking at my mother who was* standing *by the window.* It is not correct to use *sat* and *stood* in this sentence.

Index of technical terms

Acknowledgements

Cover illustration: *Pluie*, by Auguste Herbin. Private Collection, Switzerland.

The Publishers would like to thank the following for permission to use photographic material:

Julian Andrews: p.145. **Arable and Bulb Chemicals**: p.67. **Aspect**: p.60. **Basingstoke Gazette**: p.148. **Nick Birch**: p.100 top right. **Jane Bown** (*Observer*): p.157 top. **Braun**: p.53. **British Telecom**: p.129 top left. **CoSIRA**: p.125. **Format**: S. Gray p.180; J. Matthews p.22 top left; R. Page p.158; B. Prince p.180; V. Wilmer pp.14, 84 btm, 165. **Gamma**: p.100 btm right. **Keith Gibson**: pp. 129 top left, btm right, p.134 all. **Gollancz**: pp. 68, 69 all. **Richard and Sally Greenhill**: pp.47, 84 top right, 100 top left, 109, 150, 151, 189, 199. **John Haynes**: p.89. **Health Education Council**: p.136 top left. **Chris Honeywell**: p.128 btm left. **Geoff Howard**: p.157 btm. **IBM**: p.129 mid left. **Imperial Tobacco**: p.136 top right. **Douglas Jeffery**: p.49. **Rob Judges**: pp.164, top, btm, 151, 193 top, btm. **London Fire Brigade**: p.184. **Mansell Collection**: pp.56, 128 all except btm left. **Network**: Mike Abrahams p.183; Roger Hutchings p.155; Barry Lewis pp.22 top centre, top right, btm left, 65, 129 btm left; Judah Passow p.133 left; John Sturrock p.7 top left, 84 top left. **Natural History Photographic Agency**: p.133 right. **Ike Onuordi**: p.15. **Pixfeatures**: p.179. **Jill Posener**: p.22 btm right. **Rosie Potter**: pp.11 all, 18, 20 all, 21. **John Powell**: pp.26–7 all. **Jeffrey Tabberner**: pp.34, 182, 211. **Thomson Holidays**: p.192. **Thorn EMI**: p.52. *The Times*/**John le Carré**: p.143. **John Topham**: pp.61, 100 btm left. **Simon Warner**: pp.62–3, 72–3 all, 86, 146. **Widener Collection**: p.131.

Illustrations by: Rupert Besley; Simon Dorell; Penny Ives; Marie-Helen Jeeves; Jan Lewis; Maggie Ling; Ian Miller; Liz O'Sullivan; Nick Sharratt; Brian Walker; and Brian Wall.

The publishers would like to thank the following for permission to reprint copyright material:

John Ardagh: extracts from *The Book of France* and *Rural France*. Reprinted by permission of Century Publishing Co. Ltd. **W.H. Auden**: extract from 'Some Say That Love's a Little Boy' from *Collected Poems*. Reprinted by permission of Faber and Faber Ltd. **Lynne Reid Banks**: 'Trust' first published in *The Real Thing* by the Bodley Head. Reprinted by permission of Watson, Little Ltd. **Stan Barstow**: extract from 'One of the Virtues' from *The Desperadoes*. Reprinted by permission of Michael Joseph Ltd. **John Berger**: from *Boris*. First published in *Granta* 9 (1983). **Alan Bleasdale**: from *Love is a Many Splendoured Thing*. Reprinted by permission of Harvey Unna and Stephen Durbridge Ltd. **Ray Bradbury**: 'The Aqueduct' and 'The Leave-Taking' both from *The Stories of Ray Bradbury 2* (1981) (Granada Publishing Ltd.). **Brothers Grimm**: 'The Old Man and His Grandson' from *Brothers Grimm: Fairy Tales* (n.e. 1975). Reprinted by permission of Routledge and Kegan Paul Plc. **David Campton**: 'Night Watch' from *On Stage* (J. Garnet Miller Ltd.). **Sean Carey**: 'Gunfight at the Crown and Leek' from *New Society* 21.6.84. Reprinted with permission. **John le Carré**: excerpt from *Smiley's People* (1980). Reprinted by permission of Hodder and Stoughton Ltd. **Rachel Carson**: from *Silent Spring* (Hamish Hamilton Ltd., 1963). Reprinted by permission of Laurence Pollinger Ltd., on behalf of the Estate of Rachel Carson. **Charles Causley**: 'Ten Types of Hospital Visitor' from *Collected Poems* (Macmillan 1975).Reprinted by permission of David Higham Associates Ltd. **Roald Dahl**: from 'The Cane' from *The Wonderful Story of Henry Sugar*. Reprinted by permission of Jonathan Cape Ltd., for the author. **Dhumektu**: 'The Letter' from *Lambailey* (OUP, 1980). By permission of Dr. G.G. Joshi. **The East Midland Regional Examinations Board**. 'The Real West' from the East Midland Regional Examinations Board 1983. With permission. **Buchi Emecheta**: from *Head Above Water*. Reprinted by permission of the author. **James Fenton**: 'Nothing' from *Children in Exile*, Salamander Press 1983. Reprinted with permission. **A.N. Forde**: 'Sunday with a Difference'. Reprinted by permission of the author. **Robert Frost**: 'Tree at My Window' from *The Poetry of Robert Frost*, edited by Edward Connery Latham. Reprinted by permission of Jonathan Cape Ltd., on behalf of the Estate of Robert Frost. **William Golding**: from *Lord of the Flies*. Reprinted by permission of Faber and Faber Ltd. **V. Ramsamooj**

Gosine: from 'The Bird Catchers' from *Steel Nocturne*, (Longman Caribbean, Trinidad). Reprinted with permission of the Publisher. *The Guardian*: 'Strip Cartoon Romances' from *The Guardian*, Autumn 1979. Reprinted with permission. **Hertz**: 'Teaching a Girl About Hertz is Teaching Her to Say Yes'. Advertisement in *The Times* 12.10.72. **Ernest Hemingway**: from *The Old Man and the Sea*. Reprinted by permission of Jonathan Cape Ltd. on behalf of the Executors of the Ernest Hemingway Estate. **Ruth Prawer Jhabvala**: excerpt from *The Householder* (1960). Reprinted by permission of John Murray (Publ.) Ltd. **Jenny Joseph**: 'Warning' from *Rose in the Afternoon* (J.M. Dent 1974). Reprinted by permission of the author. **Just Seventeen**: extract from *Just Seventeen* 29.12.83. Reprinted with permission. **Yashar Kemal**: 'The White Trousers' from *Anatolian Tales* (1968). Reprinted by permission of Collins Publishers. **Anne Lee**: from *Faust and Furious* (1982). Reprinted by permission of Cambridge University Press. **Dennis Lee**: 'Oilcan Harry' from *Nicholas Knock and Other People*. Reprinted by permission of Macmillan of Canada, A Division of Canada Publishing Corporaton. **Laurie Lee**: 'Leaving Home' from *As I Walked Out One Midsummer Morning* (1969). Reprinted by permission of Andre Deutsch Ltd. **Ian McEwan**: First published in *Granta 7*. (Reprinted by permission of Deborah Rogers Ltd.) **Eric McGraw**: 'Feeding The World' from *Population Today*. Reprinted by permission of William Heinemann Ltd. **Bernard MacLaverty**: from *Secrets and Other Stories* (Blackstaff Press Ltd., 1977). **Edwin Muir**: 'The Way' from *The Collected Poems of Edwin Muir*. Reprinted by permission of Faber and Faber. **Jörg Müller and Jörg Steiner**: from *The Sea People*. Copyright © 1981 of the original German edition (Die Menschen in Meer) by Verlag Sauerlander, Aarau/Switzerland and Frankfurt am Main/Germany. English translation Copyright © 1982 by Victor Gollancz. By permission. **Eckehard Munck**: 'The Milgram Experiment' from *Biology of the Future*. Reprinted by permission of Schreiber. **The Observer**: 'Ethics and Ethiopia' from *The Observer* 28.10.84. Reprinted with permission. **George Orwell**: from *Nineteen Eighty Four*. Reprinted by permission of A.M. Heath & Co. Ltd., for the Estate of the late Sonia Brownell Orwell and Martin Secker and Warburg Ltd. **Dorothy Parker**: 'By the time you swear you're his . . .' from *The Collected Dorothy Parker*. Reprinted by Permission of Duckworth & Co., Ltd. **Brian Patten**: 'Sometimes it happens' from *Vanishing Trick* (1976), and 'In the high rise Alice dreams of wonderland' from *Grave Gossip* (1979). Reprinted by permission of George Allen & Unwin (Publ.) Ltd. **Salman Rushdie**: 'The Golden Bough'. Copyright © 1983 by Salman Rushdie. First published in *Granta 7*. Reprinted by permission of Deborah Rogers Ltd. **Willy Russell**: 'Memory of Childhood' from *Politics and Terror*. All rights whatsoever in this play are strictly reserved and application for performances etc., should be made before rehearsal to Margaret Ramsay Ltd., 14a Goodwin's Court, St. Martin's Lane, WC2. No performance may be given unless a licence has been obtained. **Carl Sandburg**: from *The People, Yes*. Copyright 1936 by Harcourt Brace Jovanovich, Inc., renewed 1964 by Carl Sandburg. Reprinted by permission of the Publisher. **Stephen Spender**: 'My parents kept me from children who were rough' from *Collected Poems*. Reprinted by permission of Faber and Faber Ltd. **Fritz Spiegl**: extracts from *Keep Taking the Tabloids: What The Papers Say And How They Say It* (1983). Reprinted by permission of Pan Books Ltd. **Paul Theroux**: 'New York Subway' from *Subterranean Gothic*. First published in *Granta 10*. Reprinted by permission of Gillon Aitken. **Dylan Thomas**: extract from *Under Milk Wood* (J.M. Dent 1954). Reprinted by permission of David Higham Associates Ltd. **Jack Trevor Story**: extract from *The Trouble With Harrey* (T.V. Boardman, 1949). Reprinted by permission of Macdonald and Co. (Publ.) Ltd. **True Magazine**: 'It happened like this' from *True Magazine* February 1984. (Copyright *True Magazine*. Reprinted with permission). **Peter Ustinov**: extract from *Dear Me* (1977). Reprinted by permission of William Heinemann Ltd, for the author. **Kurt Vonnegut**: extracts from 'Address to a Graduating Class at Bennington College 1970' and 'Teaching the Unteachable' both from *Wampeters, Foma and Granfalloons*. Reprinted by permission of Jonathan Cape Ltd., for the author. **Arnold Wesker**: extract from 'Roots' from *The Wesker Trilogy*. Reprinted by permission of Jonathan Cape Ltd., for the author. **Which?**: 'The Real Thing?' from *Which?* 1984. Reprinted by permission of the Consumers' Association.

Every effort has been made to trace and contact copyright holders but this has not always been possible. We apologise for any infringement of copyright.